# ADVANCE PRAISE FOR
## — *TRAIN BEYOND THE MOUNTAINS* —

"[A] rolling meditation on trains... Railway buff
Antonson is a knowledgeable guide and his grandson,
Riley, offers a youthful perspective on their travels."

**FRANCES BACKHOUSE**, author of *Once They Were Hats:
In Search of the Mighty Beaver*

"Antonson takes us ... on a fascinating journey
through train lore... for anyone who loves
twists and turns explored by an inquisitive mind."

**ROSEMARY NEERING**, author of *Down the Road:
Journeys Through Small-Town British Columbia*

"Antonson's travels with grandson Riley
remind me of John Steinbeck's classic, this time exchanging
the open road of America for steel rails rolling through
Canada's vast geography and history."

**MICHAEL MCCARTHY**, author of *The Snow Leopard Returns:
Tracking Peter Matthiessen to Crystal Mountain and Beyond*

### PRAISE FOR OTHER BOOKS BY RICK ANTONSON

**Walking With Ghosts in Papua New Guinea:
Crossing the Kokoda Trail in the Last Wild Place on Earth** (2019)

"*Walking With Ghosts in Papua New Guinea* is among
the best travel narratives I have read. I highly recommend
this book to armchair travelers anxious to experience life
in a truly wild, and in many ways, primitive world."

**JAMES P. DUFFY**, author of *War at the End of the World*

**Full Moon Over Noah's Ark:**
**An Odyssey to Mount Ararat and Beyond (2016)**

"A book filled with the enthusiasm of discovery,
the delight in accomplishment, and the relief of return."

**KIRKUS REVIEWS**

"This tasty, spicy feast of a book could have gone
beyond its 350 pages. Once picked up, it is hard to put down;
it would serve well any library's bookshelf."

**LIBRARY JOURNAL**

**Route 66 Still Kicks: Driving America's Main Street (2012)**

"One of the best books of the bunch."

**NEW YORK TIMES**, roundup of holiday travel books

"The most impressive account of a road trip I have ever read."

**PAUL TAYLOR**, publisher of *Route 66 Magazine*

"A middle-age Woodstock in motion, an encounter
with an America that isn't as lost as we think … in the end Antonson
proves that Route 66 indeed still kicks—as does America."

**KEITH BELLOWS**, editor in chief, *National Geographic Traveler*

**To Timbuktu for a Haircut: A Journey Through West Africa (2008)**

"Rick Antonson's classic travel memoir…"

**CHICAGO TRIBUNE**

"Anyone planning a trip to Africa should put
Antonson's book on their packing list right after malaria tablets."

**NATIONAL POST**

"In the magical-travel-names-department,
Timbuktu undoubtedly holds the trump card—Marrakesh,
Kathmandu, or Zanzibar are mere runners-up—but Rick Antonson's
trek to the fabled desert city proves that dreamtime destinations
are found in our minds just as much as on our maps."

**TONY WHEELER**, co-founder of Lonely Planet
and author of *Bad Lands: A Tourist on the Axis of Evil*

# RICK ANTONSON

# — TRAIN —
# BEYOND THE
# MOUNTAINS

## Journeys on the
## Rocky Mountaineer

GREYSTONE BOOKS
Vancouver/Berkeley/London

Greystone Books Ltd.
greystonebooks.com

Cataloguing data available from Library and Archives Canada
ISBN 978-1-77164-486-0 (cloth)
ISBN 978-1-77164-488-4 (epub)

Editing by Lesley Cameron
Copyediting by Lenore Hietkamp
Proofreading by Alison Strobel
Indexing by Carlisle Froese and Stephen Ullstrom
Jacket and text design by Fiona Siu
Jacket photographs courtesy of Rocky Mountaineer
Maps by Eric Leinberger

Printed and bound in Canada on FSC® certified paper at Friesens.
The FSC® label means that materials used for the product have
been responsibly sourced.

Greystone Books thanks the Canada Council for the Arts,
the British Columbia Arts Council, the Province of British Columbia
through the Book Publishing Tax Credit, and the Government of
Canada for supporting our publishing activities.

Greystone Books gratefully acknowledges the xʷməθkʷəy̓əm (Musqueam),
Sḵwx̱wú7mesh (Squamish), and səlilwətaɬ (Tsleil-Waututh) peoples on
whose land our Vancouver head office is located.

"It is well-known that the train is the last word in truth drugs."
PAUL THEROUX

*This book is dedicated to grandparents,*
*mine among them, who took one of the world's most*
*important train journeys, that of immigrants.*

*Gramma Mina Antonson (née Krislock), from the United States*
*Grampa Sigurd Antonson, from Norway*

*Nana Belle Fleming (née McInnis), from England*
*Pop Hugh Fleming, from Scotland*

**MAP 1: CANADA'S ROCKY MOUNTAINS AND THE PACIFIC COAST**

The *Rocky Mountaineer*, on the Pacific coast of Canada, is one of the most famous trains in the world today, travelling on heritage tracks that run primarily between the Rocky Mountains and Vancouver.

# — CONTENTS —

# — LIST OF MAPS —

# — AUTHOR'S NOTE —

AN EARLY DECISION for any traveller is whether to go alone or go with someone else.

I've ridden the rails in more than thirty-five countries, travelling thousands of miles through places as varied as Belarus, Mongolia, Iran, and North Korea.[1] With my two sons, Brent and Sean, I've circumnavigated the Northern Hemisphere by train. Wrapped in the romance of railroads, I proposed to Janice, now my wife, aboard the *Sunset Limited* in Alabama, heading to New Orleans. Alone on a train in Senegal, I bonded with three local men with whom I shared a roomette for two days, forming relationships I would never have developed if I had brought a travel companion. Over a sleepless night on a train in eastern Turkey, I traded my food and conversation for those of an elderly farmer in the compartment we shared using languages we didn't, and discovered his homemade Noah's Soup, of which there was sufficient for him to share with one lone traveller. The dilemma of going with a travel companion or going alone is very real for me.

My plan for this particular journey was to board the westbound *Rocky Mountaineer* in Banff, Alberta, to take the train beyond the mountains.[2] Later, I'd depart from Vancouver, British Columbia, aboard another train bound north by northeast, venturing back for a spell in the Rocky Mountains. My first impulse was to go solo, as that makes it easier to get into those awkward situations where stories live. Yet to be on one of the world's great trains was too special not to share. My motivation was to enjoy the simplicity of train travel: meandering through

5

time to the soothing rhythm of the tracks, with few responsibilities. Such a temptation begs for an accomplice. Spontaneously, I invited my ten-year-old grandson. Riley was eager from the start: "You'll be so happy to have me along, Grampa."

A few years earlier, my grandson, my son, and I had taken Amtrak's *Coast Starlight* on the two-day journey from Los Angeles to Seattle. I learned that having a kid along on one's travels defines responsibility. Riley was a great travel companion then: inquisitive, self-entertained, prone to short answers and long silences, and wide-eyed about people and encounters. How had he changed since then, I wondered. How had I?

Train travel is an ongoing moment. It is the continual unfolding of anticipation and understanding. I got more of those than I envisaged when Riley and I were aboard *Rocky Mountaineer*'s bi-level coach. Often he'd say, "Let's head to the back of the train, Grampa." There, on the lower level's open-air observation deck, Riley would lean into the summer wind, tousle-haired, eyes alight, as the train rolled down the tracks of time. His grin reflected the pure joy of a child's ability to live in the now. He'd squint at the trees ("What's that one, Grampa?"), frown at dilapidated farmhouses ("That's sad."), or offer insights ("You're not as easy to travel with as I'd hoped.").

I wanted to share the gifts of train travel with my grandson: the gift of unexpected relaxation (it's like a long walk without the footwork); the gift of discovering new friends (each with a story to tell, or a secret to hide); the gift of time to think (or, for a kid, to play video games on a tablet). And I wanted to see everything anew through Riley's eyes, one-seventh the age of mine.

TRACKS ARE TO TRAINS what roots are to trees. The *Rocky Mountaineer* travels over bands of steel that nourished a whole country and formed part of the national drama that nurtured Alberta and British Columbia with settlement, all the while displacing and disrupting the lives of Indigenous people. I realized our travels would bring us face to face with what Wallace Stegner expressed as contradictions between the West of the past and the West of the present, and that solidified the importance of my travels with Riley.

THE LAG OF TIME between a travel experience and the story's publication in a book is measured in years. Things change during that time.

As this book goes to print I note differences in Riley. He was ten years old during our travels, and he'll be fourteen when he gets to hold a finished copy. That he flourished in soccer, grew to be more than six feet tall, and became an engaging teenager in the intervening years will surprise no reader, nor will it that he talks of this as "our book."

Riley said to me one day, "Grampa, you need to write in our book about the terrible fire in Lytton after the year we passed through. And what about the flood you told me only comes every seventy years and just showed up and ruined the Fraser Valley?" Importantly, he also urged me to write about a tragedy. "You have to tell readers about the Kamloops residential school and the graves of the missing Indigenous kids." Those, and also the unforgettable fact that for two years people put their travel lives on hold for a virus.

Pandemics like COVID-19 are sadly not new to the lands the *Rocky Mountaineer* wanders through. Ramifications of the 2020 outbreak in the Pacific Northwest pale in comparison to those of epidemics that arrived with European explorers in the 1700s, diseases the Indigenous inhabitants had no protection against. Tuberculosis, influenza, measles, cholera, smallpox, and other illnesses decimated the population.

The COVID pandemic forced Rocky Mountaineer to suspend their 2020 schedule. The Fairmont Banff Springs Hotel closed temporarily. Travellers stayed home. Restarting in 2021, Rocky Mountaineer operated with sporadic passenger numbers. In that period, climate change wreaked havoc in the province, unleashing fires and floods. As travel restrictions eased in 2022, borders reopened, and tentative bookings grew, the company remained wary of potential government-dictated disruptions.

On the *Rocky Mountaineer*, passengers journey through the village of Lytton, where the Thompson and Fraser Rivers meet. In the summer of 2021, wildfires burned it to the ground. Due to extended dry periods that year, B.C. faced the third worst fire season on record. Fires around the province approached targets and then retreated; threatened First Nations communities then altered course, teased danger, then abated. On June 30, the day after Lytton set the highest temperatures ever documented in Canada (121.3° Fahrenheit; 49.6° Celsius), flames so quickly advanced on the village that residents had thirty minutes' notice to evacuate. Ninety percent of Lytton was razed within the hour. Homes and shops of the 250 residents were left as smouldering timbers or charred husks of vehicles. Museums with one-off historic relics and local stories were destroyed. The train bridge burned. It's unclear how long it will take for Lytton to rebuild.

Passing through the Fraser Valley on the *Rocky Mountaineer* brings a sobering reflection on nature's wrath. In Sumas Prairie, a lowland created by a drained lake, potential floodwaters are ideally contained by dikes and berms and pump stations when everything aligns favourably. When they don't, water goes where it wishes to, cascades over embankments and runs deep across ranches and townships—and that's what occurred in the fall of 2021. An atmospheric river—long, winding band of moisture-laden air—brought record-setting heavy rain to B.C., walloping the Fraser Valley, destroying farms, and triggering mass evacuations. Communities and landholders had prepared for a serious flood every fifty or seventy years, with the last in 1948. However, they could not cope with this severe flood, amplified by a changing climate. The water has now receded, but its threat remains.

When the *Rocky Mountaineer* traverses the east side of Kamloops, the former Kamloops Indian Residential School comes into view. In 2021, the unmarked graves of as many as 215 Indigenous children were discovered there. Many were the ages I'd just had the joy of watching my grandson grow through, a privilege denied to their parents and grandparents. These children died during their forced attendance at the school and went missing, their deaths not registered. Often their families were not notified, their gravesites left anonymous. Residential schools were the creation of Canada's government and predominantly the Roman Catholic Church (though also Anglican, Baptist, Methodist, Presbyterian, and United Churches), with this one operating from 1890 to 1978. These schools aimed to rid Indigenous children of their customs, language, eating habits, style of dress, their family ties, and their rich culture. Canada's 2015 Truth and Reconciliation Commission report deemed their effects to be "cultural genocide."

History encountered through travel is especially important when it is hard to comprehend and damning. Canada's Governor General Mary Simon sombrely said, "It's unimaginable that a place of learning could be so cruel."

For a spell, uncertainty about the future was reflected in Riley's words, "Will the *Rocky Mountaineer* run again?" And when it finally did: "Now people are travelling through land that needs healing." Everything that has happened since our journey attests to a hidden truth of train travel: the traveller will eventually see the unexpected or overlooked, the shied-away-from or the concealed—as well as bear witness to landscapes and learn to really see them and the people who live there. And it's the traveller's duty to learn from those experiences and use them to bring good to the world.

The pandemic jostled all of us: we should never again take for granted the freedom to travel. As a result, today there's a fresh eagerness to confront the traveller's age old quandary: "If not now, when?" I hear the answer in Riley's voice, "Let's go!"

# — PROLOGUE —

BEFORE THE ROCKIES became the Rockies... Around 75 million years ago, the dinosaurs roamed the verdant wetlands of what is now the Alberta Badlands, blissfully unaware of how much their life was about to change.

They foraged their way along a relatively thin band of land that stretched from modern-day Alaska to halfway down Central America. To the east, today's Alberta, Saskatchewan, and much of the American Midwest (think Minnesota) were covered in water; to the west was a vast ocean. Miles beneath the Earth's surface, a tectonic plate was also on the move, creeping northwestward toward plates moving eastward underneath the ocean. Although their rather energetic introduction to each other would lead to the cataclysmic creation of the Rocky Mountains, we won't blame the dinosaurs for not noticing what was happening beneath their feet. This was the Laramide orogeny period. The plates moved 4 inches (10 centimetres) a year, or about the width of a single strand of hair every day, slowly enough that there was time for something even more dramatic, and more mysterious, to happen before the Rocky Mountains emerged. Whether because of a massive meteoroid hitting the Earth or a series of air-choking volcanoes, dinosaurs became extinct 66 million years back—4 million years before the heavy lifting of making the Rocky Mountains began.

This may seem forever ago, but in the grand scheme of things it was quite recent. If you were to condense the story of planet Earth from its beginnings to today into a twenty-four-hour period, the Rocky

Mountains did not make their presence known until 23:30 hours. They are geological babies.

Eighteen hundred miles (3,000 kilometres) long, they are direct descendants of the Ancestral Rockies, which rose from under the seas 300 million years ago. As those mountains then eroded, the resulting sediment kept building in layers where it flowed and settled, getting so heavy it created a basin down the middle of what we now call North America. Covered in water for tens of millions of years, the resulting rock layers were eventually thrust skyward when the plates pushed up against one another, which is why you can find prehistoric fossils high atop the Rocky Mountains in Burgess Shale.

In the midst of all that brutality, rocks fractured, creating pathways for the magma underneath the plates to ooze its way up. That magma, when hardened, left rich veins of gold.

Astounding? Yes. Yet the Rocky Mountains would not be the marvels they are today were it not for subsequent monumental periods of glaciation. As the glaciers formed and receded, they carried with them rocks and pebbles that gouged deep grooves in the bedrock. The Cordilleran Ice Sheet, from 2.6 million years ago to 10,000 years ago, played a significant role in the evolution of the landscape. The slow strokes of ice age carving created the photogenic, jagged-edged peaks known throughout the world—without it, they may have been round and undulating—and added the bedazzling turquoise of the local lakes by grinding "rock flour" silt and suspending that silt in the water, through which light reflects back to us in a hue unlike anything else in nature's palette.

The evolution of the Rocky Mountains is carved in stone, elements of it attributable to human behaviour. While there are still about 17,000 glaciers in B.C. and 800 in Alberta, a recent study predicted the Columbia Ice Field portion within the Rockies could disappear in little more than seventy years if carbon emission rates related to human activity remain unchanged. During that time, B.C.'s Coast Mountains will lose half of their glacier volume. Only dinosaurs should be surprised.

See the Rockies while you can.

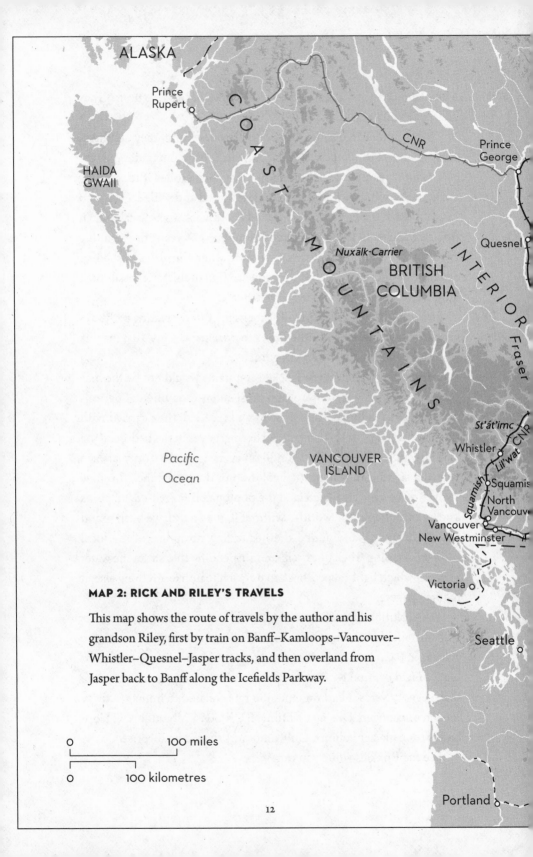

ALASKA

Prince
Rupert

HAIDA
GWAII

COAST

MOUNTAINS

INTERIOR

Fraser

CNR

Prince
George

Quesnel

Nuxälk-Carrier

BRITISH
COLUMBIA

Pacific
Ocean

VANCOUVER
ISLAND

St'át'imc

Whistler

CNR

Lil'wat

Squamish

Squamis

North
Vancouv

Vancouver
New Westminster

Victoria

Seattle

**MAP 2: RICK AND RILEY'S TRAVELS**

This map shows the route of travels by the author and his
grandson Riley, first by train on Banff–Kamloops–Vancouver–
Whistler–Quesnel–Jasper tracks, and then overland from
Jasper back to Banff along the Icefields Parkway.

0 ⊢————⊣ 100 miles

0 ⊢————⊣ 100 kilometres

Portland

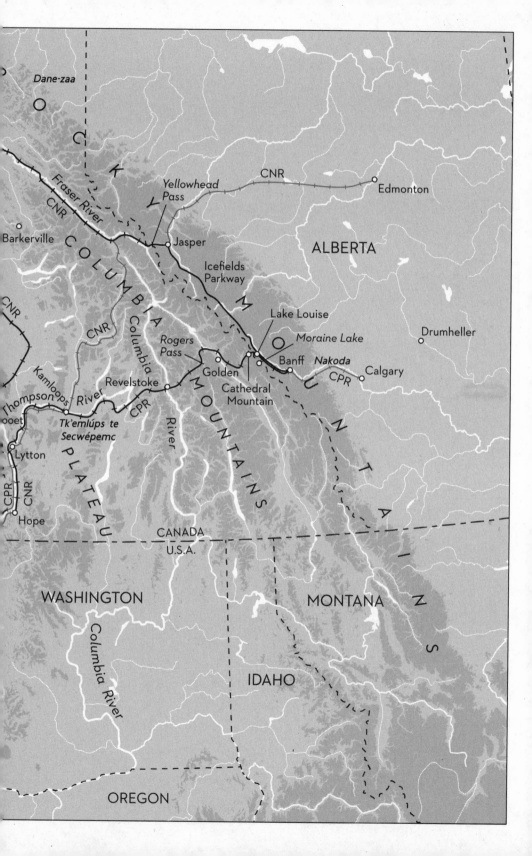

# – I –

# JUNCTIONS

"Everything is a railway junction where
past and future are sliding over one another, not touching."
**TIMOTHY MORTON**, *Humankind: Solidarity
With Nonhuman People*

# — 1 —

O N A 1920S SUMMER DAY at Chicago's Grand Central Station, the platform bustles with train passengers. At the far end, a locomotive pulses with excitement, shrouded in steam, a fire roaring in its belly. Its oiled drive shafts are poised for that first mechanical order from the throttle to apply power to the wheels and turn them against the rails. The train displays a round logo, a badge of honour that streaks THE MOUNTAINEER in block capitals at an angle and boasts the wording "Chicago–Vancouver" and the railway company names Soo Line and Canadian Pacific.

This huge Pacific steam locomotive is about to lead the train on the first leg of a journey across the Great Plains and into Canada, thence through the foothills and the Rocky Mountains to Vancouver, more than 2,000 rail miles (3,200 kilometres) away.

The flutter and fuss are palpable. Redcap porters load suitcases, some bearing names such as Milwaukee Stamping Co., into the baggage car. Canada's T. Eaton & Co. catalogue featured two dozen pieces of luggage that year in recognition of the travelling public's interest in style, and several passengers carry such pieces. The popular canvas-covered stateroom trunks are also in evidence. Sophisticated women in long dresses or twill suits search for their sleeping cars, taking the hands of platform staff as they step up into their rolling home for the coming days and nights. Gents resplendent in their Broadway hats and moleskin coats stand by gamely, letting railroad staff do their jobs. Relatives wave fond farewells to people waving from the coach windows.

Walking along the platform, newsboys hawk their wares, offering the latest headlines for "two pennies a paper." A few travellers buy a broadsheet, anxious to see advertising from Sears-Roebuck's new retail outlet in Chicago or from the new automobile manufacturer in Detroit, Chrysler Corporation, or to check the score of baseball games played in New York's recently built Yankee Stadium or at Chicago's Cubs Park. Some passengers carry copies of the recently published *Great Gatsby*, by F. Scott Fitzgerald.

A voice booms from the public address system, talking over the travellers and staff: "*The Mountaineer* will depart in five minutes for St. Paul/Minneapolis, Fargo, Minot, Calgary, Banff, Kamloops, and Vancouver. All passengers should now be on board the train."

This train has two tony sleeping cars built by the Pullman Company in the United States, three slightly less luxurious sleeping cars with cushioned seats that give way to curtained-off bed settings at night, and a deluxe dining car fitted with amber-glowing table lamps and white tablecloths, on which cut-glass decanters and silverware are already in place. Each car is resplendent in the deep-green livery of *The Mountaineer*. At the front is the gleaming engine and tender. The sleek appearance is the epitome of North America's elegant rail travel. In the fast-paced years to come, *Rake* magazine would nostalgically describe it as a time when "changing locations was an inherently glamorous endeavour."

And then, with the time-honoured cry of "All abo-o-o-ard!," the conductor signals the engineer that it is time to move out. With a blast from the steam whistle and a huff of steam through the powerful cylinders, the engineer releases the brake and the train begins its slow departure.

The Pacific locomotive, built by the American Locomotive Company, has an ideal wheel configuration for traction: four smaller wheels on the "leading truck," six 75-inch (1.9-metre) "driving wheels," followed by two smaller wheels on the "trailing truck." In common parlance that makes it a "4-6-2," as it's known under the Whyte Notation, a steam locomotive classification proposed by mechanical engineer Frederick Whyte.[3] Sixteen tons (14,500 kilograms) of coal in the tender and 11,000 gallons (41,000 litres) of water will together work in the locomotive to convert heat into steam. It is the latest example of technology's triumph over territory. This style of locomotive has been developed specifically for passenger travel, offering speed, power, stability, comfort, and smooth transport across both open terrain and demanding mountain passes.

The advertising of the route calls it "the train of two countries." It will take passengers up the shore of Lake Michigan, over the northern reaches of the United States. The trackage slips across the U.S.-Canada border at Portal/North Portal, different towns in different countries, but only a few yards apart. There the train will merge with a Canadian Pacific Railway (CPR) train for the rest of its journey across the Prairies and through the Rockies to Vancouver, which had recently displaced Winnipeg from its position as Western Canada's largest city. Along the way, travellers will hear unfamiliar place names, such as Estevan, Moose Jaw, Hope, and Langley. The train will pass freight trains waiting on sidings, giving priority to the railway's passengers. With stops for refuelling along the way, this trip will take the better part of four days.

Passengers will be enthralled by the rhythmic clickety-clack of wheels travelling over plates joining sections of steel track, the receding view for those in the last car, and the change from lakeside to flat countryside to rolling hills to vaulting mountains with precipitous cliffs. When *The Mountaineer* traverses the Rocky Mountains, following the path of river valleys set among craggy peaks, the travellers will soak up some of the most magnificent scenery in the world. Great rivers flow under high trestles, and passengers will look out the windows and gasp in amazement at their height above roiling waters. Dramatic snow-laden peaks hover menacingly. Mountain meadows filled with riotously coloured wildflowers—fireweed, purple fleabane, bristly prickly poppy, and Rocky Mountain pussytoes—provide feasts for Midwestern eyes made weary by industrial landscapes.

THE MOUNTAINEER OF THE 1920S represented an appeal of train travel that still enthrals travellers a century later.

# 2

ONE RECENT SUMMER MORNING at the Banff train station, I stood beside twenty-two freshly washed coaches headed by a powerful diesel engine idling on a track. Each coach was adorned with a wave of white, topped with a blue swoosh below its rooftop's gold ribbon, broken only by its bent-glass ceilings. I could imagine the entire train seeming to undulate as it moved along the tracks. The engine had an emblem with mountain-sharp R and M lettering merged into a graphic with "Rocky Mountaineer" printed below.

Three decades ago, I was vice-president of the Great Canadian Railtour Company (GCRC) for the first three years it operated the *Rocky Mountaineer*. I was responsible for sales and marketing, reservations, and loose ends, of which there were many. The entire time I worked with the company we were on the brink of bankruptcy. I once knew this train and from whence it came; I wanted to see what it had become since that era, this time as a passenger. It struck me how much had changed since then, even at a superficial level: the coaches had matured from rust and tarnish to gold-and-blue beauties. Well over half the coaches were two-level dome cars with seats on the upper level under a glass roof, and a dining room on the lower level, where I could see the places set for breakfast. The rest were mid-century coaches updated in style, and with enlarged windows that arched at the roof, and seating that would let one "take it all in." There were no sleeping cars: everyone onboard would stay in hotels overnight at the midway town of

Kamloops. This ensured the entirety of our two-day trip would be in daylight, thus avoiding the major complaint about earlier train services passing through some of the most stunning scenery at night. There were no baggage cars, as everyone's main luggage had already left in a truck to be reunited with travellers when they arrived in their hotel rooms that night.

The *Rocky Mountaineer* has no equivalent in North America. Its few comparable one-of-a-kind train experiences along heritage tracks are found on other continents. Elegant train travel has, by way of revival, come into its own in recent decades, often with the retrofitting of a once grand train, or a renewed interest in legendary routes, or, more rarely, the launch of elaborate and unexpected new trains.

"We should have done this years ago," an elderly man said, watching a family with two teenage kids pose for selfies. "We could have brought *our* kids before they got so busy."

"We're here now." His wife smiled. "Best we get on board. It'll be two days before the next departure."

I WAS SHIELDING a cup of hot chocolate against a cool mountain breeze. At moments like that I often contemplate the old saw: "Each day lies before us as a blank page. What will we do to write its story?" The answer, of course, is to take the first step.

"Let's go, Grampa," chided my now constant companion, Riley, "or me and this train will leave without you."

There was a confidence in Riley as he stepped aboard the *Rocky Mountaineer*. What put that spring in my grandson's stride? Was it the sense of freedom so prevalent among train travellers?

Riley's grin echoed my own childhood excitement about a train jaunt I had made more than sixty years ago with my grandmother through the Rocky Mountains. Today that journey evokes a wistfulness I hope to never lose. The refrain from an outbound train, or being wakened in the middle of the night by a distant train horn, stirs in me the want of being elsewhere.

Riley is tall for a kid his age, which has thinned him for the time being. He has his mother's looks, which, speaking as his father's father, are the better set of genes for that. A spike of his blond hair flares blue. He's an able camper; we've slept out under the stars. Soccer is one of his sports, video gaming another. Impatient for life (and with people), he's up for adventure, and he has no known fears. (A year before, he'd plummeted 171 feet (52 metres) off a bridge on a bungee cord.) It interests him to be unpredictable.

Growing up, I was encouraged to run toward life, to not measure what one had done but rather to assess what might be on the horizon. My father said to my siblings and me that you often have to make a choice: "You can *do*, or you can *have*." I'd made up my mind to *do* whatever experiences I could, forsaking the possessions. It had worked out favourably, so far—and I wanted to pass that lesson along to Riley, particularly the meaningfulness of travel experiences. While there is much left for me to learn, I'm aware that travel is the world's synapse. By connecting people from around the world, it takes down barriers to understanding. Travel lets us celebrate our differences. I once heard a cabinet minister in India say, "Travel sits on the right hand of peace." If it can do that for countries, what might it do for a grandfather and a ten-year-old?

There was a hum among passengers as the diesel horn sounded its boarding announcement, nudging those still standing in awe of the station's surrounding mountains. Little did they know they were staring at appetizer scenery. More awe lay around the bend: the unremitting beauty of the landscape enhanced by the meeting of fellow travellers, and the enjoyment of gourmet meals and a level of service seldom encountered in today's world of trains. This was not a checklist trip. This would be a defining trip, their journeys filled with meaning and purpose.

A discussion on the platform interrupted my musings. Two couples of a certain age were jousting over their upcoming week. There was camaraderie in the air around them, friendly but combative. Someone was about to lose an argument.

"I told you so," said one of the men. "It's going to be great."

"It's going to be slow," said a woman. "Two days to Vancouver. We could fly there in an hour."

"And what would you see?" the man asked.

"The back of someone's head," she answered. "But only for sixty minutes."

"Oh, I love trains," said the other woman, laughing at the exchange. "I was on a train in the '90s with my first husband. Nothing like this one, though."

I was unsure if she was comparing husbands or trains. Eyes front, I told myself. The second man joined the verbal pile-on. "I've travelled on elegant trains all over the world. Last year we were on Peru's *Andean Explorer* to Cusco, before that we went to Lhasa from Beijing on the Qinghai to Tibet Railway, and now..."

"And now *this*...," the first man interrupted, spreading his hands and giving a half bow of respect toward the train. Their banter transported me back decades in my own little world of trains to a time when I was a sponge for new stories, particularly those from old codgers who had travelled widely, especially if they had done so by train. The two couples echoed what I sensed: even though I'm now an old codger myself, one can glean much about life rolling along on a train, day after day, distracted by fresh vistas of the mind as well as of the eyes.

"Let's go," Riley said again, disappearing onto the train. I placed my foot where Riley's had been and followed him aboard.

We found our seats and settled in. The train horn blew its farewell. Our engine pulled. Our train tugged. We were leaving the station and heading into the blank pages of the stories that lay ahead. Bystanders and Banff station staff waved us off. Fellow travellers greeted us. Riley nodded goodbyes and said hellos, as would a seasoned traveller. I had no doubt he'd want me to explain the landscape and talk him through the local history, and share the lore of international rail travel. He'll be hanging on my every word of wisdom, I thought. He must know how lucky he is to have me along to amuse him.

"Grampa, please pass me my tablet."

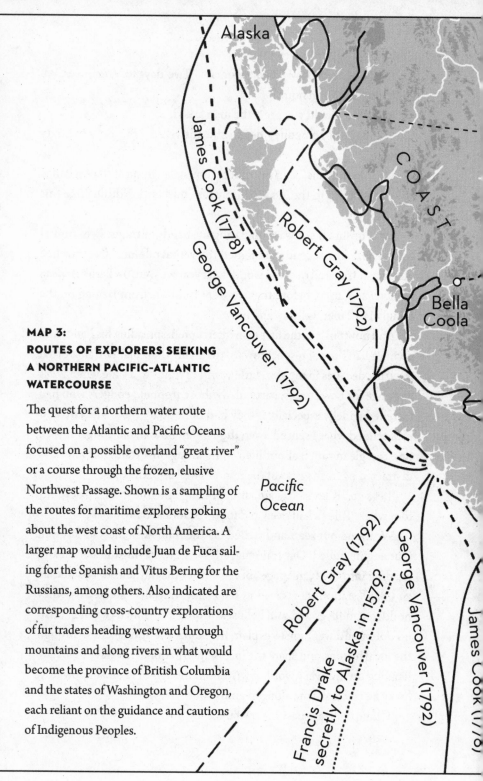

Alaska

James Cook (1778)

Robert Gray (1792)

C O A S T

George Vancouver (1792)

Bella Coola

**MAP 3:**
**ROUTES OF EXPLORERS SEEKING**
**A NORTHERN PACIFIC-ATLANTIC**
**WATERCOURSE**

The quest for a northern water route between the Atlantic and Pacific Oceans focused on a possible overland "great river" or a course through the frozen, elusive Northwest Passage. Shown is a sampling of the routes for maritime explorers poking about the west coast of North America. A larger map would include Juan de Fuca sailing for the Spanish and Vitus Bering for the Russians, among others. Also indicated are corresponding cross-country explorations of fur traders heading westward through mountains and along rivers in what would become the province of British Columbia and the states of Washington and Oregon, each reliant on the guidance and cautions of Indigenous Peoples.

Pacific Ocean

Robert Gray (1792)

Francis Drake secretly to Alaska in 1579?

George Vancouver (1792)

James Cook (1778)

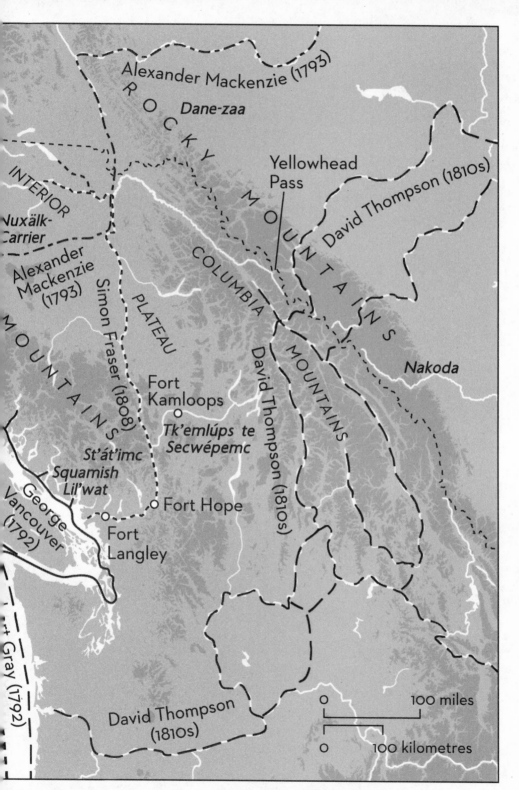

Alexander Mackenzie (1793)

Dane-zaa

R O C K Y  M O U N T A I N S

Yellowhead
Pass

David Thompson (1810s)

INTERIOR

*Nuxälk-
Carrier*

Alexander
Mackenzie
(1793)

Simon Fraser (1808)

PLATEAU

COLUMBIA

David Thompson (1810s)

M O U N T A I N S

Nakoda

M
O
U
N
T
A
I
N
S

Fort
Kamloops

*Tk'emlúps te
Secwépemc*

*St'át'imc*

*Squamish
Lil'wat*

George
Vancouver
(1792)

Fort Hope

Fort
Langley

Gray (1792)

David Thompson
(1810s)

100 miles

100 kilometres

# — II —

# WESTERING

"I really think we are spoiled for travel
else where, after the beauty & interest of the Rockies
for no where else is there such a wealth of beauty
and interest, and I conclude that the haunts so attractive
to the world have no attraction for me."
**MARY VAUX**, American naturalist and artist,
letter to Dr. Charles Walcott, March 11, 1912

# — 3 —

A WESTERING TRAIL OF IRON lay ahead. The sky stretched full of platinum clouds above the arc of glass that canopied our train car. I oriented myself: we were in the upper level of a domed coach with windows everywhere. With seats for seventy-two guests, it gave the feeling of airline business class but with extra elbow room and more leg space. Passengers relaxed in twos on either side of an aisle used for service and sauntering. The lower level held the dining room, with seating for thirty-six guests at tables of four. To the front of the dining room was a fully equipped kitchen. At the back of the coach's lower level was an outdoor viewing platform, or "deck," as passengers took to calling it, maybe 9 feet by 9 feet (3 metres by 3 metres), sheltered below the upper level's floor and open to the winds and scenery, with waist-high chrome railings.

"Finally," said Riley, as the *Rocky Mountaineer* departed Banff. The coaches took up slack as the train displayed its slow-motion strength. I'd like to say we "chugged" because that's in the lexicon of train imagery, but instead we gracefully left the station behind and accepted the mountains' invitation to explore.

"Welcome aboard," said Kim, the first of the onboard crew to introduce herself formally. Her right hand casually motioned to the woman beside her. "This is Ariel. She, too, will be with you today and tomorrow."

"First formalities this morning are about your safety," said Ariel. "After that, it's about your comfort. Then we'll talk food." We were under

28

the care and watch of professionals with an outwardly casual demeanour aimed at earning the confidence of travellers while instructing us in the protocols of companionable group travel. Importantly, they were also trained in case of schedule irregularities.

"Soon we'll take everyone in the front half downstairs to the dining room for breakfast," said Kim.

"That's us," piped Riley, loudly enough to override the public address system. "We're right in the middle."

"That's right," smiled Ariel, looking straight at him. "From the young man forward, we're *seating one* for today's breakfast and lunch. The second group follows on later. Not to worry, we've lots of warm goodies to keep you happy while you're seated up here."

Kim added, "Tomorrow you switch. Those of you in the back half of this upper level will then have first seating at both meals."

Ariel walked the aisle handing out hot towels as Kim strolled behind her with a tray of choices: champagne, juice, water, coffee, tea, or a morning smoothie.

"Could I please have another?" asked Riley as he downed his blended fruit drink before Kim had moved on.

"Have as many as you like, Riley," said Kim, unaware she'd usurped my grandfatherly oversight of Riley's penchant for the beverage. Her mind was on everyone else's enjoyment as well. "Make sure your eyes are alert, because morning is a good time to see wildlife. Keep watch for bears."

Right then someone called, "Moose," as another said, "Elk," and a third claimed, "Bighorn sheep." Ariel gently clarified: "It's a whitetailed deer."

KIM PROVIDED COMMENTARY as the train wound along the tracks through the Sawback Range, making it clear where cameras should be pointed: Castle Mountain[4] (with its obvious bastions and embrasures fortifying it against all forces of nature and humankind); Mount Temple (surprisingly, named after a man named Temple, not a religious structure); Morant's Curve...

Wait, I thought. On that I want more. One can't adequately grasp the magnificence of Morant's Curve from onboard. Fortunately, I had previously seen from a distance this section of the Bow River as it bends beneath the sweep of mile-high mountain peaks. I was on land, with a train coming toward me, offering me the same view Nicholas Morant captured when he photographed CPR trains, beginning in the early 1930s. The CPR embedded the compelling pictures in its promotional materials around the world, and made famous what is more prosaically called Milepost 113 in this railroad subdivision. A little more poetically, *Classic Trains* magazine called Morant's Curve "one of railroading's hallowed places."

OUR HOSTS MILLED ABOUT answering questions (in at least four languages that I heard) and ensuring we were each at ease. How could we not be? The atmosphere was a mix of goodwill and cozy. I felt like a kid again while being intent on bonding with a real one. The tantalizing promise of breakfast—caramelized pancakes and crispy bacon—almost wafted up from the menu itself.

I was struck by the demographics of my fellow passengers. My expectation had been that most folks would be from the cassette era, so the age spectrum pleasantly surprised me. A gentleman across from us, and up a bit, wore a perky hat festooned with the pins of other railways. I suspected he might know a thing or two about trains. A young couple clinked champagne glasses. The family with two teenagers I'd noticed in Banff was seated ten rows behind us. An elegant Japanese woman of about seventy had two seats to herself, whether by design or circumstance I didn't know.

Riley wiggled a loose tooth, undaunted by being the youngest on our coach. He swivelled excitedly in his seat even more than I did. "Where do you think everyone's from? I'd like a glass ceiling like this in my bedroom at home. How many tunnels do you think we'll go through?"

Usually, I prefer knowing only the basics about where I'm going on travels. I like being naïve about what's around the bend, even being lost. But for this trip, I had Riley along and it had seemed wise to give his parents an itinerary. Before Riley and I left home, I fawned over maps charting history, routes, and geography, and pawed through books. A ragged, off-kilter circle emerged on my mind's map to outline our forthcoming journey, largely dictated by the route of rails.

Stories about nature and history, European explorers and Indigenous Peoples, flowed from our train host's onboard commentary as surely as the annual snowmelt flowed into creeks that fed the three rivers that shaped our route: the Columbia, Fraser, and Thompson.

NORTH AMERICA'S PACIFIC COAST, particularly along the part American schoolbooks call the Pacific Northwest, was once the most sought-after geography for explorers, seeking the Northwest Passage, whether over land or by ocean. Stories of their searches serve as bookends for British Columbia's "discovery" by Europeans upon their arrival on the lands of Indigenous Peoples. One such bookend features the ocean-going escapades of mariners in the Pacific Ocean; the other is of those on foot who wondered what riches lay on the western side of the Rocky Mountains. Early interest in charting this part of the world was motivated by the belief in a navigable passage of water that could dramatically reduce trade travel time between Europe and Asia, eliminating the need to round the tip of South America. Between the 1500s and the 1800s it was thought such a waterway might be a "Northwest Passage" of continued sea in the Arctic, or possibly a "great river" connected waters from Hudson Bay to the Pacific. Discovery of such a northwest passage would address one of Europe's biggest geographical questions of the era, on a par with efforts to find Timbuktu or the source of the Nile River. But those are just the facts.

WERE IT NOT FOR fog and secrets, two candidates for the Great River—the Fraser River and Columbia River—would have been "discovered" long before Europeans finally first navigated them.

Englishman Francis Drake, seaman extraordinaire and circumnavigator of the globe, was commissioned by Queen Elizabeth, and provisioned five ships that departed from Plymouth in 1577. The *Golden Hind* was his home southbound, through the Strait of Magellan, and then northward as he probed the west coast of the Americas. He brought musicians for dinner entertainment, a well-stocked wine cellar, and fancy-dressed waiters, as one would. Was he on a secret assignment? His official account states he went no further than the 48th parallel north, but more recent studies support he possibly reached 56 degrees north, in Alaska, before ice turned him back. If so, his achievement and resulting charts would predate recorded European progress that far by two hundred years. That thesis suggests Drake's sailing success and impressive charts were kept secret to prevent the Spanish knowing. However, Drake's log records that "either there is no passage at all through these Northern [*sic*] coasts, which is most likely, or if there be, that is unnavigable."

The Greek explorer Juan de Fuca appears not to have wanted his exploits kept a secret and may have embellished them with the claim that his Spanish-owned ship's journey from California north along the Pacific coast in 1592 found an entry inland by river. A stretch of water bears his name (compliments of a British captain passing through later), but historians generally feel he never sighted the entrance to either the Columbia or Fraser Rivers.

Peter the Great of Russia was envious of the Pacific Ocean exploits of other countries. He therefore sent Danish scientist Vitus Bering overland to the Pacific coast of Russia, where Bering built two ships and ventured to Kamchatka peninsula, Alaska, in 1728 and again in 1741. Bering went in search of a land bridge between Asia and America, but instead identified open waters between the two continents, to which he lent his name. Bering's caper has been called "the world's largest, longest, and best financed scientific expedition of all time." It ended in a foggy shipwreck on the Island of Blue Foxes, off the Alaska coast, where Bering, ill and malnourished, shivered to death.

The legacy in Western Canada of the British sailor James Cook has its roots in his 1778 visit. Landing at Nootka Sound, and sailing along the coast, he jostled with Spanish explorers for recognition about what was seen, and by whom, though none of them reported having inspected the coastline closely enough to find a river with the potential they sought.

One of Cook's midshipmen returned to these waters in 1792. Captain George Vancouver's ships, the *Discovery* and the *Chatham*, were blown away from shore, where he would otherwise have had a decent chance to sight a significant river's mouth two weeks before Robert Gray, of the United States, saw it. Captain Vancouver also bypassed the mouth of the Fraser River, which was wrapped in fog.

Gray, having sailed out of Boston, found and named the river in question for one of his ships, the *Columbia Rediva*. At the mouth of this Columbia River, the lands, soon to be called Oregon, became American possessions. When Captain Vancouver ventured into the Columbia's mouth during his return south, he erroneously wrote: "It does not appear that Mr. Gray either saw or was ever within five leagues of the entrance." His mistaken claim of the area in Britain's name (which would have been valid a few weeks earlier) sharpened territorial disputes. Gray and his notable achievements are often lost to popular enquiry, despite an open sharing of his discoveries at the time.

Another sailor for whom recognition remains in a modest mist is José Narváez, sailing out of Spanish-held Nootka in 1791. He was the first explorer recorded as entering the muddy waters where the Fraser empties into the Pacific, a discovery for which he is overlooked, largely because Spain kept it secret for fear rival nations would use the information to further their territorial competition.

The Columbia and the Fraser (and the Thompson) Rivers influenced the route Riley and I were taking. They defined the geography, and thus the telling of stories. All three rivers originate in the mountains of B.C. not far from one another, and explorers coming overland in search of one found all three.

WHAT WAS IT about three teenagers in the late 1700s that set them in motion to become Western Canada's most important explorers? They were only a handful of years older than Riley. Alexander Mackenzie emigrated from Scotland to New York City and arrived in Canada in 1778 at the age of fourteen, and joined the fur-trading North West Company (NWC), the Nor'Westers. Fourteen-year-old Simon Fraser, born in the United States but of Scottish ancestry, apprenticed with those Nor'Westers in 1790. Six years earlier, fourteen-year-old David Thompson had left the banks of the River Thames in 1784 for Rupert's Land, the vast territory yet to be called Canada that was governed by the fur-trading behemoth Hudson's Bay Company (HBC). Thompson later made his reputation after he crossed over to his competitor, the NWC, for his chance to cross over the Rockies. Each of these men set out overland on a quest to find the Great River, believing it to be the as-yet-unnamed Columbia, and intending to trace it to its Pacific Ocean mouth.

Let me put this in context: when Alexander Mackenzie reached the Pacific Ocean by an overland route in 1793, he was twenty-nine; that same year Simon Fraser was seventeen and David Thompson, twenty-three. Three men in search of one river found four rivers, one of which is unrelated to our train journey but critical to Canada's development. Mackenzie called it Disappointment River, only to have the 1,100-mile (1,800-kilometre) route, Canada's longest, renamed in his honour: the Mackenzie River in the Northwest Territories. Fraser named the Thompson River after his fellow shareholder in the brigade company, David Thompson. Thompson returned the favour by bestowing Fraser's name on the province's longest river.

Remembering that the elusive Columbia River was named after an American ship coincident with establishing an American presence in the area, it is reasonable to assume that without Mackenzie, Fraser, and Thompson, westernmost Canada as we know it today may well have become an American state. Without these three men, there may not have been lands claimed for Britain that demanded the making of an all-Canada railway to keep British Columbia from joining the United States. And that came closer to happening than most people realize.

IN 1793, ALEXANDER MACKENZIE was sent to find and then travel down the Great River imagined as connecting Hudson Bay with the Pacific Ocean. The river first believed to fulfill these requirements (the one that was eventually called the Columbia) actually begins in a remote part of the Rocky Mountains and flows southward to where it marks today's boundary between Oregon and Washington states; it is half again as long as the Fraser River. Picture Mackenzie's handsome face set with determination, a head of heavy curls extending to whisker-sideburns and a narrow nose, all punctuated by a cleft chin, his eyes bright with anticipation. His task was to find and follow this river to the sea and establish a British fort there. When Mackenzie found a substantial river, he thought he was on the upper reaches of the Great River. (He was actually on the Fraser River.) He decided against following it farther after hearing stories from local Indigenous people of impassable gorges. He believed he would more likely find the Pacific Ocean if he kept moving due west overland. Thus, he and his crew travelled 240 miles (400 kilometres) on trading routes through rainforest and on rivers. Members of the Nuxälk-Carrier, the local First Nation, guided him.

At one point Mackenzie's crew refused to keep going through the dense forests. Mackenzie wrote in his diary, "I would not abandon my design of reaching the sea." He cajoled them onward and westward with the lure of future recognition, and the difficulty of turning back without him. Rightly, he felt his reaching the place where land and sea met was to be a singular achievement, yet that would turn out to be true only in terms of a land crossing. Indigenous people they met along the way told them stories of white men on the oceans, sailing "huge canoes with sails like clouds." In camps, Mackenzie recognized European trading goods—left behind by whom? Soon he smelled salt air. He arrived in the village of Bella Coola, halfway up the Canadian coast, only to learn that Captain Vancouver had been there forty-eight days earlier. One could imagine their utter astonishment had their visits overlapped. *"You're from where?"*

Mackenzie became the first European to traverse the North American continent from the Atlantic to the Pacific, twelve years ahead of a similar accomplishment by the famous American explorers Lewis and Clark. Indeed, given that Indigenous Peoples had little need to traverse such a great distance, Mackenzie was likely the first person ever to do this. He mixed grease from a bear's gut with a pigment of red ochre to paint word of his achievement on a large rock: "Alex Mackenzie from Canada by land 22$^d$ July 1793." Surveyors later etched his lettering into the stone. The elements have not washed away this scrawl of immense importance. Oh, what we'd give for a selfie.

I've often wondered what drove Mackenzie to such an extreme. Was it a wish to return to Scotland and live in the financial comfort of recognition? Might it be an intuition for greatness? Or does the universe compel certain individuals toward an apex of place and good record keeping? What if he'd been required to keep the success a secret?

FIFTEEN YEARS LATER, in 1808, Simon Fraser embarked on the same quest for a major river route as had Mackenzie. Of coincident importance, in 1802 the president of the United States, Thomas Jefferson, read the account of Mackenzie's journey to the Pacific, *Voyages From Montreal*, and subsequently instigated a U.S. overland expedition, led by Captain Meriwether Lewis and Captain William Clark. Lewis and Clark reached the Pacific in 1804, further establishing those lands under claim of the U.S.

In his 1808 trip down the river that would bear his name, Simon Fraser found occasions to question map references noted by Mackenzie (who had by then been knighted), which overlooked geographical factors Fraser would have found helpful. Frustrated by the omissions, his comments bordered on the irreverent. Once he noted, "It does not appear to have been noticed by Sir A.M.K. as he used to indulge himself in a little sleep... I could prove he seldom or ever paid the attention he pretends to have done, and that many of his remarks were not made by himself..."

Believing he could be on the Columbia River, Fraser stayed the course. When he noticed a good-sized river flowing to join with the river he was on, he bestowed on it the name of his fellow Nor'Wester, mistakenly thinking David Thompson must be farther eastward on that same river. Thompson (who never saw the river that bears his name) was actually on the Columbia.

As Fraser's canoes eventually entered a valley and approached a delta nearing the river's mouth, the explorer realized he was too far north for the river he travelled to be the Columbia. He noted the nearby 49th parallel in his journal. His disappointment must have been gut-wrenching. As he reached the river's mouth, he wrote, "I must again acknowledge my great disappointment in not seeing the main Ocean..." He was closer than he could imagine; only islands blocked his view.

THE THIRD OF THESE EXPLORERS, David Thompson, travelled the Columbia River to its mouth in 1811, where he learned the Americans had established a fort thanks to Robert Gray's maritime exploration and Lewis and Clark's overland trail blazing.

When I was at Riley's school level (Grade 5), I encountered a book titled *The Map-Maker*, by naturalist Kerry Wood. It was about David Thompson's development as a cartographer. The book's cover is etched in my mind: a man standing in mountains with a sextant held to his eyes, above high cheekbones; he had a stylish haircut and wore high boots and a leather jacket with decorative fringes falling away from his shoulders. I've long credited that book and David Thompson with inspiring my interest in maps, geography, and the interrelated life of travel. Now, on the *Rocky Mountaineer*, Thompson reappeared in my thinking as a pivotal figure in Western Canada's story. He identified options for trade and transportation routes and surveyed them before there were railways to consider their use. I pledged to buy Riley a copy of the book—whether he wanted it or not.

NO ONE FOUND a navigable Northwest Passage or the Great River.

Other changes were happening to affect the speed of trade between Europe and Asia. By the 1830s and '40s railways were being incorporated in pockets of America, laying the groundwork for linkages into transcontinental networks. And France began work on the Panama Canal in 1881.

As in the United States, railroads may have been the great enablers of Canada's settlement by immigrants from Europe, Asia, and elsewhere, but they also significantly altered the landscape and dynamics of the country, disrupting existing territorial ownership and the lives of people who had lived there for centuries. While estimates by academics vary, the Indigenous population of the territory we now call the country of Canada (a name derived from the Iroquois kanata, meaning "settlement") may have peaked around 500,000 before European immigration exerted its colonial influence, though some estimates from anthropologists run nearer 2 million. By 1900 the number of Indigenous people in the country may have dropped to as low as 117,000. In the year 2020, more than 1.6 million Indigenous people—identified as Métis (those whose ancestry is both Indigenous and European), Inuit (here meaning northern Canada's Indigenous Peoples), and First Nations (groupings of independently administered Indigenous Peoples) lived within Canada. There are today 45 First Nations in Alberta and 198 in B.C. Most were happily settled long before Europeans took a fancy to their lands and casually changed oral place names that had been in use for five thousand years or more.

Among those traditional territories that the train Riley and I were on would travel through are those belonging to the Secwépemc (formerly Shuswap; pronounced Shoo-shwahp), the St'át'imc (anglicized as Salish), the Stó:lō (pronounced Staw-low), the Squamish Lil'wat (pronounced Squa-mish Lil-watt), and the Dane-zaa, which, in but one example of a recurring linguistic situation, can be found spelled as Dunne-za, Danezaa, Tsattine, Tsa-tinne, as well as Tsaa-dane, and Tza-tinne. (Many dialects are "tone languages" in which pitch—say a rising or falling tone—is important to pronunciation and therefore meaning, as is a pause in the middle of a name or original characters, such as "ąą" or unfamiliar "nasal vowels," all of which led me later to online alphabet and syllabary in a search for understanding.)

A lexicon is also helpful to track railway names. Railroads crawled west in search of prosperity and revenue, attracting schemers and dreamers along the way. Most start-ups evolved into mergers or bankruptcy. The *Rocky Mountaineer* trains that Riley and I travelled on over the course of our entire journey rolled mostly over tracks laid by the two major railroads that survived and thrived through a century of changes: the CPR and the Canadian National Railway (CNR). The latter's makeup in 1919 also included the Canadian Northern Railway, and, soon afterward, another major line, the Grand Trunk Pacific Railway. Another set of tracks we trained over was pushed north from Vancouver along the west coast with the geographically confusing name of Pacific Great Eastern (PGE), before it too came under proprietorship of the CNR. (It can be a little confusing to keep track of the tracks.)

# — 4 —

HAPPENSTANCE IS A traveller's best friend. The two couples from the station platform were seated across from one another, not far from us on the train's upper level.

"Now this is what I call 'private varnish,'" said the man who kept taking the conversational lead.

"Excuse me?" said the other man's wife.

"Train talk," he replied, a bit flippantly.

"He's full of it," his wife said. "Makes up railway lingo as he goes along."

"'Private varnish' sounds like a cocktail," said the other man.

"Or a bikini wax," came an Australian stage whisper from farther up the aisle.

On this matter (not the wax), I could help.

THIRTY YEARS AGO I'd stood in a CPR heritage coach at what is now Pacific Central Station in Vancouver. It was parked in preparation for an evening reception with which I had no connection. "Act like you belong" was one of the few helpful pieces of advice I'd ingrained into my sons, as it often places one in interesting circumstances. I had come upon the coach and strolled nonchalantly onboard the one-hundred-year-old business car uninvited, pretending I belonged.

A volunteer railroader was buffing the mahogany interior while waiters set up around him. Everywhere—ceiling, sides, and alcoves—

shone with the gloss of wood. I watched his affection for the shine he'd created. "Private varnish," he said, knowing he'd caught me unaware with a phrase coined in the 1950s to reflect glamorous excursions in private train coaches.

I was unsophisticated in the nuances of train culture, unfamiliar with its clever phrasings, and inexperienced when it came to previously fashionable things. Yet the man spotted my interest in the coach he was fastidiously caring for. "That's what opulent train travel used to be called," he said. "Private varnish—an expression forgotten by anyone who's never experienced such extravagance, or who doesn't like to dine out on obscure words."

"Well, I'm none of the above, except maybe I like words," I said.

"This coach was the pride of CPR executives." His role had seamlessly morphed into that of tour guide. "It ran for decades. It carried corporate types most of the time. Big shots usually, along with a steward to attend them."

He walked toward the other end of the coach, beckoning me to follow along.

He pointed to a portion of the wall. "See the inlay of different woods?" I could detect hues next to the mahogany but not species. "That's birch," he said pressing a knuckle against irregular pieces of wood perfectly aligned with the surface. "There's walnut. Those are slivers of maple." He made the trees' contributions to the décor sound crucial. He applied polish on his cloth and buffed away the smudge where he'd pressed a finger against the inlaid forest.

The man wore a railroader's bib and pants, which could have made him look like a caricature except he seemed right at home—or at work—dressed like that. "I spent a lot of years as a railway engineer. Even pulled this coach behind me once," he said. And without missing a beat he spieled, "You'd not know it, but there's eighty thousand hours of restoration work put into this car. We brought it back from neglect to look spanking new. Retired railroaders did it. Guys like me."

Looking at the reconditioned coach, I said, "That'd be the way to travel. If you could afford it."

"Oh, they could afford it all right. Like I said, it was towed behind the train's consist—that's what coaches and the engine are called: consist. In the U.K., it's called the 'rake,'" he said. He slowed to let my mind absorb his jargon. "This coach was for those who respected the luxury of time."

I enunciated each word: "*Luxury. Time.*"

"Ha, you got it," he said, as though he believed they equalled one another.

I extended my hand in a thank-you. The man plunged his hand with the polishing cloth into my open palm, and shook it, the rag wrapping my wrist in an odour I savoured for days.

"LAKE LOUISE," announced Kim as the *Rocky Mountaineer* pulled through a lovely station. The lake she referenced nestled nearby but out of our view. "Stunning," exclaimed a fellow traveller who had ventured here the day before. "It's the most famous lake in the Rockies." Even in photographs taken by amateurs, the lake's emerald colour looks as if it was professionally tampered with for the picture.

Here for the moment, you'd be forgiven for confusing Canada's Rocky Mountains with Russia's Ural Mountains. Movie director David Lean needed them to stand in for the Russian range in his 1965 film of Boris Pasternak's novel *Doctor Zhivago*. With its historic aura, this location became the remote train station in revolutionary Russia. The Soviet Union had banned distribution of the novel, and Western filmmakers were unwelcome in that country at the time the movie was made. Most of it was filmed in Finland and Spain, but the star of the show (well, aside from the script, Omar Sharif, Julie Christie, and the score) was the stunning scenery we were passing through, albeit without snow.

The Rockies have long been the scene of dramas, for both the movies and those making them. A young Marilyn Monroe tore ligaments in her ankle while filming *River of No Return* in Banff, having earlier sprained her foot falling through ice near Jasper (to the rescue: co-star Robert Mitchum). It is said that male Banff Springs Hotel staff competed for the job of pushing her wheelchair. Unnecessary assistance, of course, when boyfriend and baseball magician Joe DiMaggio was onsite.

Originally, Lake Louise was known as "lake of the little fishes," a literal translation of the Stoney Nation name, Ho-Run-Num-Nay. It's possibly one of North America's most recognizable geographical landmarks, although words and photographs don't compare to actually seeing it.

SHORTLY AFTER, we were at what Ariel called "the literal high point of our journey": 5,332 feet (1,627 metres) above sea level. As altitude goes it is nothing compared to the nearby peaks over two times that height. But as elevation goes for a train ride, it's up there.

What makes this passage from the province of Alberta into B.C. of special note is it coincides with the Continental Divide of the Americas. Our train was on this Great Divide that extends from the southernmost tip of South America to the northernmost part of North America: 6,745 miles (10,855 kilometres) along the ridges of the Rocky Mountains, Sierra Madre, and Andes.

I looked down on Divide Creek, named for what it does, which is follow along the contour of the Continental Divide for a ways. It is not a long creek, and eventually divides as it splits with one fork heading down the eastern slope to the Bow River and eventually to Hudson Bay, draining to the Atlantic Ocean as creeks and Canadian rivers do on that side of the mountains. The other fork heads west to join with the Kicking Horse River and eventually delivers its waters (or what is left of them after they become part of the Columbia River) into the Pacific Ocean, along with the water from the other creeks and rivers on the west side of the divide. No river actually flows "across" this physical statement. There are, however, lakes that straddle the setting and drain down both sides.

About 60 miles (100 kilometres) north of our train's position was an anomaly to these geographic conventions: Mount Snow Dome. Journalist Ken Jennings termed it a "hydrological apex," saying that it identifies a single point where three different watersheds meet. He noted that the Arctic Divide and the Continental Divide cross over one another at its peak. He made clever sense of the dynamic in *Condé Nast Traveler*: "So, for a snowflake drifting down onto Snow Dome, three destinies are possible. If it falls on the western side of the peak, it's headed—eventually—to the Pacific via the Columbia River. A few inches north, and it'll be going to the frigid Arctic Ocean instead. A smidge east, and it'll be routed east to the Atlantic via Hudson Bay."

IT WAS NOW TIME for us to enjoy one of the most spectacular descents of any train journey in the world. We were approaching Cathedral Mountain with enough notice from Kim for the camera hawks to get into position and select shot angles. I pointed away from it, past the Kicking Horse River flowing far below, and across to the north, telling Riley, "Toward the end of our travels, we'll spend a night down there in a lodge tucked in the woods."

"Looks like it's all trees," he said. "You sure there's a lodge?"

"Yup. Cathedral Mountain Lodge would be a great place to wrap up our trip."

"Whatever..." His feigned indifference was surely inherited from me. Despite my years of practice, though, he was closer to perfecting it.

Riley waved to attract Kim's attention to ask if he might have another smoothie. Smiling a promise, but not distracted, Kim announced we were about to enter a long tunnel that would turn us 270 degrees *inside* Cathedral Mountain. This was the start of the slow-descent Spiral Tunnels (at the preferred 2.2 percent grade), a product of Swiss ingenuity that in 1909 replaced the original route of 1884, the dangerously steep Big Hill (a staggering 3.5 to 4.4 percent grade, difficult to ascend or descend with steel on steel). The Spiral Tunnels would take us through their curves within Mount Ogden as well. "The new circular route doubled the hill's original 13 kilometres, that's 8 miles of track, adding immeasurable safety," said Kim.

That it was an engineering marvel didn't much impress Riley. What mattered was that he got to the observation deck in time for a ride through the tunnel. He knew kids under the age of twelve were not to be outside alone, so his hand grabbed my sleeve. "Come on," he said, "this is like the longest tunnel in the Rockies." (I opted not to mention that the Connaught Tunnel, near Revelstoke, is much longer...)

James Hill, one of the early Canadian-American railway executives, did not share Riley's enthusiasm for a tunnel here. "What we wants [*sic*] the best possible line, shortest distance, lowest grades, and least curvature we can build. We do not care enough for Rocky Mountains scenery to spend a large sum of money developing it." Hill retained a profanity-spewing American engineer, "Hells Bells" Rogers, to undertake surveys and route recommendations. Not all of his ideas were greeted with enthusiasm by those responsible for construction. When crews reached this point in 1884, they ignored Major Rogers's recommendation that they drill a 1,400-foot (425-metre) tunnel, build across rockslides with house-size boulders, and figure out a way to tunnel under a glacier without destabilizing it. Howling winds and winter blizzards brought temperatures to -40° Fahrenheit (also -40° Celsius). Even more unacceptable was the year-long delay Rogers's proposal would mean. The builders opted for running the rails (and future trains) straight down Big Hill to the new town of Field.

All that would change after mishaps made ongoing operations untenable. But when first constructed, the tracks on Big Hill heralded an era of misfortune and derring-do. "It was the beginning of a quarter-century of hell-bent-for-leather railroading, when engineers rode the wood-burning engines with one hand on the gear bar, the other on the sand valve, and brakemen used an axe handle to set the hand brakes," wrote journalist Vera Fidler in *Canadian Frontier* magazine in the 1970s. Her story comes to mind every time I hear of a train mishap. A relative of hers, engineer Jimmy Fidler, once safely took a runaway train the length of Big Hill, an adventure she recounts in the same article. He pulled whistle blasts to warn the switch-tenders he was "Coming through!" The prescribed speed for descent was 8 miles (12 kilometres) per hour over an expected forty-two minutes. Fidler's runaway train made it in seventeen minutes. In a telegram marked "Rush," he was fired for his efforts.

ZEB (SHORT FOR ZEBULON) served as guest services manager with Rocky Mountaineer. "My childhood dream," he told me, "was to work for *National Geographic*. Their photographs epitomized a worldliness I could only imagine."

He then told me about a *National Geographic* photographer who had been a passenger.

"If I understand this correctly," she said to Zeb, as the eastbound train they were on approached the lower entrance for the Spiral Tunnels, "the train goes over half a mile inside Mount Ogden. And it goes nearly two-thirds of a mile within Cathedral Mountain. Right?"

"That's it," said Zeb. "It curls, then straightens, and curls again. From above, it can be seen crossing the river and going under the highway between the two mountains."

"That's the shot I want!" said the photographer. "How would I find the most unusual place to see tomorrow's train heading west through these tunnels?"

"It's a bit of a hike," Zeb told her. "But I could take you to an amazing overlook."

"Will you?" she asked. "I can pay you."

The next day Zeb guided the photographer on a deer trail to an outcrop with a view of the train threading the tunnels. She took superb pictures. As they were packing up to leave, two young hikers arrived off the trail. One said, "It's a surprise to see anyone else up here."

The photographer replied, "*We* are with *National Geographic. We're* on assignment."

Zeb says it was the highlight of his career. "I worked for *National Geographic* for a day. And *our* photograph was published in *National Geographic Traveler* magazine."

RILEY STOOD ON the observation deck as the train rattled through the mountain's interior of rock and rail. He had his phone's camera ready to go during the entire ride inside Cathedral Mountain. He recorded black rock being turned grey by the interior lights of the coaches. His audio recorded grinding wheels. He glimpsed a glow from the train's distant headlamp as our elevation slowly lowered by 50 feet (15 metres). We could practically smell the fumes when we watched his video later.

The current train manager, Ira, was standing beside Riley. "You're about to get great pictures of the railway and the highway." Riley would not let the train's snaking under the highway or crossing the river distract him. Enthralled and focused, he was propped in position for our upcoming entry into Mount Ogden's tunnel.

Minutes passed, Riley's eye to the camera the entire time. "I didn't feel like we were turning," Riley said to Ira as the train emerged again into daylight, having actually circled twice on our spiral descents and ended up heading west, as had been our direction upon entering higher up.

RILEY AND I took our seats in the dining car for a breakfast served by Jennifer and Jeremy. "Grampa'll eat anything except onions," Riley announced when they offered him a menu. I've read that our bodies— not our taste buds—determine what foods we intensely dislike by way of warning us away from allergies, if we listen. I listen anytime a chopped or diced or sprinkled onion appears. Yet, incongruously, I salivate at the delicious smell of fairground fried onions.

Two women from Austin, Texas, sat across from us. They appeared as two frames from a time-lapse picture. Colleen, middle-aged, offered her name, and said, "Mom has wanted to be on this train for years. I've been busy with my career. I run an auto parts company. My brothers and sisters couldn't get away with her for long trips. Then, I realized, this isn't long. And we shouldn't keep putting it off. So, here we are."

Mom, who didn't offer her name, nodded. "This train's popular talk in Texas. Might be famous around the world, I guess. We've got Rocky Mountains in the States, but they're not as grand as these. We've got no train like this one either."

"Americans know how to make businesses work," said Colleen. "But Amtrak's numbers have fallen over the years. They don't make money. Always need government subsidies. I like Amtrak. It's just not fancy travel, is all."[5]

"Amtrak's noble," I said. "They have a mandate for dedicated routes, and that's a tough way to make a profit. I've ridden them often—most recently the *City of New Orleans*, and I liked that particular journey a lot. Well, not the food."

Jennifer appeared with our meals right on cue. The blueberry pancakes went in front of Colleen, with a splash of colour courtesy of the grilled tomatoes. I smelled my cheddar soufflé before it was at the table. I once heard a chef say, "Aroma is the soul of a meal." I jabbed at the roasted potatoes the moment the plate landed.

"This food, the views. It's all so different from other trains we've been on," said Mom.

Colleen looked around and said, "I'll need this image as therapy next week when I'm back riding my desk in Austin."

Mom had heard Riley mention we had stayed in Banff for two days. She and Colleen had been at the Whyte Museum in Banff, and when I mentioned we had too, Mom said, "Do you realize Catharine Whyte was a society girl from Massachusetts? She used to date John Rockefeller the third. Then she moved to Banff."

Mom, it turned out, used to be a schoolteacher. That explained her ability to sound as if quoting verbatim. I welcomed her rendition: "Catharine Robb met Peter White—with an 'i' not a 'y'; not sure why he changed the spelling around that time—at Boston Arts School. She was a debutante. He was the son of a railway worker from Banff. It was 1925.

They fell in love. She moved to the Rockies. They painted. Hiked. He photographed. They climbed. Painted more. They collected artifacts. Now you have the Whyte Museum, built around their original log home."

There was more. The Whytes' paintings portrayed wilderness settings new to European eyes, or indeed any eyes except those of the Stoney Nakoda who guided their expeditions.

Riley added, "There was an old bearded guy in one of the museum photos. Well, lotsa old guys... One looked like Grampa so I told Grampa to grow a beard on our trip. See..." He scuffed the stubble on my chin, and we both laughed.

"Whyte intrigued me," said Colleen, ignoring my beard—and Riley's interruption. "Many women travelled in these mountains in the late 1800s, early 1900s. They were extraordinarily independent of family, of men. Did you come across a Mary Vaux?"

I'd not.

"She was one of them. About my age. She was out of Pennsylvania. She climbed mountains around here, writing, chipping at rocks, and taking photographs, sketching. Her husband, Walcott, had something to do with the Smithsonian in D.C., but she was here before they were married. I saw a picture of her with a camera, and I wanted to be the woman in that photograph," said Colleen.

Mom chipped in, "The mountains were populated by Indigenous women who trudged hillsides not for sport but for necessity; not to take photographs but to survive; not to sketch but to find berries for their family."

Mom was on a conversational roll. "I've come to respect three American women I'd never heard of until two days ago. Mary Vaux came to the Rockies from Philadelphia with her family as a youngster and made repeated trips as an adult after 1887; Mary Schäffer also came from Pennsylvania, making her first visit to the Canadian Rockies in 1889; and Catharine Whyte arrived from Massachusetts in 1930. They rode horseback, and made men try to keep up with their climbing.

stamina. They wrote memoirs. Think about those skilled, determined, independent women."

I waited a triple drumbeat, accurately anticipating what Mom said next: "Just like Colleen."

# — 5 —

WE WERE IN MOUNTAINS once thought to be impenetrable, and therefore inhospitable to the notion of railway passage. The tenacity of explorers, surveyors, engineers, and construction workers carving a way through proved otherwise.

The tunnels and passes have names to honour many of the Caucasian men (no women, and few non-European people or labourers) who played a role in the CPR's development. I regret there is not one named after surveyor Alfred Perry—perhaps someone may petition to have Rogers Pass renamed Perry Pass. Historian Richard Thomas Wright told me that he'd once met Perry. Or, more properly, Wright said he'd "met what sense of him remains 120 years after his death."

As Wright saw it, "sometimes explorers come close to having their hunches validated, their paths followed—and their names embossed in history books. Sometimes surveyors get overlooked despite being the first to walk into passes that bear the name of someone who came later but walked farther."

Alfred Perry missed out on the recognition lottery. Wright "met him" when "digging dusty," as he terms riffling through newspaper clippings, card files, obituaries, letters, reports, trial bench notes, and reminiscences about the man—all manner of documents except a photograph. "Right before my eyes emerged a fully formed image for one of Canada's forgotten mountain men, a 'well-known explorer' to his contemporaries," said Wright. "Now? Who talks of Perry?"

In 1858, Perry was among the settlers known as the Overlanders who traipsed across the mountains in search of new lives. He left scribbled journals he'd jotted beside his campfires, and they depict the charm of exploring and the drudgery of travel along routes known only to Indigenous hunters. He sought mountain passes that could be used for trade, be that via pathways, roads, or eventually railway routes. His contemporary prospector Timoleon Love said, "Perry? Sure I knew him, a downright, down east Yankee, the most determined fellow I've ever met. I met him on the Quesnel River in '60. He had a claim there but got kind of fed up and kicked his rocker and tools into the river." Another prospector, Pierre Pambrun, said, "Perry and I found gold near Jasper's House. Everyone knew him. He was what you'd call a 'celebrated character.'"

Celebrated? Not now. Almost, though.

In 1865, Perry worked in New Westminster as assistant to Walter Moberly, a thirty-three-year-old engineer who had gone broke building part of the Cariboo Wagon Road and later became assistant surveyor-general to oversee explorations east of Kamloops. Moberly said, "When Perry worked for me, he was between gold rushes." The egotistical, short, impulsive Moberly could not have chosen a more opposite associate. In Moberly's words, Perry was "a powerful man, tall, lean, kind of quiet spoken," befitting his mountain-man persona and extensive knowledge of the region.

The government tasked Moberly with locating a trade route suitable for a road, perhaps a railway, from Fort Kamloops east to the Columbia River and beyond, already surmised to be a critical portion of any eventual mountain passage. Moberly and Perry headed east from the north arm of Shuswap Lake. Reaching the Columbia River, they embarked in a hollowed-out log on a swift and dangerous river journey that ended at Big Eddy, now Revelstoke. Moberly noticed bald eagles flying westward up a stream. So they pushed west, discovering and naming Eagle Pass. Moberly blazed a tree, and with surveyor's chalk wrote, 'This is the route for the Overland Railway.' Twenty years later the CPR ran steel through where Moberly and Perry had hiked.

Wright told me that in June 1866 Perry and Moberly were again out searching, this time for an eastern pass through the Selkirk Mountains. While Moberly lay sick with mountain fever, Perry went up the Illecillewaet River. "Moberly and Perry had investigated this river the previous fall. At a fork they'd chosen to turn north, and found it unsuitable," Wright said. Eight months later Perry hiked only partway along the easterly fork. "Quite frankly, he blew it," said Wright. "Perry decided the route was not suitable, and went no further. He was wrong."

Years later when the CPR came through this pass at the Illecillewaet River headwaters, Moberly became miffed by Major Rogers being widely recognized for recommending the pass, which, unsurprisingly, became known as Rogers Pass. Moberly argued that he and Perry had first detected the route. Alas, Moberly's earlier report was clear—they had given up before determining a pass. History can be unflattering to explorers who don't leave their names as markers: both the CPR and the Trans-Canada Highway today use Eagle Pass, another missed opportunity for attribution by Moberly or Perry.

AFTER BREAKFAST, we were back in our upper-level seats. Riley scoured the scenery hoping to spot a lynx or cougar. I nagged him, "Having a good time with Grampa?"

"Barely," he'd replied, twitching his nose to gently alert me that I was veering toward self-congratulation.

He moved into video game mode, which bothered me given our magnificent surroundings. I nudged him, thinking that would distract him from the screen and make him look outside the window. After an hour he surfaced like someone who'd been submerged under a waterline. I worried he might get gamer-bends if he re-emerged too quickly. But he was happy, and my opinion irrelevant.

The woman ahead of us peered into our space. Apparently she didn't feel her opinion to be irrelevant. "There were a lot of women and kids your age living in hard circumstances in these mountains," she said to Riley, uninvited.

He sat upright, paying polite attention. "Grampa talked about women in the mountains over breakfast." His tone was respectful but clearly did not invite further comments from her. She sat down. Riley relaxed, curled into his seat, and cuddled up to his tablet as one would a teddy bear.

WITHIN MINUTES, Riley had passed between my knees and the seat in front of me to get to the aisle. "I'm heading to the deck. Wanna come? Or are you going to sit here with your nose in a book?"

As soon as we stepped outside, Riley snuck into the corner railing spot vacated by a man my age who turned to talk with us. Riley hugged the railing as though it was part of his personal journey toward independence. The train's movement blew his hair wild and made his eyes watery. He'd found his place in the sun.

The man he'd displaced smiled. He was the one I'd noticed earlier, wearing a hat in the style of railroad engineers, and covered with buttons and pins. They represented at least a dozen trains from around the world.

"Have you been on all of those?" I asked, eyeing his display.

"I wish," he said, though it sounded tinged with intention rather than regret. "Name's Ray," he said, shaking my hand. "I like slow travel."

"What'll be your next train?" I asked.

"Well, South Africa's *Blue Train* is a traveller's dream. To board in Pretoria and find you've got one of the suites with a standalone marble bathtub..." He paused, imagining, I supposed, either the twenty-seven-hour journey or the pleasurable scene he described. "It's long, it's sleek, and it's blue... a five-star appearance for a five-star train. It's almost as exciting to watch it roll by Kruger National Park as to be onboard. Well... not quite." Canada's mountains surrounded Ray, but his mind was rolling into Cape Town. "Right now," he said, eyes closed, "I'm playing backgammon in the club car, and in walks Omar Sharif..."

He blinked.

"Ah, and then there's the *Great Southern*," said an Aussie woman standing with her husband, both pulled our way by Ray's talk. "Australians do trains pretty well, though we've none like the *Rocky Mountaineer*. Finest of ours is the *Great Southern*. But it's not always available. When it runs, it's top drawer. A first-class sight, she is." Her husband added, "Our mates were on it. Splendid nights. Lush drinks. You sleep on board. You get out in the Hunter Valley for wine tours." The woman closed off their promotion: "Who wouldn't want to travel by train between Brisbane and Adelaide?"

"New Delhi to New Delhi, for me," piped up a man in his mid-twenties, his companion's arm entwined with his. "The *Palace on Wheels*, eight days out, Jaipur, Jodhpur, Agra... More... Return... We were on it a year ago. We'd go back, except there are too many other trains to ride."

Ray responded as if he were the moderator of a quiz show. "There are lots of trains in India. The refurbished ones are posh. They're quite into rail tourism there. What is the best one?"

"We rode the *Maharajas' Express*, a few years back," said the man's partner, his French accent adding a touch of elegance to his description of the train. The pair was from Atlanta, Georgia, and the same age; their wedding rings looked shiny new. "There's a reason the country markets itself as 'Incredible India.' Train waiters wore turbans with tufts. Six nights of train dinners, and we couldn't get enough. The train's won those 'Best of...' awards by the pail-load," he said. "Likely for the spicy cuisine."

"If you want style, you want the *Royal Scotsman*, a whole train known by the name of its engine," said Ray, conjuring images of being on a train in the Highlands, sipping scotch, feeling the glamour of being inside "coaches painted in polished ebony."

Ray turned my way. "Actually, *The Flying Scotsman*, that's one you should take your grandson on. He'd learn how trains got started in Wales, how England made them work, and how Scotland refined them. Then the world followed on. Get him on it from London to Edinburgh. It's a rolling time capsule." Watching Riley hang over the railing, his hair trailing wind, Ray said, "He looks like he doesn't want to miss a thing."

It was fine to muse about other train experiences, but I wanted to be in the now. I thought Riley's smile—and indeed those of other guests—reflected what Lady Macdonald, the wife of Canada's first prime minister, felt travelling here, below "lofty peaks smiling down on us, and never a frown on their grand faces!" I took in the setting as we roared over some of the most improbable railway tracks in the world, ones that made a country.

TRAIN TRAVEL IS a swaying conversation about past and present. It gives you time to ponder questions you couldn't entertain in the rush of a workday, such as, What if you asked for a wagon road and got a railway?

As Canada's Fathers of Confederation spent the summer of 1867 celebrating creating a country of four provinces—Nova Scotia, New Brunswick, Ontario, and Quebec—the United States was simultaneously expanding its own nation by purchasing Alaska from the Russians. As a result, the Colony of British Columbia had Americans to its north and south. To the west was the Pacific Ocean, and to the east were the Rocky Mountains and Rupert's Land, a swath of territory controlled by the HBC. The provinces of Alberta, Saskatchewan, and Manitoba did not yet exist as such.

The risk of the colony being consumed by its expansionist neighbour was real; the U.S. vision for a continental system of government was taking root. Culturally, British Columbians, like the United Empire Loyalists who fled to Nova Scotia, New Brunswick, Ontario, and Quebec following the American Revolution, still felt strong ties to the British Empire. But those ties needed a knot.

In the spring of 1870, a three-man delegation set off from B.C.'s capital, Victoria, for a visit to the distant Dominion of Canada's capital, Ottawa. To understand the delegation's mandate—*build us a wagon road to link us with Canada and we will become your newest province*—you need to understand their journey. They travelled from Victoria to San Francisco by steamer and took various trains, including the Union Pacific Railroad, to cross the United States before turning north to Ottawa. If they had wanted to stay in British territory for their journey, they would have had to travel by horse-drawn carriage, canoe, cart, boat, and, if the weather turned, dogsled.

The delegation planned to pitch their wagon road idea to Sir John A. Macdonald, but Canada's first prime minister was suffering from one of his numerous bouts of illness, so his minister of militia and defence, Sir George-Étienne Cartier, took the meeting. Much to the delegation's astonishment, Cartier promised more than a road. He said Canada would build a cross-country railway within the next ten years.

Although Macdonald was a keen railway proponent—his government had already hired Sandford Fleming to survey a possible route—it was Cartier who recognized the power of railways as a societal and economic driver. Twenty years earlier, as a politician in the government of what is now the province of Quebec, he had introduced a bill for the creation of the Grand Trunk Railway of Canada (GTR), which linked Montreal with what is now southern Ontario. And in 1872, it was Cartier's name on the bill to create the CPR. In part because of Cartier, Canada became a nation sewn together with threads of iron.

The Pacific Scandal (think of it as bribes to elected officials in attempts to influence the awarding of lucrative government contracts) brought down Macdonald's government after revelations that the privately owned CPR had funded Macdonald's Conservative Party in an effort to win the construction bid. This coincided with a major recession in the nascent country, making politicians quiver at the financial burden of building Cartier's promised railway. The rest of Canada, faced with possibly ruinous expenses with few tangible rewards, was tempted to let B.C. secede from the confederation it had just joined.

However, "Old Tomorrow," as Macdonald was known for his ability to achieve elusive consensus, found his way back to power. If the railway could be built as promised, B.C. would stay a part of Canada.

Macdonald turned to George Stephen, the president of the Bank of Montreal, who forged a syndicate of investors behind the vision.

The deal was finally done. Let the construction of the Canadian Pacific Railway begin.

IT'S BEEN SAID that writers should avoid alliteration, always. And here I encounter storytelling with Smith, Stuart, Simon, and Stephen unavoidably slipping off my fingertips. Let me sort them out. Donald Smith arrived in Canada in 1838 as an adventurous eighteen-year-old with nothing in his pocket aside from a letter of introduction from his mother's brother, John Stuart. Stuart had been Simon Fraser's assistant when tasked with finding a supply route over the Rockies, and his stories filled young Donald's imagination with aspirations of a life beyond that of working in a clerk's office. A day after Smith arrived in Montreal, he had a job grading beaver pelts for the HBC; eventually, he would become the HBC's governor and primary shareholder.

During his stint as the HBC's chief factor in Labrador, Smith finally met his first cousin, George Stephen, who also grew up in Banffshire, Scotland. Smith looked every bit a man from the northern wilds. By contrast, the elegantly dressed Stephen, a respected textile businessman in Montreal, embodied his earlier job as a draper's assistant. And yet they recognized in each other the canny knack of knowing how to make money make money. A decade later, Smith introduced Stephen, by now the president of Canada's Bank of Montreal, to James Hill, the aggressive one-eyed Irish steamboat entrepreneur who'd built a name for himself on the Red River. Smith and Hill wanted Stephen to invest in a struggling rail line, the St. Paul, Minneapolis and Manitoba Railroad. Their eventual success gave them the confidence to bid for the contract to build the CPR. The investment later threatened to be disastrous, but as a result of their acumen and courage, Smith, Stephen, and Hill became three of the most influential men in Canadian history.

Prime Minister Macdonald gave them one rule, from which they could not waver: the entire railway route had to remain in Canada. This, mythmakers have said, was Macdonald's "national dream," a phrase unequalled in describing a vision that became a country.

Hill thought an all-Canada route was too expensive. However, given the mandate, he lobbied to keep the line close to the 49th parallel that identified the Canada–U.S. border. There is an accepted truth: where-goeth the train so goeth the fortunes of land speculators and entrepreneurs, n'er-do-wells, and city builders. Hill knew the Americans were relentless in their drive to dominate North America's western economy, and if the CPR didn't occupy that terrain, the Americans would find a way to co-opt it.

There were two main route options to a Pacific Ocean terminus once across the Rocky Mountains and the new provinces interior: broadly, a choice between Bute Inlet and Burrard Inlet. The route that didn't happen would have taken the railway through the Rockies via the Yellowhead Pass, and eventually alongside Bute Inlet, across a bridge to Sonora Island, and another span to Quadra Island and on to Vancouver Island, where it would head southward to terminate at Victoria. The route that did happen was 120 miles (200 kilometres) south of that and came alongside the river, canyon, and valley all named after Simon Fraser, to terminate in Port Moody on the eastern shore of Burrard Inlet (from where it would eventually move farther along the inlet to Vancouver).

To achieve his preferred approach, Hill hired the legacy-obsessed, tobacco-chewing "Hells Bells" Rogers to find a southern route through the Rockies instead of the more northern Yellowhead Pass. Hill also encouraged Stephen, as chair of the CPR, to lure William Cornelius Van Horne from his management post with the Chicago, Milwaukee, and St. Paul Railroad to become general manager of the CPR. And the decision was made to task American Andrew Onderdonk with constructing 300 miles (500 kilometres) of track, from Port Moody eastward to meet the rails being built westward from Montreal.

The national dream was underway.

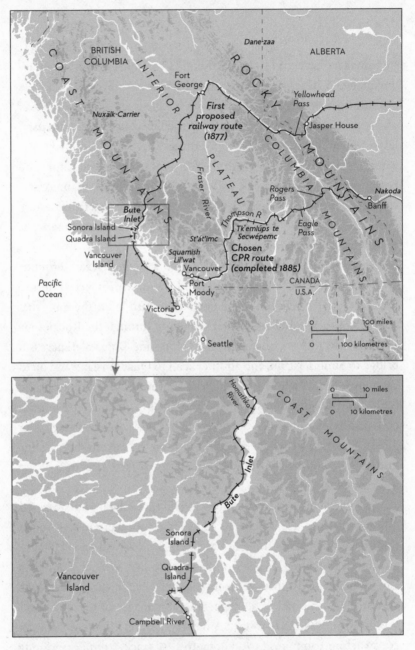

**MAP 4: PROPOSED AND APPROVED RAILWAY ROUTES THROUGH THE ROCKIES TO THE PACIFIC OCEAN**

In 1877, Sandford Fleming proposed a railway route through the Rocky Mountains via the Yellowhead Pass for the Canadian Pacific Railway, which declined it in favour of a route closer to the border of Canada and the U.S. Portions of Fleming's original idea were later developed for the Grand Trunk Pacific Railway as well as the Canadian Northern Railway, both eventually becoming part of the Canadian National Railway, though the island-hopping proposal never happened.

# — 6 —

OUR TRAIN TRAVELLED over an imaginary line in the wilderness. After we passed through the town of Field at the base of the Spiral Tunnels, Kim announced our shift between two of the world's twenty-four time zones. She advised us to adjust our watches by one hour "back in time," and we happily extended our day as we relinquished Alberta's Mountain Time Zone and accepted B.C.'s place in the Pacific Time Zone.

ACTIVE PICTURE TAKERS David and Susan from Melbourne, Australia, were seated beside us. Many of the highlights pointed out by the onboard staff were "train left," which was their side of the train. There was often a general leaning of passengers from one side of the train across their neighbours' chairs if that provided a better vantage for taking pictures. The opposite also occurred. As a result, Susan would often make her way over to our spot, or I would move into their space. I realized they were getting some great shots, ones that I'd enjoy having, so I asked if they'd send me a few of their pictures once they were home. A bouncing Riley said, "Use AirDrop," as he took my iPhone and activated it before I could ask what AirDrop was. He asked David if he could have his phone, and to "open it, please." Riley next borrowed Susan's phone and did likewise. "You're all now on AirDrop. Here's how you use it." He took a photo as we entered Golden, and showed three neophytes how to hold our phones close to one another and within his view, letting selected pictures transfer into the other person's collection.

OFTEN, TRAVELLING BY TRAIN feels as though the setting varies dramatically within miles or even minutes, bringing different terrain and fresh stories. That's what happened when we entered a valley in the Rocky Mountain Trench, its floor less than 2 miles (3 kilometres) wide at its narrowest and only five times that at its widest. Its length from Yukon to Montana is around 1,000 miles (1,600 kilometres). And the story the new setting brought to mind is alarming.

In the 1950s the U.S. Army Corps of Engineers proposed flooding significant portions of this trough where our train travelled; it was known as the North American Water and Power Alliance (NAWAPA) plan. The thinking went like this: Commercial and population demands of a growing economy in the United States could benefit from higher water flows through rivers such as the Colorado and the Yellowstone. The newly generous rivers could then be used as economic pumps. Mindful of the plentiful water supply in the state of Alaska that could provide the desired increase in water flow for those two rivers, American engineers focused on what lay between them: Canada's Rocky Mountain Trench.

It's simplistic to say that the proposal was, "Let's flood this part of Canada as a feeder route for American water heading south to American rivers." It was more like: "Let's build three hundred projects, many of them dams, along with rerouting natural river courses, displacing communities and Indigenous people's heritage sites, *and then* flood this part of Canada as a feeder route for the massive volume of water heading from Alaska into, and consistently swelling, the Colorado and Yellowstone Rivers, and use them for an endless supply of water and power." (I paraphrase . . .) Along with diverting major rivers, it would have created a 500-mile-long (800-kilometre) reservoir, which would have become as much an identifying feature of the land as are the mountains.

Enter environmental groups on both sides of the 49th parallel. Add thoughtful and forceful community leaders in both countries. Exit the NAWAPA planners.

The benefits of not proceeding with NAWAPA extend to my grandson's generation. Instead, Canada and the U.S. negotiated the Columbia

River Treaty, signed in 1961, which enabled more modest dam construction in the name of power supply as well as flood control, and with a nod to an emerging environmental awareness. A review of that plan's future is underway. While there is no expiry date, either country can give ten years' notice to abandon it, acting unilaterally, anytime after 2024. What isn't talked about anymore is the distortion of the Colorado River or the Yellowstone River that would have happened under NAWAPA, or the damage to the lives and livelihoods of those whose homes and families populate the Rocky Mountain Trench through which the *Rocky Mountaineer* was currently travelling.

OUR TRAIN CAME OUT OF a mountain's shadow. Sunlight glanced off the train. Riley swirled around from his perch on the deck, squinting into his camera. He lowered it, smiled at me, and then pushed his face back into the wind.

Ray, as ever present in his spot, as was Riley in his, said, "I'm happy rolling along."

"What makes you say that?" I asked.

"When I was a kid a little older than Riley, I read a story about a man named Van Horne who came to Canada to build this railway. It sounded like the toughest job in the world, full of adventure. I dreamed of seeing things when I was young that I'm only getting to enjoy when I'm older. No one can understand our train travels today without knowing the story of Van Horne."

Ray's British accent intensified into that of a storyteller, implying, *I know a bit about people who make trains run.* I was willing to listen.

IN 1856, ABRAHAM LINCOLN'S nascent campaign to become president of the United States brought him to the town of Joliet, Illinois. Students enrolled in a telegraph school at the city office were tasked with composing a report of his visit. One of them was thirteen-year-old William Van Horne.

Just before deciding to become a telegraph operator, young William drew a caricature of his school principal that earned him a beating

so severe that he decided never to return to school. He determined
to be in charge of his own education, a decision reinforced by a letter from one of the railroading men he encountered. "Your destiny
mostly lies in your own hands," the letter read. "Have some grand
and glorious object in view and not live as some live to eat drink
and sleep."

In railroading history, few men reached the pinnacles of success
enjoyed by William Cornelius Van Horne. It could be argued that without him, Canada's ambition of uniting the country from coast to coast
would have been thwarted by frustration. It's hard to imagine the skills,
stamina, and sheer stubbornness necessary to overcome one seemingly
insurmountable obstacle after another. Whether it was sinkholes that
swallowed train engines whole in Northern Ontario, mountain passes
that claimed the lives of men blasting their way through, an envious
mentor who hated being eclipsed, or politicians and investors who
balked at the rising costs, Van Horne tamed them all by dint of his
disposition.

After becoming the youngest railway superintendent in the U.S.
at the age of twenty-seven, Van Horne oversaw larger and larger train
companies. His innovative ways were brought to the attention of
George Stephen, the president of the CPR, which had just won the bid
to construct the railway—including a cash grant of $25 million and
25 million acres of land (over 10 million hectares). Stephen needed
Van Horne to push 650 miles of track (1,000 kilometres) through the
untamed Canadian Shield, 850 miles (1,300 kilometres) of prairie, and
500 miles (800 kilometres) of mountain in B.C.

By May 1881, Van Horne's predecessors had advanced only 131 miles
(210 kilometres) in the company's first year. Beginning on January 2,
1882, Van Horne worked feverishly to make good on his promise that
500 miles of track would be laid in the second year—even though it
drove his crews to mutinous exhaustion.

In today's idiom, Van Horne would be a micro-manager. No detail
about running a railway was too small for him to learn about. Unhappy

with the food on one of his train trips, the portly railwayman came up with a fancier menu that served CPR's guests for decades. He knew where every cent was spent. Prescient in his understanding of the railway's future, he ensured passengers enjoyed the spectacular views in comfortable coaches. He later launched the CPR's telegraph and mail service and hotel chain (today's Fairmont Hotels).

His contemporaries may have appreciated Van Horne's disdain of self-aggrandizement, but it has left the generations that followed with a gap in our knowledge. Had Van Horne allowed someone to interview him for a biography, maybe then we'd know what he was thinking that morning of November 7, 1885, when he posed for a picture of the last spike being hammered into the rail that joined the CPR's westward and eastward construction projects.

The last spike did not mark the end of Van Horne's decision making. Soon, he visited the western terminus, Port Moody. While there, he became enchanted by the lands to the west, nestled along Burrard Inlet, and between Coal Harbour and English Bay, where pods of civilization were putting down roots with home-spun names such as Hastings, Granville, even Deadman's Island, and epithets such as Gastown. "This is destined to be a great city," wrote Van Horne, "perhaps the greatest in Canada."

To the disappointment of Port Moody's bustling community, Van Horne secured that destiny by moving his terminal city to the coastal mill town, declaring, "We must see to it that it has a name commensurate with its dignity and importance." He named it Vancouver, after Captain George Vancouver. The provincial government deferred to Van Horne, granting 6,000 acres (2,400 hectares) of land to the CPR by way of encouragement. While Port Moody and Victoria each grieved their loss of stature as the railway's proposed Pacific terminus, Van Horne's deep-water port at Vancouver also prepared to become home docks for the CPR's steamship empire.

# — 7 —

EVERY TRIP BEGINS with dreams. I knew nothing of Riley's, but my own included one shaped by his presence. I wanted the trip to make a difference to his life. Trains move across a geographic stage with actors coming in and out of scenes, prompting thoughts about where one is going, physically and life-wise. Train travel brings out unexpected truths because it enforces spells of pondering. Have I pursued the dreams I had when I was Riley's age? Would ten-year-old Rick approve of mature Rick's life? Would mature Riley decades hence acknowledge that ten-year-old Riley's train journey had influenced his life? I realized that my own train journey as a youngster motivated my wanderlust, and a balking at being ordinary. Such truths can hide from an adult, but not from a child. I'm old enough to ask if I had let go of my dreams, but not bold enough to suggest anyone else has.

THE *ROCKY MOUNTAINEER* pulled off the main tracks onto a siding and slowed to a stop.

"We've a freight train to let pass," said Kim. "We'll get to see what it's hauling."

"Why do we wait for it?" asked one of the Aussies.

"Sometimes freight trains move on through, especially if they're on their way to meet a ship waiting at harbour. The railways give our passenger trains priority whenever possible, though, which is most often. We work well together. CPR moves a lot of westbound goods from eastern Canada and the Prairies along these tracks, much of it heading to Asia." Depending on the time of year, those goods could be grain from Saskatchewan, rock-oil from Alberta, or forest products from B.C. Given their comparative safety and speed, trains are also the preferred means of transport for eastbound imports from Asia.

Riley swayed theatrically in his seat as an eastbound train went by, his perception of rocking coming from the swiftness of the passing train. "Whew…" he breathed. Closed containers and boxcars hid their cargo.

"As we get closer to Vancouver you'll often see empty coal cars eastbound to mines for reloading and returning to the coast for shipment across the Pacific," said Ariel. With that, the rumbling stopped. Calm arrived in the tailwind of the train that had passed. With a shunt, our train took up slack and gained speed. We re-entered the main trackage.

I'd asked Ray to join me for a coffee, and Riley came along, bribed by a smoothie, despite my growing unease about how he'd burn off all that energy. We settled into an empty booth in the vacant dining room.

"The whole idea of rails is to keep something on an intended course," said Ray, with a look to Riley.

I knew that. Who didn't? I wanted to move the conversation along. "You said trains first happened in Britain in the early 1800s. What happened next?"

"Whoa," he said. "We've had tubs on wheels in grooves long before that. The Romans had them. The Greeks had them twenty-seven hundred years ago. An animal pulling a wheeled cart through gutters was the grandfather of modern trains."

"Grandfather?" asked Riley.

"Forerunner then," said Ray. "If you think train travel began with steam engines, you're wrong. Train travel began in dirt ruts."

OK, I was wrong.

"And another thing," he said. "You think trains began with steel rails? Not so. There were wooden rails in the 1500s. People stacked goods on flat surfaces atop wheels, and pulled them along the rails. Austria had them."

He recited the evolution of the track system: "Rutways, cartways, tramways, wagonways, trackways, *then* railways." He explained that mining had played a significant role. They'd have a cave of coal or tunnel of ore and need to get the motherlode down the side of a mountain. A barrow on wooden rails kept it from falling away. Engineers of the day added flanges on the side of wheels to keep them from slipping off. "Where'd you think the handbrake came from?" he asked.

I hadn't.

Ray chuckled in anticipation of his explanation to Riley. "Boiling water had been tossing the lid off English pots for centuries before anyone thought to harness the power of a steaming kettle. Once the Brits caught onto that in the 1700s, building a steam engine wasn't far behind."

This all made sense to me: steam-pushed pistons force a drive wheel to rotate and in doing so push coupling rods to in turn push the main arms that rotated locomotive wheels along the tracks. I simplify, but that's the gist of it.

"A British engineer made the first steam train chug in 1804. That was on a cold February day in Wales. Man's name was Trevithick."

Why don't we better celebrate such an easy to remember name? Ray turned to Riley. "Look at pictures of Japan's bullet train, the Shinkansen, as the network's known, or Europe's *Train à Grande Vitesse*—French for high-speed train and truncated to TGV—and think of how far we've come in the two hundred years since Trevithick."

"I was on the TGV," said Riley. "It went 300 kilometres an hour."

I did the math: 300 kilometres is 185 miles per hour, but I'd read that under test conditions, the TGV has topped almost twice that speed.

"And it no longer shakes itself apart like the old locomotives did," said Ray, with an acknowledging smile to Riley. "Trains once had names like *Puffing Billy* and *Catch Me Who Can*, but no one ever thought they'd go very fast. A *Tom Thumb* locomotive pulled America's first public train along the Baltimore and Ohio Railroad in 1830. That's B&O, one of the railways in Monopoly." In my prejudgment that kids today ignore board games and fairy tales, I waited for Riley to ask, "Who's Tom Thumb?" and "What's Monopoly?" But I was wrong.

While getting goods to market highlighted the value of the new invention, the real excitement came with passenger travel. Ray said, "To the average person, the thrill was not watching the new gizmo, but the chance of riding one." Soon, a 30-mile (50-kilometre) town-to-town service was sufficient to encourage building private coaches for personal use. Britain, France, and most of the rest of Europe caught passenger train fever. The United States was not far behind.

The U.S. improved upon the locomotives, enhanced passenger and freight cars, and for the next century took a lead in transcontinental railways, developing networks around hub cities. Cross-Atlantic sharing (or stealing) of ideas, patents, and progress was constant. The age of trains had arrived—particularly the glamorous era of passenger rail travel.

OUR TRAIN STOPPED at Revelstoke, where the operating subdivision shifts. Mountains loomed around us. Everyone gazed through the glass roof at peaks in every direction. You could see everywhere. "The Glass Train," one of the Aussies called it. Then he added something I caught but didn't fully appreciate at the time: "You can see your way through history."

A RAILWAY'S SPUR LINES are like a river's tributaries. They flow into the main, swelling the major course with the movement of people. At first glance, spurs and tributaries seem the lesser story. They are not; they are just less well known. Spurred commerce and resulting travel helped settle the young province of British Columbia with fascinating pioneers, most of their contributions lost, forgotten, or unfairly neglected. The photographer Mattie Gunterman, for example, made her way to just south of where our train rolled, and it was a spur line that helped her community develop.

Mattie Gunterman would have loved Instagram. She'd definitely be an influencer—someone whose photos of themselves pulling off exciting escapades in far-flung places inspire thousands of followers to live big. Born in Wisconsin in 1872, such immediate fame was not to be, which is not necessarily a bad thing. Her surviving photographs—half of which we'd call selfies—have earned Gunterman something far less ephemeral than thumbs-up likes and heart-shaped emoticons. They immortalized her life, and the lives of the decent and tough men, women, and children around her.

Take Mattie's portrait of her and her husband, Will, in the spring of 1899. In an age when most photos were taken in a studio with painted backdrops filling in for real life, she set up her four-by-five plate camera on a "corduroy road" laid down through the spindly forest. Will is her pack mule, heavily burdened with all the gear they'd need as they camped and worked their way from Seattle to their new home in B.C.'s West Kootenay mountain ranges, a journey of almost 700 miles (1,100 kilometres), all on foot. Mattie's long, heavy skirt would have protected her somewhat from the swarming blackflies and mosquitoes, but her stylish hat is a reminder that societal norms followed women into the wilderness. A childhood illness had made her frail, but on one shoulder is a canvas bag with their clothes, and in one hand is the camera case she lugged from snow-covered mountaintops to the depths of silver mines. Neither Mattie nor Will is smiling in this photograph.

As they literally worked their way into British Columbia—Mattie as a laundress and cook at logging and mining camps, Will doing physical labour—the region at the end of their trek was experiencing a boom, thanks in large part to the CPR's decision to build a line from Kootenay Lake to the south end of Trout Lake. Although the line was shorter than first promised, its construction employed hundreds of men and made possible the development of a hundred silver mines that provided work to thousands more. Construction workers melded in camp with hewers of the region's natural resources.

The miners and loggers earned perhaps $3.50 a day and got to enjoy Mattie's cooking. Although her photos reveal both the heavy toiling and fun times of the camp, her starkest image is of two dozen men lined up outside a hotel. A rope links them together, as if they were horses about to pull a nearby sleigh through the snow. In the sleigh were the bodies of two miners who had been killed while trying to rescue a fellow miner overcome by noxious fumes.

Incredibly, Mattie took these photos simply for personal fulfillment. Most of her collection was destroyed when an arsonist set fire to her home in 1927, but luckily, she had always made second albums of her photos for her son Henry, who had also kept 300 of her glass plate negatives. Finding Gunterman's art nearly a century after it was created was a fluke that eventually ensured recognition of her as a noteworthy part of settling this province. Those photographs and negatives would have remained buried in Henry's attic were it not for three enterprising men who travelled to Beaton, B.C., in the early 1960s in search of stories and photos of a place that was about to be flooded to feed a new hydroelectric plant near Castlegar. One of them was Ron D'Altroy, the historical photograph archivist at the Vancouver Public Library, where the collection is preserved and Gunterman's skill recognized.

"CONSIDER THE CRAFTSMANSHIP required to build trains that people would travel on in comfort and style," Ira, the onboard train manager, told a group of guests deep in conversation about the olden days. "Making coaches was as difficult as making engines."

The exposed trucks of locomotives, the multiple wheels and iron bolts, and greasy parts on a locomotive always look in photographs like they want to rattle loose. By comparison, the exterior of even modest passenger coaches of the era look refined. Uniform siding on all coaches was a cost-efficient way to buy materials and offered visual continuity. Painting coaches all one colour meant one mix of paint, a budget-satisfying bulk purchase that applied a sleek, attractive march of matching coaches.

One of the Atlanta men said, "Assuring comfort when travelling is my main concern. I bring along my pillow, even on trains."

"'Travel and Sleep in Safety and Comfort' is something we take for granted on overnight trains," said Ray. "But the saying came about as trains improved from a reputation for ache-inducing jolts to pleasant transportation. You can thank George Pullman for that."

GEORGE PULLMAN STOOD OUT from other railway coach manufacturers right from the beginning. He set the standard, and was associated with commodious railway travel in North America and Europe by the mid-nineteenth century and well into the twentieth. At the peak of the railway boom, more than 25 million passengers a year travelled on train coaches built by the Pullman Company. Pullman's eye for finery soon caught the attention of the man who would build the *Orient Express*, which eventually deployed a version of Pullman's "Palace Cars" in Europe.

Train coaches did not travel great distances until stronger engines, supply depots for water and coal, and restaurants along the routes were in place to cater for passenger needs. For the first overnight journeys, most passengers slept sitting up, crumpled, hunched, and uncomfortable. In 1853, just such an overnight experience—45 miles (70 kilometres) along Lake Erie between Buffalo and Westfield— spurred twenty-two-year-old George Pullman to design seats that unfolded into berths. He added a unit that pulled out from the ceiling to give an upper berth, thus maximizing the space. Curtains for privacy completed the transformation of overnight train travel.

Pullman refined his construction techniques for years before forming a company in the 1860s with the express purpose of offering comfortable travel in carpeted coaches with upholstered seats. He re-engineered wheel systems for quieter rides. And his coaches were respected for their courteous porters resplendent in company attire. Often they were former slaves, intentionally given a chance at earning good money and respect.

The Pullman Company, founded as the Pullman Palace Car Company in 1867, introduced dining rooms and parlour cars with deluxe appoint-

ments. Their talented waiters and chatty conductors told tales, many
made up on the spot to suit the passengers' interests—something I wondered about aboard the *Rocky Mountaineer*. What would it have taken
for someone to spontaneously point out "Mount Riley" if an inquisitive
kid asked too many questions about too many mountain names?

Pullman interiors were special. Seats were wide, adorned with
armrests, and able to recline. They were positioned for viewing out the
windows (which may sound obvious now but wasn't always a consideration in those days). Buffed wood, tooled leather, soft drapes, and the
ubiquitous steward heralded the care and attentiveness all high-end
train services provide today.

A SCOTSMAN WAS standing beside me on the observation deck. He'd
told me he suffers from "airport fatigue" and has taken to avoiding
them. He was short and had a sassiness I liked. "You all think this is a
wonderful train," he said to half a dozen of us, as we passed through a
forest of cedars. "I know wonderful," he claimed. "This here is smooth.
You want wonderful? I'm a steam train man. Give me belching smoke,
unsteady tracks, grit in my eyes, and a beer in the vestibule."

One man's rugged elegance is another man's anguish. We laughed
with him; the images he conveyed were easier on the mind than in reality.

"Riley," he called, not the first grandparent-of-others to take casually
to grandparent-sharing with me aboard the train, "we're coming to a
place where a kid not much older than you witnessed completion of
this mighty railway."

"Witness . . . like for the FBI?" asked Riley.

"I mean he watched the comedy show when they drove the last
spike. A teenager, he was. Just a kid."

WITH HIS MUDDIED RIGHT BOOT on a wooden tie, left thumb hooked
into his pants pocket, the boy in question looks as if he felt he had
every right to be posing alongside some of the men who, against all
odds, had wrestled a wilderness into a country.

Cheeky devil.

It was 9:22 on the morning of November 7, 1885, and the last spike was about to be hammered into the ribbon of rail to join B.C. with the rest of Canada. Edward Mallandaine, born in the year Canada became a country—1867—stood directly behind Sir Donald Smith, who had his left foot perched on a rail tie. But unlike Edward, Smith had reason to steady himself. The CPR's chief financier had botched his first attempt to drive home the iron nail to mark the place. The polite crowd did not laugh out loud, but many were amused. He needed to be more careful the second time. Smith leant over the railbed, spike maul in hand.

Edward was determined to sneak into this photo precisely because he had failed in his first attempt to be part of Canada's history. His dream had been to help quash the North-West Resistance led by Louis Riel. In May 1885, when word came that Riel had surrendered, Edward was still high in the Kootenay mountains that separated him from his imagined chance at glory hundreds of miles to the east on the Prairies. As a younger boy, he'd devoured books of derring-do. Now, unable to fulfill boastful promises he'd made when leaving his home on Vancouver Island, his impending return made him feel like a failure.

Sure, Edward could tell family and friends about getting his scalp singed as he ran away from a forest fire. He could brag about meeting the Governor General of Canada, who offered Edward a job on his estate in England as a reward for thwarting three thieves. He could tell them he was coming home with $200 in his pocket and his virtue intact despite months among the hard-drinking men who risked life and limb to cut a rail path. That wasn't enough for Edward. He wanted a demonstrated moment in history.

Edward had been in Farwell, now Revelstoke, when he heard there would be a ceremonial driving of the last spike, 30 miles (50 kilometres) east in a place called Craigellachie.

If ever there were a rallying cry for the obstinate and stubborn, it was "Craigellachie!" The name of a fiercely defended rock in Scotland, it was mentioned in a poem much loved by Donald Smith who, when taunted with the futility of building a railway through the Rockies, would respond with that one word. To his friend William Van Horne, Craigellachie became synonymous with belief in the railway's eventuality. Van Horne arbitrarily created a station called Craigellachie, determined it would be the spot where the crews coming from the west and east would join together the last 23 feet (7 metres) of rail. He didn't have a place predetermined, just its name.

Edward's resolve to be in Craigellachie strengthened when he bumped into Duncan Ferguson, who had a contract to provide ties for the railway. Edward and Ferguson had met on the boat from Victoria to New Westminster on the first leg of Edward's journey. Ferguson admired the boy's pluck.

Ferguson regaled Edward with descriptions of the dignitaries arriving on CPR locomotive No. 148 for the driving of the final spike. Sandford Fleming, the surveyor and engineer who found a route through the Rockies, would be there, as would Major Rogers, whose Selkirk Mountain pass had won the day, and Sam Steele of the North West Mounted Police. Steele's force had worked dawn to dusk, and well into the night, to protect workers and the railway.

While these notables would ride to Craigellachie in comfort, Edward's only option was a flatcar carrying the final load of rails. It was a horrible, sleepless journey. The railbed had been newly laid, giving it no time to settle for a smooth ride. The snow was so wet that the engine couldn't make it up the grade into Eagle Pass. The engineer decided to leave Edward's flatcar behind to lighten the load. Undaunted, Edward jumped onto one of the two remaining railcars and shivered his way to Craigellachie.

That morning he found himself standing beside Ferguson as Rogers's crew put the last rail in place, and the official photographer, Alexander Ross, readied his camera. It wasn't hard to tell that Edward didn't belong among the top-hatted titans realizing the "Canadian Dream" of a national railway. Someone shouted at him to get out of the way.

"Let him in, he can stand right there," replied Ferguson. And, giving Edward a moniker that would secure his place in history, Ferguson said, "Don't you know that's the Craigellachie Kid?"

WE HEARD KIM'S ANNOUNCEMENT that our train would slow to "roll-by speed" because of a cairn that marked "The Last Spike." We slowed to 5 miles (8 kilometres) an hour out of respect for everything it symbolized.

AFTER OUR TRAIN RESUMED SPEED, the Scot smiled at his own story. "I laugh when I hear about the CPR's last spike, as though a single pin hitched the country."

"It was pretty impressive," said Brenda, a woman whose trimly cut hair seemed in keeping with her clipped Midwest American accent.

"Ah, that's not what I laugh about," said the Scot. "What's funny is that there were five last spikes for Craigellachie! Count 'em. Five."

THERE WERE INDEED FIVE "LAST SPIKES": one was bent by a gaffe, one was tapped home then removed, one was driven separately a little down-line from the main event, one ceremonial spike didn't make it to the event and stayed in Ottawa, and—well, the fifth isn't much written about. So, where is it?

If you close your eyes, you can almost hear the "clang!" of metal against metal as Donald Smith hammered at the *first* last spike placed in the final foot of rail. Listen for the silence that came afterward when everyone realized the sixty-five-year-old had bent the iron nail—not the best way to symbolize the coming together of a nation. That *first* last spike was wrest from the frozen ground.

Smith cautiously tapped a *second* last spike into place, pausing just long enough for the photographer to take the most referenced picture in Canadian history. Holding the spike in place was "Hells Bells" himself. "He was so gleeful," remembers the Craigellachie Kid, "that he upended a huge tie and tried to mark the spot by the side of the track by sticking it into the ground."

Some of the navvies whose muscled arms and practised swings had helped pound 30 million spikes to build the railway weren't impressed with Smith being their representative for the pounding of notional spike 30 million-and-*one*. They posed for their own "last spike" photo up the rails, not too distant from the official proceedings. And their spike was hammered in without a miss. There was not a grey beard or top hat to be seen among those workers as that *third* "last spike" of the day hit home.

The *fourth* last spike never made it to the ceremony. It was in the possession of the country's Governor General. Lord Lansdowne, Queen Victoria's son-in-law, had hoped to do the honours by driving in a specially prepared silver spike. But he had to be in Ottawa that day, and the spike stayed with him.

Before the train left Craigellachie, the roadmaster, Frank Brothers, sensed that Smith's second spike was destined to become a collector's item. He didn't want the hassle of dealing with treasure hunters, so he removed it. (It was later presented to a future president of the CPR.) Understandably, it needed to be replaced by a workman in order to secure the rail. When that *fifth* last spike was knocked into place, the conductor yelled, "All aboard for the Pacific!" Canada's first transcontinental train rolled westward over the *real* last spike.

As the dignitaries celebrated on board, hundreds of workers stared at the departing train. Many could determine which spot held the last spike. Equipment for removing and replacing spikes lay all about, and most of them knew how to use it. Surely someone had the idea: "There sits the *real* last spike. I think I'll remove it and pass it along to my grandkids..."

So, where do you think the last spike connecting Canada coast to coast might be?

RILEY LED ME to the deck again. Brenda and her husband were there, quieted by their contentment. South of Shuswap Lake's shore is the semi-arid Okanagan wine region that stretches down B.C.'s dry zone into Washington State's fertile desert valleys. Skirting Sicamous we saw dozens of boats with cabins built atop a barge-like base—houseboats, floating about on the long, narrow lake like a loose village.

Watching Riley, Brenda said to me, "I've three grandkids and I've been thinking I'm going to take each of them travelling with just me. Friends *talk* about doing things like that. I'm going to be one of the ones who makes it happen."

A FRIEND RECENTLY TOLD ME that a log cabin he'd built in the hill to the east of our train tracks was going up for sale. It was made of large fir logs, with about 600 square feet (56 square metres) of living space. It would be an exciting escapade to buy it and move it to Silvertip Mountain near Hope where my wife and I have a secluded piece of land. I pointed out the general whereabouts of the cabin to Riley as the *Rocky Mountaineer* went by.

"We should build a log cabin, Grampa."

"One day," I said.

"You have a lot of 'one days...'"

AS WE APPROACHED Horseshoe Curve, my attention was drawn to a man whose confident bearing showed in his unyielding legs and a half-smile on a weathered face. He had a slight tan, which nicely set off eyes that absorbed rather than stared at the scenery. Ruffled slightly by the breeze, his sports jacket and pressed slacks seemed more fitting for an office. With his hands in his pockets, he looked calmly ready for whatever might come his way in life. I was lost in my own thoughts when I heard him ask, "What do you think of your travels with Riley?"

His phrasing brought to mind *Travels with Charley,* John Steinbeck's book about a journey with his compatriot dog. For the first time I thought of Riley as my sidekick, or me his. Turning, I replied, "You might better ask him what he thinks of his travels with Rick."

"I had a lucky summer as a child," said the man. "I was alone with my grandparents for two weeks. It didn't mean much to me then, except freedom from my parents. Looking back, it's when I took on my grandfather's confidence and my grandmother's patience."

He was not done. "Time passes so quickly now. I want to put my feet out and dig my heels in to slow it down. That's the lovely thing about train travel. Time slows. You can take in things you'd otherwise miss. Like this," he added, "Notch Hill."

"Why do they call it Notch?" Riley asked, suddenly making me aware that he'd been listening to the conversation between two "old" men.

"Because it goes through a notch in the hillside," he answered. "They lengthened the tracks to lessen the decline." The train seemed to pause with him. "If only we could do that in life."

The Japanese woman I'd noticed earlier with the empty seat beside her was there on the deck, leaning unobtrusively against a post. Her hair had a streak of black within a glamorous grey, and her travel suit was the burnt orange of a happy sunset. She had the allure of being the most widely travelled person aboard the train. I thought her name should be Michiko, which means "beautiful, wise child," even though her mysterious stance reminded me of Greta Garbo's infamous misquoted line, "I want to be alone."

ARIEL ANNOUNCED THAT we were approaching the mouth of the 110-mile (177-kilometre) -long Adams River, another tributary that lends its waters—and small fry—first to the Thompson River, then to the Fraser River and, eventually, the Pacific Ocean. There, each year's sockeye salmon swim in a convoluted but ultimately circular oceanic migration over their three to five years of life. Then—in a display of nature's marvel—they find their way back to the Fraser's muddy waters, swim upriver, hurl themselves over rapids and up fish ladders, and return not only to the Adams River but also to the specific stream that was their birthplace. They come back in order for the females to spawn eggs. That magic of migrating salmon has become so well known it's almost casual science.

What is perplexing to scientists is this: A hundred years ago the average survival rate of fertilized eggs becoming fry was four in one hundred. Today it is one in one hundred. The drop is concerning and a specific cause has not been identified. We do know there has not been a notable growth in the number of ducks or other fish that are predators, but they can also fall victim to warming water temperatures or smothering in silt in low water levels. Maybe they have not been fertilized, or maybe pollutants or a changing climate are compromising their chances of survival. Reversing any of those factors requires changes in public policy and prudent harvesting of salmon at sea.

WHEN WE ARRIVED in Kamloops, rain dampened our evening expectations of a walk about town, although the drizzle felt refreshing. A sign at the station informed us Montreal was 2,682 miles (4,300 kilometres) to the east and Vancouver 263 miles (423 kilometres) to the west.

As we transferred to the hotel, the self-identified "old boy" driving our bus said we should ignore the rain and walk anywhere we wished. "Most nights hundreds of people go for live music in the park. The band's name doesn't matter. Music does."

"Let's go find a steak for dinner, and then hit the park," I said to Riley when we settled into our room.

"I've got WiFi," he said. "I'm online with friends. We've got a game underway. You go."

"Come on..."

"No, thank you. I've got friends I haven't talked to in days. I organized this game. I gotta be there. Bye."

I was learning to share my time aboard with Riley's tablet entertainments, trying to see them as a simple differential in our ways, as real as the sixty-year difference in our ages.

The previous Christmas, Riley, his younger brother Declan, and his parents flew to Frankfurt, where Janice and I were living. On a train returning us from an overnight stay in a restored castle where Janice had taken all of us as her present, I commented negatively on the parents' frequent use of tablets to mute the children and give themselves time alone without interruption. Two weeks later, unbeknownst to me, Janice sent Sean and Hilary a picture of the *International New York Times* open fully and with me buried behind it. Her note to them said,

"It works just like the tablets for Riley & Declan. I bring home the newspaper each evening, give it to Rick, and I get a quiet hour alone without interruption." Touché.

I ordered room service, steak and salad. Riley's verbal commands to his competitors online sounded like assaults until I understood it was today's version of young leadership. He was shouting them into action using his deft geo-game wizardry. I heard their responses through his headset and realized his commands were respected like those of a general. I'd learned leadership skills on a sports field, in Scouting, and at summer camp. Was his development of similar skills with comrades any less valid because I didn't understand it? I'd long ago learned to admire anyone who can stick with something long enough to win, so why not accord that respect to someone sticking with electronic victories?

Riley was falling asleep within the hour—drained from relaxing too much? To close the evening, I said to him what his great-grandfather had always said at the end of time he spent with family: "Sure do love ya, ya big dumb nut."

# — 8 —

THIS IS TRAIN COUNTRY. The morning's boarding was on schedule, as were we. I was determined never to repeat a childhood experience of a train nearly leaving the station without me. I was on an eastbound trip from New Westminster through the Rocky Mountains to Wynyard, Saskatchewan, with my grandmother; my older brother, Brian; and our mom. Brian was five at the time and a model of wisdom to me, a four-year-old with early signs of an inclination to wander. I'm told the train stopped for a station break—perhaps it was Jasper—one evening in the dark, and we went into a café across the street where we sat at a long counter. Suddenly, my grandmother realized the train was about to pull out of the station without us. My brother tells me we made a mad rush for it, Nana pulling him, Mom dragging me. We were separated in the rush and ended up in different coaches. Brian said later, "I was worried sick that I would never see you guys again."

"YOU READY FOR our wanderings?" I asked Riley, as he smiled at the Kamloops station disappearing behind us, his mind open to the coming day.

"Wonderings?" asked Riley, enjoying his play on words.

"That'll work," I said.

In a world of uniformity, where every major city is starting to look and feel similar with ubiquitous retail outlets and streetscapes, train travel is a constant unfamiliar.

THE WIND WAVED at our train, fluttering a flag. We had unstructured time on board, as our breakfast was during the second seating. Ariel walked the aisle with freshly baked treats for those of us waiting as the first seating headed off for whatever assortment of fruits and pancakes and crispy goodies they could imagine. She had a coffee for me and a smoothie for Riley—without his having requested it. There's something nice about having your anticipations anticipated. Riley left his electronics in his backpack, pushed under the seat in front of him. He gazed out as the North Thompson River and South Thompson River became one, and the train followed along.

Upbeat jazz over the speakers gave the morning momentum. I scratched at my itching beard. Riley played with his loosening tooth.

"I'm going to the deck," said Riley.

"Let me finish my coffee," I said.

"Bring it with you."

"I can't."

"Then leave it here."

His grin reassured me his sarcasm was harmless. Before I could swallow my mouthful of coffee, he was up from his seat, over me, and smiling his way down the aisle of enabling passengers, one of whom turned to me and said, "See you at breakfast, Rick."

There was no one else outside. Other guests were either getting ready to move down for a meal in the dining section or easing into their morning on the upper level. Riley took to a corner, putting down a stake like a miner's claim. His head was over the railing, sucking the wind. His shirt blew about. He braced his feet tightly together against all that, his mind open.

On the train's left side was Kamloops Lake. It went on and on. The expanse felt a little more real without glass between it and us, and perhaps that's what Riley sought. Across the tracks and up the hill on our right was a dilapidated building. It wasn't the first we'd seen worn by the rain and the dry, its wooden siding curled away from the studs by fifty seasons of snow. Riley pointed to it. "Where's the family?" It was then that I intuited Riley's motive for being on this landing; he wished to breathe as one with those of the land; he wished for a way to understand what had happened to people hereabout. I felt it was not for me to explain, but for him to work out that the place had been left behind on purpose.

Knowing I may be writing about our trip, Riley pointed to another empty home and said, "There's a story, Grampa. I wonder what it is..."

Might the story be about owners who lost possession in tough financial times? Or were they farmers who gave up after years of poor crops, and with little hope in their foreseeable future? Were they pioneers with resources to build the home but not to stay, thwarted by circumstances outside their control? Whoever they were, they once had a place to be proud of. The walls were high enough that friends would have been needed to help raise them, to pull on the ropes winched through pulleys. They'd have yarded hard to draw the frames into place where others could nail them. Staring at the disappearing story, I imagined the day when the siding was finished and the neighbours gathered around the family that stood in front of their new home and said, "Now, look at what we've built. It'll last a lifetime." The poet John Greenleaf Whittier wrote, "Of all the sad words of tongue or pen, the saddest are these: 'It might have been.'"

"Does that make you sad, Grampa?"

Riley looked at my face and knew the answer. He put his arm around my waist and gave me a snuggle that I hoped helped him, too.

RILEY POINTED TO where the tracks curved and we could see the engine and the first of the sun-glossed coaches ahead of us. Then he motioned behind us to where the end of our twenty-two-coach train followed. He stared back and forth at the bending train, unblinking. With a youngster's typical one-word observation that stands in stark contrast to our adult urge to needlessly elaborate, he breathed a slow "Nice."

A couple in their late thirties, from Rochester, New York, came outside with two kids. Teenage vibes abounded. "I wonder how old the kids were who lived in that fallen down house," said the girl, concerned about a place no longer in sight. "Bet they wouldn't have had WiFi," said her brother. "They probably did chores all day. Then went horse-back riding. That's what I'd do." He was young enough to gallop in place, but old enough to slow to a trot.

"We travel together a lot," said the mother with a smile that could have stopped a train. "Keeping kids amused can be tough." I'd noticed them earlier, seated in the empty dining car around a board game, Ticket to Ride. The gist was to gain control of all the tracks while amassing an empire of coaches—a guide to unbridled free enterprise, with the periodic counter punches of unions, competitors, and bank-ruptcy. I'd gotten the game for Riley in a fit of my own interest. It hadn't been a success. Grampas can smother a kid with enthusiasm.

The family was dressed as though they'd never imagined all four of them being in the same place that morning: one kid in plaid shorts, one in a paisley top, father in striped sweater, mother wearing a dotted blouse. Otherwise they were in harmony. They liked each other.

"People often say they leave a job to spend more time with their family, but don't," said the father. "I'm a recovering workaholic. I turn forty next week. We wanted a family refresh, and chose to be on a train away from phone calls and pestering texts."

"And the kids? They want that, too?" I asked.

"They're awed by the mountains and waters. The novelty of a train suits them. Maybe they thought it'd be Disney-on-tracks, but they're getting used to the slow discovery and relaxed wonder of train travel. They'll have the best summer stories when they return to school."

A PARADE OF TILTED POSTS lined the tracks. They were former tree trunks stripped of limbs and bark. Their high crossbeams were dotted with upside-down glass jars. Wires hung from them like a collapsed spider web. These were the remnants of a once crucial telegraph line, the Internet of its day.

I said to Riley, "Lots of old stuff around us today, like telegraph poles and cabins."

"And grampas," he said.

That netted him a grin from me, and my continuation. "The wires between those poles carried news and ideas and train dispatches."

"Patches?"

"An early version of texts," I said. "It's called Morse code."

TO THE UNTRAINED EAR Morse code sounds an incoherent mix of dots and dashes, long and short taps, repetitive or singular. The sounds didn't mean a thing until they did. Telegraphs marked the beginning of the modern communication age.

"What hath God wrought!" read the first telegram sent by Samuel Morse in 1844. (Did he anticipate social media?)

The invention of telegraphy had a profound impact on the operation of railways. Purpose-built poles with glass insulators and copper wires stretched across the Canadian and U.S. landscape for thousands of miles. In the case of the CPR, the tracks weren't in place when businesses began to demand telegraph service. To complicate matters, when Canada's government changed in 1874, the new prime minister didn't much like his predecessor's commitment to building the CPR. That federal government sent J. D. Edgar to secure B.C.'s understanding that there was no way to meet the deadline for construction of the railway. Instead, Edgar offered a wagon road accompanied by telegraph poles. B.C.'s response was emphatic: its status may have changed from colony to province, but perhaps B.C. would leave confederation and join the U.S. after all . . .

That possibility was forestalled. Macdonald was re-elected prime minister and the CPR charter of 1881 gave the company rights to build and own a telegraph service. "The railway and telegraph [had become] synonymous," wrote Robert Burnet.

Operated as a separate department within the CPR, the telegraph service was made available to the public. It was a lucrative sideline. Charges for non-CPR-related messages were by word count and distance. A ten-word transcontinental telegram in the latter nineteenth-century might cost $8 (more than $200 in today's currency). Multiply that by ten for a transatlantic telegram. Punctuation cost money, so messages were commonly unpunctuated until the word "STOP" was permitted, free of charge, to mark the end of a sentence.

Many railway dispatchers and telegraphers were women, frequently located in remote station houses along the railway. The job of a telegrapher required cracking speed, technical skill, and attention to detail, plus stamina and the ability to send and receive in code. Some men claimed they could recognize a female telegrapher by the "femininity" of her touch. The women, who were paid less than their male counterparts, laughed and proved them wrong. Young women were admitted to the profession later than young men, many of the latter starting as twelve-year-old messenger boys, encouraged to learn code in their spare time. Girls were not hired as messengers, and did not begin their training until age eighteen, at which point they lagged behind in opportunity. That didn't "STOP" them.

In Canada and the U.S., women telegraphers had to "hoop" train dispatches. They received these dispatches in Morse code, translated them into railroad English, and copied them clearly in duplicate before standing on the platform to hand them to the train's conductor and the engineer as the train passed through the station. An American telegrapher named Sue Morehead recounted her first "hoop" in her journal: "Common sense told me that I should have a light of some kind. I found an old hay-burner lantern, of the type car inspectors use to throw a spot. The train was nowhere near the station when I went out and placed myself entirely too close to the track, lantern at my feet and hoop in the air. By the time the extra got close, my arm ached and my whole body trembled. The big 5000 coming toward me with its headlight shining in my eyes loomed larger and larger. I had a moment of paralyzing fear."

Sara Anne McLagan was the first woman telegrapher in B.C. Belfast-born, she learned Morse code from her father, a member of the Royal Engineers in New Westminster. In 1868, at the age of twelve, she tapped out her first message: a call for help when a forest fire threatened her family home near Mission. Two years later she was hired as a telegrapher by the New Westminster station.

The *Rocky Mountaineer*'s passage beside the dilapidated poles was a reminder of the transition from telegrams to text. Van Horne sent a Morse code telegram over wires on similar poles to Prime Minister Macdonald when the last spike was driven at Craigellachie: "Thanks to your far seeing policy and unwavering support the Canadian Pacific Railway is completed the last rail was laid this (Saturday) morning at 9.22 W.C. Van Horne."

If Riley were to translate that into one of his text messages it might read: "THX 2 U CPR work all dn Sat morn 9:22. WCVH ☺"

AS WE ROLLED ALONG, I got to thinking about how the *Rocky Mountaineer* ended up on these tracks.

The 1986 World Exposition on Transportation and Communication, more memorably known as Expo 86, was Vancouver's *ta-da* moment, putting a six-month international spotlight on the city during the World's Fair. But what happened before Expo 86 also had wide-ranging impact, notably on the world of train travel. The theme for Expo 86 was transportation; indeed, the fair was originally called Transpo 86. In the run-up months, railway enthusiasts organized a "celebration of steam," bringing heritage locomotives to Vancouver's train station. They called it Steam Expo. Families, including my own, flocked to the exhibition, enamoured of the allure of train travel from bygone days. Some kids towed along grandparents who told stories of riding on such trains, especially through the Rocky Mountains. At the time, however, train excursions across Canada travelled through the spectacular Rockies at night, which was a source of frustration for passengers. In 1986, the government-owned VIA Rail Canada's services on the Jasper–Vancouver and Banff–Vancouver runs were losing money. Was there a link?

In Alberta, Harry Home and Patricia Crowley needed no convincing that the Rockies + passenger service = a wonderful experience, and could be made financially viable *if* they could make the Rocky Mountain train experience an all-daylight journey. Harry was a Jasper-based engineer with CNR, Pat was deeply involved with the national park's growing tourism efforts, and they were both keenly aware of Steam Expo's revival of public interest in train travel. "Wouldn't it be incredible," they imagined, "to run an all-daylight train from Jasper to Vancouver, stopping overnight in Kamloops?" Harry remains clear where credit goes: "It was our brainchild, but it was Pat's idea that travellers would not have to sleep while going through the Rocky Mountains!"

As a trial run, they arranged to have Steam Engine 1944, *Old Bullet Nose Betty*, pull heritage coaches filled with dignitaries and passengers from Jasper to Vancouver. Their marketing angle was that it would be a two-day, all-daylight experience. That was *their* unique selling proposition.

They pitched the idea to CNR, which owned the trackage. "They said, take it to VIA Rail," remembers Harry. So they approached VIA Rail and laid out their idea in detail, including all of their operation and marketing ideas, seeking support for their initiative. The response was silence. Months later, however, and with great fanfare, VIA unveiled a new initiative: Vancouver–Kamloops (overnight in hotels)–Jasper, an all-daylight train trip featuring the Rockies.

VIA had the financial resources, the coaches, and access to the route. To make sure everyone knew that VIA had now addressed the main passenger complaint of travelling through the Canadian Rockies in darkness, the replacement service was called Canadian Rockies by Daylight. To position their new product, VIA revived "*The Mountaineer*" name, dormant since retirement of the brand by the CPR and Soo Line in 1960. In a whimsy of trademarking, VIA's marketing folks added the caricature of a full-curl mountain ram in a new logo, and christened the mascot-as-train the *Rocky Mountaineer*.

On June 5, 1988, the inaugural departure left Vancouver with dozens of handpicked passengers on board as part of VIA's plan to gain promotional support and profile. One of the guests was thirty-five-year-old Peter Armstrong, an executive with the Gray Line motor coach company, which had the contract to shuttle VIA passengers between the train station and their Vancouver hotels. VIA's management may have soon regretted the invitation. Armstrong raved about the onboard experience while seeing countless ways to improve it. He might not have known much about trains but he recognized happy passengers. That trip transformed him into another in the long line of dreamers who thought they could tame the mountains with a railway. First, though, he'd have to acquire the train from his host.

VAN HORNE HAD KNOWN the driving of the last spike was only the beginning of railway wins and woes in the Rockies. It took heroic efforts to lay the tracks, but earning revenue to pay for it all with freight cargo and passengers consumed even more of his energy.

Given how wealthy CPR's founders became, it's not surprising that others wanted in on Canada's train game in the early 1900s. New railways started up but weren't able to generate sufficient cash flow to survive. With too many miles of track linking too few people in such a vast country, the federal government was enjoined to provide subsidies, costing taxpayers millions of dollars in bailouts for unprofitable railways. A 1917 royal commission recommended that all the lines not owned by CPR (most of them tied to the northern route through the Rockies via Yellowhead) be consolidated. The Canadian National Railway (CNR) undertook that consolidation, anxious to bolster profits, particularly from the increasingly viable freight services.

A railcar of coal has few demands; a coach of people has many and constant demands. At the time, passenger services all over North America struggled to balance revenue and expenditures. The CPR ran *The Canadian* from Toronto to Banff to Vancouver. CNR ran the *Super Continental* from Toronto to Jasper to Vancouver. A country rich in natural resources needed trains in order to reach far-flung markets, but its people no longer needed passenger trains in the age of airplanes and automobiles. By the 1970s, plagued by unprofitable passenger services, CNR and CPR were ready for a "conscious uncoupling," as it were. The federal government created VIA Rail in 1977 and placed responsibility for passenger services within the new national network. The most alluring of all the assembled passenger routes were the two through the Rocky Mountains.

VIA's pockets were deep but apparently had many holes. Despite significant subsidies from Canadian taxpayers, over time the entity struggled to cover operating costs let alone its capital costs. The corporation suffered financially as travel trends veered away from railway passenger services. The drop in Canadians using the trains was countered in part by attracting foreign tourists, a move that rankled some tourism enterprises that did not similarly benefit from government funding support for marketing or operations, or who thought VIA had drifted off its passenger service mandate.

A year after the launch of Canadian Rockies by Daylight, the federal government began cutting operations across a spectrum of agencies as part of fiscal restructuring. VIA was expected to share in that austerity plan. The corporation's board of directors prepared to see what the private sector might offer, individual business people sniffed an opportunistic change in the air, and ideas about taking over VIA's various ventures became a hot topic.

Sensing his bosses' inclination to jettison this tourism operation in Canada's West, VIA's manager of the *Rocky Mountaineer*, Murray Jackson, began looking around for options, one of which was himself and someone else heading up a corporation to acquire the train set and operating rights. Peter Armstrong already had his own eye, mind, and pocketbook focused on just such a business opportunity. Knowing of Armstrong's interest, Jackson approached him with a pitch that they purchase the service and run it under a private company they would co-own.

In some ways they seemed a natural fit: Jackson's VIA role gave him an insider's knowledge of the *Rocky Mountaineer*'s workings, and

Armstrong's demonstrated ability to privatize and turn around a flailing government-owned bus company had proven him adept at getting happy passengers from one place to another while making a profit. However, Armstrong stepped away from the potential relationship because he perceived that he and Jackson differed in their customer-related values and entrepreneurial styles. He pulled together his own group under the name Mountain Vistas Railtour Services and determined to make a pitch for the Rockies train service if the federal government actually decided to sell it. They did. He bid.

One of the first people Armstrong turned to when setting up Mountain Vistas was his older brother, Bev. Bev was president of a real-estate development firm, and chairman of a popular restaurant chain. His mind had the speed of lightning but the patience of slow-forming clouds. Like Donald Smith in the early days of CPR, he had a "canny knack of knowing how to make money make money."

Peter Armstrong's circle grew to include Mac Norris, the retired CEO and president of BC Rail, who agreed to chair Armstrong's advisory committee for the bid, adding knowledge and name recognition highly regarded by CNR and CPR executives and VIA Rail's board.

The government received over a dozen expressions of interest to buy the *Rocky Mountaineer*. Armstrong's group advanced to the final three, along with a bid by the Carnival Cruise Line subsidiary Holland America Line headquartered in Seattle, Washington, which ran a successful Alaskan passenger train, and a submission from VIA's management group, led by Jackson. Ultimately, Armstrong and his partners found themselves owners of the *Rocky Mountaineer* train, and that year (1990) the operating company's name became the Great Canadian Railtour Company (GCRC), and not surprisingly the company was often known simply as "Rocky Mountaineer."

A coincident government decision was that VIA's *Canadian* would no longer operate Toronto through Calgary to Banff to Vancouver on CPR tracks. Instead it would only travel Toronto through Edmonton to Jasper to Vancouver on CNR tracks. By 1990 VIA Rail was fully out of the two-day, all-daylight service in the Rockies with an overnight in Kamloops.

UNBEKNOWN TO ARMSTRONG at the time he acquired the *Rocky Mountaineer*, VIA had promised to run a special train from the Pacific Asia Travel Association travel mart held that year in Edmonton to its conference the following week in Vancouver. Several hundred travel industry influencers from two dozen countries had booked passage on this hosted excursion, scheduled to take place a mere month after Armstrong became owner of the train. Armstrong's new company had two weeks' notice of this unexpected obligation.

The rookie team hastily brought the railway coaches out of winter cocoons. They contracted for railway access and found ten former VIA workers and a manager to staff the train. They commandeered friends and family to come on board to host the guests, serve food, and fix any problems—dressed in rented tuxedos. Armstrong stocked the bar with complimentary spirits with the hope of distracting passengers from any shortcomings. Former Prime Minister Joe Clark, whose electoral riding included Jasper, travelled on board to greet travellers in his role as Canada's minister of foreign affairs, addressing passengers from the front of each coach with the statement: "This is the most spectacular train trip in the world." His quote was promptly emblazoned on travel promotion materials around the globe.

Having people do whatever it took to make the *Rocky Mountaineer* live up to its lofty ambitions became critical as the company navigated one frustration after another in those early years. Mac Norris would address each new difficulty by advising, "It's all in the recovery." There were so many difficulties they became known as The Recovery Railway.

When he'd projected a modest first-year loss for the new business, Armstrong based his numbers on VIA's documented commitment to turn over 17,000 passengers they claimed had made advance bookings for the 1990 season. The actual number turned out to be approximately 7,500 passengers. Even with GCRC selling an additional 3,500 tickets once they took over marketing, it meant 11,000 paying passengers that season, not the forecasted 20,000. Armstrong was well aware that "no one had made money taking passengers through the Rockies by train for forty years." He'd just extended that record to forty-one.

With the summer season completed in September, next was the "autumn surprise," as it came to be known. The company faced possible bankruptcy unless its dozens of creditors would cooperate. That autumn, the company needed to contract suppliers such as hotels in Kamloops and Vancouver for the next year, with the final payment for 1990 rendered services being made the same month the 1991 season started.

One evening, PBS broadcast a television feature throughout the U.S. titled *Last Train Across Canada* about the cancellation of *all* passenger train services in Canada. The gist of the title was factually inaccurate but totally credible to the audience. The show went on repeat. American travel agents would argue with Rocky Mountaineer representatives, claiming "There aren't any more trains in Canada. Tom Brokaw said so on PBS." The first rule of crisis management is, "Make sure you've got a crisis." This was a crisis. To counter the misinformation, the public relations firm Leone and Leone out of California was mandated to "Get the *Rocky Mountaineer* mentioned everywhere in the U.S.A." It took two years of relentless media relations to overcome the common misperception that passenger trains did not exist anymore in Canada.

PASSENGERS ON THE *Rocky Mountaineer* those first years had no idea of the fiscally perilous journey the company was on. In the first year GCRC lost $1 million. In the second year it lost $2.9 million. After the third year of operation, the cumulative loss was more than $7 million. A fourth season looked all but impossible.

"I was pretty scared," Armstrong admits. "Hotels were tired of us by the third autumn surprise. They demanded payment." His financial backers were turning off the taps. His CFO was researching bankruptcy protocols. One staff member recalled later, "We'd leave the office wondering if creditors would have put locks on the doors when we came to work the next morning."

Armstrong's VIA-related problems hadn't ended after the first season, when their promised passengers never showed up. In the immediate contract that followed the bid, an overconfident Armstrong had agreed to onerous conditions for taking over the route. Complications compounded with his negative cash flow. VIA showed no sympathy, even sending a $10,000 invoice for changing light bulbs.

In Armstrong's eyes, VIA behaved as if its own survival depended on GCRC's failure. As he saw it, the *Rocky Mountaineer* had unwittingly become a political pawn between the federal government policymakers and the quasi-independent government entity VIA Rail. Armstrong felt the government wanted the *Rocky Mountaineer* to be a model of privatization success, and he wanted to make it so. At the same time it appeared to him that VIA feared that if the *Rocky Mountaineer* did well, the government would sell off more of its train sets.

GCRC's battle with VIA ended up in a fractious arbitration process. The mediator sided with GCRC, saying the company "has a strong case that it was misled by VIA Rail and that [it] suffered financially as a result." He recommended that VIA cover the $7.5 million the company had lost in its first three years. VIA balked at the settlement and put the dispute in short-term limbo, delaying paying any of the compensation, which risked GCRC folding as an enterprise prior to getting any of the funds.

That very week, Armstrong had $4,000 in the bank account. He faced an immediate $1 million in operational payables. Staff payday was on Friday. Advance bookings for next season provided insufficient cash flow to meet his obligations, which exceeded the $7.5 million.

One of the few remaining believers in the company's future was Peter's brother. As horrifying as it was to lose $7.5 million related to the VIA distraction alone, Bev knew fledgling businesses faced tough situations. "We can get through this," was his attitude. Bev and Peter went to the primary investor, Alberta-based Vencap Equities, which was rightly worried about its existing investment. Peter and Bev proposed that the solution to save Vencap's initial $2.5 million was to put in an additional $1 million to keep the company solvent so it could pursue success with the coming season. Vencap agreed—but its president, Sandy Slator, stipulated two conditions. First was that Peter deal with the million-dollar fee due to CNR and CPR for track used during the previous season. Second was that he make his VIA problems go away *for good*. Only then would Vencap provide the funding. Peter had only days to address both factors.

Bev left the meeting thinking that the conditions, while fair, would not be easy to fulfill. They got in the car, and Peter called Rob Ritchie, president of CPR, while Bev drove.

"Rob had once said that if I really got into trouble, to give him a call," Peter remembers. "When he answered the phone, I said, 'Rob, this is *the* call.'"

CPR and CNR wanted the *Rocky Mountaineer* to succeed under its new ownership. They had watched three seasons of struggle and progress, difficulties and decisions, initiative and integrity. Ritchie took up the cause. Both CPR and CNR agreed to defer payment dates for the trackage fees.

That left the drama with VIA, which was disputing the mediator's assessment—but that changed because the federal government did not want to see a privatization process falter because of a government agency. The board of VIA Rail Canada took the decision. VIA signed the damage settlement and GCRC received its $7.5 million resolution (which was $1,000,000 in cash and the rest in equipment and service credits to use at the Vancouver and Jasper stations and the Vancouver repair shop).

The *Rocky Mountaineer* would live to see its fourth season.

RILEY WAS LEANING OVER the deck railing, swaying in position.

"I'm heading in for breakfast," I said. "Riley..."

"I'm not going." His grin threw down a challenge, absent his mediating nose twitch.

In the tug-of-wills that followed, I nearly lost the war. He was adamant. He'd eaten a scone upstairs. Gone was any interest in food. He'd had hours of thinking whatever a ten-year-old-with-wind-in-his-face thinks and wanted to stay where he was.

"You're not eating?" I tugged.

"Only if you're quick about it," he pulled.

"This food's too good to rush through."

"Promise I won't miss a tunnel?"

Neither he nor the train would miss a tunnel, but his banter confirmed we travelled on grandkid terms, and I liked that.

OUR BREAKFAST CHOICES were plentiful, and Riley inclined toward oatmeal topped with fresh blueberries. Across from us were Carl and Hilly, an older duo from a small town in the Netherlands. Sharp, funny, and observant, they shared stories of travelling on trains. "In America, it's so different from Europe," Hilly said. "At home trains run *all* the time, but not *on* time. But here, they run so seldom it'd be hard not to get the departure time right."

"This railway—you know they call them 'railroads' in the U.S. but 'railways' in Canada—stands out from anything else we've been on. You're too young," Carl said looking at Riley, but making me feel his junior, "to remember the 'clickety-clack' of the old rails. Now it's continuous rail and no more of that wonderful sound."

"What's *clickety*?" asked Riley. It was a sound as seldom heard in Riley's world as the "tick-tock" of a clock.

Carl, being a grandfather, took a shine to Riley and ignored his friendly taunt. "It used to be a kid like you could grow up to be an air monkey on a locomotive; now they'll call you an airbrake repairman."

"I can see the monkey in you," I said, leaning in to Riley's ear. He flipped a blueberry at me, a distraction that allowed him to taste my pancakes.

Our train slowed. We felt the coaches ahead moving to the left, as the train came to a rest on a siding.

## — 9 —

PURPOSE AND BEAUTY are not always matched. "Looks like we're at the back end of Ashcroft," said Carl.

Guest services manager Ira announced we were pulled over on a siding to wait for a train limping our way with a damaged boxcar. Railway sidings are seldom in the privileged part of town. "It's not very pretty," said the woman across from us. "Not pretty at all," responded Riley. Mounds of wire destined to carry electricity to job sites were everywhere. Out-of-use long-haul truck beds were at rest, exposing their rusty bits. Wooden fence posts lay in rolls of wire ready for use when unrolled and stretched. This was commerce lying in wait. None of it got a visual lift from the dead grass. The scene was brown and yellow.

The laying of train tracks was driven by land speculation as much as the desire to build communities and businesses. Often behind an attractive train station one found the messy industrial heart of towns wanting to become cities. Here before us was such a place.

When the freight train came by, we looked in vain for the car with the limp.

AFTER BREAKFAST Riley had us outside straightaway. Using his social fenders (elbows and shoulders), he politely worked his way forward in Craigellachie Kid fashion, slowly displacing the four people between him and his corner. Once there, he tucked in, stood firm when the train stopped, looked every which way to the hillsides for wildlife, and rocked with the roll of the train when it started to move again.

Eventually the others were whisked away from the deck by the call of more coffee or a morning snooze. We were left alone, Riley and I. Then I noticed the woman I'd named Michiko. There was youthfulness in her eyes, though her demeanour conveyed a wise septuagenarian. She'd taken up position out of my peripheral vision, again leaning against the support post. I imagined her singing to herself—in a pensive voice—the Jim Croce song, "There never seems to be enough time to do the things you want to do once you find them..."

There are countless stories about train travel around the world since its beginnings a little over two hundred years ago. I realized ours was but one of them. Hers was another. What was it? Before I could ask her, other people came back outside. Her look left me regretting not having brought my parents on this train, since they'd wanted to and I'd promised I would. But I never got around to it because I was busy with less important things; they're dead now, as is the experience we would have had together.

AS THE FIRST lunch seating began, the deck emptied of all passengers except for my grandson and me. He looked around to make sure no one was watching from inside the hallway or stairway by the door.

Riley danced.

It was a leg-kicking, arm-swinging two-step of a sort. He sang loud enough that I could hear him, but it was not a song I recognized. The music gave the beat and he kept at it, placing his right hand on his forehead, making an "L" I took for a teasing "Loser" symbol, unsure if it was to make fun of me, or part of the drill he was doing. His leg crossings moved him around the deck (remember it was 9 feet by 9 feet, or 3 metres by 3 metres for the metrically inclined). He never turned his back on me, and his eyes never left mine. He smiled through the song for minutes. There came a jitterbug interlude. When the soundtrack finished in his mind, or so I interpreted, he stopped with an ever-so-slight bow. He walked to the railing, put his left shoulder to the metal of the coach, and finally faced away.

"What was that song?" I asked over his shoulder.

"It's from Fortnite."

"What's a Fortnite?"

"Grampa, there's so much you don't know. It's my favourite game. It's what I play on the tablet. The song makes me happy."

If there'd been any trip tension between us, it had come from my judgment of how he should spend his time. I'd been blissfully ignorant; he'd found that weakness and tickled at it. "If you were a bit more interested in what I'm doing, you'd know that."

Chastised, I hugged my grandson. I sometimes seek immediate resolution to a situation when I should let it coast a while ... "Let's head up for a while. Rest your eyes from the wind. Teach me Fortnite."

Riley was not moving. The train's rhythm was his rhythm. He had a sure footing, both in his stance and within himself. He hung over the railing. Twenty minutes passed.

"What are you thinking about?" I asked.

"I think about the people you're talking with all the time. I wonder who they are at home. I wonder about the people living in houses out there with nobody else around. I waved to one lady. What do they do? I think about the truck drivers at the crossings. And I saw a school bus with kids on it. I waved from the train. They waved back. What do you think about, Grampa?"

"It's lunchtime," I said. "Let's go."

"The wind took your words," he said. I wondered if he got his predilection for sarcasm from me. Why hadn't I told him that what I think about is *him*? That I wondered if he was learning and enjoying, and was glad he came along. Or that I was impatient waiting for him to say that nothing beats the happiness of train travel; that on a train your mind is freed of responsibilities except those of reflection and anticipation. Taking a slow train by choice is a chance to dream while awake; train travel is the transportation equivalent of "stop and smell the roses."

But all that sounds so grandfather-ish. Instead, I said, "Lunch. Food. Let's go."

"You can eat whenever."

"This is whenever."

"I'm staying here." He understood the philosophy of train travel better than I realized, perhaps better than I did.

Selfishly, I upped the ante. "Smoothies..."

WHEN WE WENT IN for lunch we were seated alone, waiting for others to join us. Riley asked if I'd taken a picture of him dancing.

"Yes, right here." I showed him.

"Delete it."

The comment was not at all rude. I saw in him self-awareness as disarming as it was definitive. It was not a confidence I recall having at his age. It would serve him well in life; Riley's likely the last kid in his schoolyard who would put up with a social bully.

Before lunch service began, I took a full sheet of writing paper and placed it in front of Riley, moving aside his cloth napkin. "What are you doing?" he asked.

I took the saltshaker and traced its bottom contours onto the paper with my pen. Then I took a knife and traced a line around it on the paper with my pen.

Riley laughed. "You're being silly."

We stopped there, but it was reminding both of us about our first train trip together with his dad a few years back, from L.A. to Seattle. Every Amtrak meal began with a large paper placemat before us. I'd pick up utensils one at a time and trace them out as if they were geographic features on his placemat. We'd name each result ("Knife River" or "Saltshaker Lake" or "Napkin Holder Mountain"). Then Riley would draw train tracks through the maze and sort out a routing from one end of the sheet to the other, mindful of the obstacles.

Jeremy served lunch to our table, offering fresh salmon. He accepted Riley's request for a smoothie. People at other tables sipped wine, and the crossover conversations picked up. A quiet lady across the aisle, who may have been over eighty years old, looked just as at home as if she were in her own living room. Her clothes reminded me of my stylish nana. Her blouse was frilly yet pressed. She wore a hat that was a confident touch at a dining table. She was accompanied by a gin and tonic.

Soon, three others joined her and conversation enveloped us. "I love the resurgence of train travel," said one of her tablemates, with what I thought was an Eastern European accent. "Even ones that have been around forever seem to be getting new attention, new furnishings."

"And new pricing," said the face under the hat. "I was on Spain's *Andalus Express*, which is a revival for the old darling, and they've certainly updated the ticket price as well."

"VIA Rail operates *The Canadian*," said one of the men from Atlanta who were at her table. His partner added, "We took their *Western Way* a few years ago from Toronto through Edmonton. Lovely. We came back to see the Rockies in daylight, and here we are."

I could follow the name-dropping until one of the trainspotters mentioned *Transcantábrico Gran Lujo*.

"Would you say that again, please?"

"*Transcantábrico Gran Lujo*... The train operates from San Sebastián to Santiago de Compostela."

"I don't know where that is," I said.

"Northern Spain. The scenery is nice, but the coaches are nicer. Hardwood. Private bathrooms. Showers. You're served the best in Spanish food." At that, Jennifer served four plates to their table, each a slightly different configuration tailored to individual requests.

From the corner came the well-dressed woman's contribution. "Among the peers of the *Rocky Mountaineer* when it comes to service and vistas—and," she gave a slight nod to the plate Jennifer placed before her, "the cuisine would be the *Orient Express* and the *Pride of Africa*."

"I've not ridden either," I said.

"I've ridden both," she said. She raised the G&T, toasted my way, placed it to her lips and sipped, and then concentrated on her lunch.

OUR TRAIN WAS ALONGSIDE the South Thompson River when someone shouted, "Rafters on our left!" Passengers on the right of the train stood to get a glimpse of the adventurous. There were two rafts, each with six people paddling like mad to avoid rocky outcrops and keep pace with the raging current. The rafters splashed through the danger, the rapids turning one raft clockwise.

"Can we do that, Grampa?" asked Riley.

"I did it with your dad and uncle, when they were your age."

"Not what I asked," said Riley. "You and me, can we do that?"

The responsibility for a ten-year-old in a river raft is huge, and not something I'd be inclined to take on—again. I knew the rafters were about to roar through the Jaws of Death, a gorge with a reputation for tossing rubber rafts at will. That's where our family cascaded forty years ago, dodging rocks that posed serious potential for a mishap. Riley's dad, Sean, was about six years old and his uncle Brent, ten. We were with another family, thankfully including the able raftsman (and travel historian) Richard Thomas Wright.

It was thrilling.

And what made that long ago experience parallel today's had been a train going by on the tracks above as our bouncing raft entered the Jaws of Death. We were wont to wave to the train but could not take our focus off paddling. I remember looking up as we neared the torrents of water and seeing faces pressed against the train's windows—as were those of my fellow train passengers now—both praying for the raft's safe passage and hoping to catch a mishap on film.

"You've actually done that?" asked Ariel.

What watching cannot convey is the fear a rafter feels knowing others have died on this river while doing exactly what they are doing. Nor could a viewer then have imagined the feeling in my gut when our rubber craft crashed into a boulder and heaved sideways, taking on water, soaking all rafters, and almost throwing one of my sons into the river. Richard had yelled as the oarsman, "Left! Paddle left. Now! Paddle. Paddle." I recall how that got us to avoid the gullet of the river.

I was younger then.

Today I was among the calm train folk who waved to paddlers as they howled with exhilaration. We silently applauded their safe passage.

"I asked you a question, Grampa. Can we do that?"

"One day," I said, catching myself overusing that phrase, sensing I'd want to be tethered by ropes to my grandson, each of us wearing double life jackets and motorcycle helmets, with a patrol raft alongside.

THE RAISON D'ÊTRE of the *Rocky Mountaineer* is to present Western Canada's stunning scenery in daylight. But during its start-up in the early 1990s, daylight also exposed the train's shortcomings.

"The food was cold. The train was often late departing. Even more often, late arriving," remembers one onboard attendant. "There was little heat on damp mornings. The air-conditioning was inconsistent on a hot day." Her job was to camouflage the bad bits with above-and-beyond service while reminding passengers to keep their eyes looking to the other side of the windowpane.

Early reviews were generally forgiving, but the *Rocky Mountaineer* hadn't set out to be a bus service on rail. Armstrong met Tom Rader, owner of Rader Railcar in Colorado (later renamed Colorado Railcar), one of the few companies capable of building Canada's first full two-storey dome car. The new service, branded GoldLeaf, provided meal service the calibre of *The Mountaineer*'s 1920s dining cars, with an art deco touch and contemporary cuisine. Dome cars have been around since the 1940s and '50s, but this was deluxe.

Rader asked Armstrong how much he was going to charge its passengers. He replied, "Double the regular service." Rader thought Armstrong had completely misjudged the situation (not the first one to have that opinion), but Armstrong's instincts were spot on. Before the start of the 1995 season, the dome car was sold out before it was built.

To get the new coach on the tracks in time, Armstrong relied on a GCRC employee with a track record of problem solving, Earl Simons. "We had to make miracles happen. No one else could have done what Earl did." After months of construction at the factory, and with passengers booked to travel on it in five days' time, the unfinished dome car was hitched behind an Amtrak train to haul it from Denver to Seattle to Vancouver. As the train hurtled along at 60 miles (100 kilometres) an hour, Simons oversaw a welding team brought aboard to finish their work—during the journey. After four days, the dome car pulled into Vancouver's station. Simons was on his knees vacuuming. Electricians were soldering wires.

Until that point, the longest passenger train in Canada had been the CPR's twenty-seven-car *Dominion Train #3* in 1965. GCRC set a new record with the thirty-seven-car *Rocky Mountaineer* in 1995. Three locomotives pulled the train, and the train consist included twenty-seven passenger coaches, three power cars, three baggage cars, and one lounge/smoking car (the last year smoking was permitted onboard). Kamloops didn't have enough beds for everyone. Staff gave up their rooms. Some bunked at the home of Doug and Flo, the couple who oversaw the train cleaning in Kamloops. Passenger numbers had come a long way since the first season when some trains were so short they'd be visually swallowed whole by snow sheds.

In 1996, GCRC moved into offices at Vancouver's VIA-owned Pacific Central Station. With plans to double the frequency of trips, Simons purchased nineteen railcars from VIA, to be gutted and retrofitted. And more dome cars were on their way from Colorado. With success came the threat of competition from their landlord. VIA lobbied its government owners for an expanded schedule through the Rockies, and to let it back on the Banff–Vancouver run.

David McLean, the former CNR chair and a friend of Prime Minister Jean Chrétien, was adamant: "When you sold someone something, you can't come back through a government-subsidized company and compete with them. It just didn't seem fair."

Armstrong found himself back in Ottawa, fighting to protect his company's livelihood. "GCRC in fact benefitted by VIA Rail being obstinate—it gave Peter a reason to get up earlier every morning," said Armstrong's confidant, Jess Ketchum, who coordinated the lobbying strategy (one part defensive, two parts offensive) during numerous trips to Ottawa. "It created the opportunity for us to generate tremendous support." Kamloops hoteliers were firmly in the company's camp, as were the premiers of B.C. and Alberta. In February 1997, the minister of transportation announced that VIA would not be allowed to double its mountain capacity and had to stay off the Banff–Vancouver route.

Freed to invest in growth without government-subsidized competition nipping at it, GCRC added three new GoldLeaf dome cars and fifty-four new departures. Two years later, it beat its own record for longest train when forty-one cars pulled out of the Vancouver station. After surviving seven years in business, Rocky Mountaineer had earned its reputation as an overnight success.

I WAS WALKING to the coach's centre stairwell heading down from the upper level when the crowd at the back caught my attention. Merriment is as Australian as kangaroos. One of the Aussies shouted my way: "How's the grandson to travel with?" They motioned me over to their end of the coach, Riley trailing. There were a dozen of them around my age.

"Anyone want to rent-a-grandson?" I asked.

Hands went up. "Happy to take Riley if you need a break," said a woman from Cairns. "Mine are at home and I'm missing them every time I see you two kibitzing."

"How's your trip?" I asked them.

"We've travelled heaps," said a man who looked to be from the Outback. He wore a sports cap with the words "Bergen Railway" (the one in Norway between Oslo and Bergen) sewn on. "But I've never experienced anything like this train. We come from a country where the scenery is endlessly the same. Here it changes with every curve of the tracks."

"Most of us are from Adelaide," said another. "There are trains through there that you should take your grandson on. Tracks head across our country, and up to Darwin, so they're long journeys." Riley always nodded politely when someone suggested he and I take another train trip.

The longest distance you can travel on one train ride is the *Trans-Siberian Express* between Moscow and Beijing (with two alternative routes: the one entering China from the north is somewhat longer than through Mongolia, or the all-Russia one to Vladivostok, each being seven days of rail travel and layovers). The second-longest is between Halifax and Vancouver with hiccups requiring short bus transfers where the original tracks have been pulled up, and, all-in, it's six days. It is operated by VIA Rail with the Toronto–Edmonton–Vancouver portion known as *The Canadian*, featuring Silver & Blue class. The third-longest takes five days across Australia on the *Indian Pacific* from Perth to Adelaide to Sydney.

"Of course, the overall service is not like this one," affirmed the man with the cap.

I would agree. Janice and I travelled aboard the *Indian Pacific* with much anticipation in 2014 and were a tad disappointed. For instance, their beautiful logo art on the train's exterior was peeling away. It was one of those first impressions that leave you wondering about the parts you can't see. Our occasion for travel was a benchmark birthday. Janice booked us in Platinum Class, which we found didn't exist in terms of differentiated service. The meals were indistinguishable from the regular ones. The roomette, while slightly larger than their Gold Class offering, had seats covered in tired cloth, and without any fixture and fittings you'd care to talk about. Marketing executives hype pre-trip impressions with terms such as Platinum Class, but a company should never create expectations they are not prepared to deliver. We live in a time of "adjective travel," and travel marketers should be chastised when they misuse terms such as "exotic" or "lavish." One of the Aussies I spoke with summed it up perfectly: "The *Orient Express* is black-tie elegance, the *Rocky Mountaineer* is snappy casual elegance, and the *Indian Pacific* is blue-jeans elegance."

FORMER TRAIN ENGINEER Harry Home would want me to draw your attention to this part of the ride: "The scenery from Spences Bridge to Hope, in my humble opinion as a railroader, is among the finest in the world." Starting in the mid-1880s, Spences Bridge and vicinity was frequently home to James Teit, a mostly forgotten Scot who married into the Nlaka'pamux community. Over decades Teit learned various Indigenous languages, earned respect of geographically diverse First Nations' leaders, and tirelessly translated their words and ambitions to petition governments as a spokesperson seeking recognition of their rights, sovereignty over their lands, and authority over their lives.

Riley and I were on the deck when I overheard fellow passengers talking about Avalanche Alley: "Kim was explaining upstairs that we're heading to an area with a reputation for landslides and snowslides, so there are manmade overhangs that protect the tracks." It was the New York State couple relaying information to their two kids.

Trains react poorly to sliding mountainsides, which tend to push them off the tracks, or take the tracks away. Early trains through here—indeed this actual trackage—was often disrupted or shifted as a result of nature's surprises. With experience came the ability to predict where—although not when—these were most likely to happen. That led to the construction of sheds strong enough to absorb the falling rock or snow, and slide it off and away, missing the tracks entirely.

"There are dozens of sheds," said the mother. The kids were more interested in gossip. "Any trains go missing? Any snow-buried trains they couldn't find? Ever!"

The answer was no, but the potential was real.

Riley was distracted, one ear taking in this banter. Mostly his eyes searched up the cliff. He looked to be calculating how anyone had been able to build these tracks in the first place. A straightaway with several snowsheds came into view. He aimed his camera.

"Quick, Grampa. My storage is full. Give me your camera. Hurry."
He opened my phone, turned his back on me, and leaned into my chest
for balance.

Awareness struck: the outside deck was where Riley absorbed the
landscape, and himself; inside the coach was where he absorbed his
fellow travellers.

BRENDA HAD TAKEN UP position near Riley, the two of them often
pointing out sites to one another without exchanging words. "I didn't
expect today to be as good as yesterday, but it's so different, it's almost
better," she told me. "It's like going through six countries, with all the
variations. One morning you've got the tallest of trees upside the tallest of mountains. That afternoon you've got scanty trees and wide
lakes." She claimed that in between you sense a country of cabins, then
one of farms, another of ranches, places so remote you wonder how
tourists ever find them, if they do. We'd gathered outside as the train
approached the town of Lytton (on June 30, 3021, a wildfire destroyed
Lytton as mentioned in the Author's Note, and it is being rebuilt). Kim
had advised, "The Fraser and Thompson Rivers meet here at Lytton,
and you'll see their different colours at the confluence."

"I'd never heard the word 'confluence' until now," said Brenda.

"It means the coming together of differences," said a man's voice.

Brenda's reference to *confluence* prompted me to think of our coach
of passengers. We were own confluence of New Zealanders, Germans,
Americans, English and Scots, Brazilians, Koreans, Australians, Canadians, Italians, and Japanese. We were the United Nations on rails,
brought together by the serendipity of travels.

MICHIKO REAPPEARED ON the deck and set her back against the metal
post, definitely unconcerned if grit or grime would soil her expensive suit, which today was a cream tone, a cotton that reminded me
of a nomad's sailcloth tent in the Sahara desert (never once has anyone asked my fashion opinion, but it was striking). She watched Riley

while I in turn observed her from the corner of my eye. All three of us squinted in the swirl of air. Her coiffed hair gave way, spiking its black wave within the grey. Her face was furled with stories, and their secrets folded into a smile. Like so many people her age, she looked as though she knew what she knew, and was about to share it.

"This trip means the world to you today," she said with a hint of wistfulness in her tone. It would be silly of me to nod, as she wasn't looking to see that. In fact, she wasn't even looking at me. She kept her eyes on Riley. "And in twenty years this trip will mean the world to him."

I wanted to ask about her journey. (I'm a nosy traveller, but respectful.) I suspected something gnawed at her. Was it a missed opportunity to have done likewise with one of her kin? She walked off through the door as I hesitated.

"SOON WE'LL BE AT HELL'S GATE," said Kim to those of us seated under the dome. "Keep your eyes open. It's terribly rough water. The coho and spring salmon swimming upriver find it treacherous, so there's a fish ladder that helps them bypass the turmoil. They jump one long step at a time to get up river and spawn a new generation."

After hours on the deck, Riley chose that moment to indulge his tablet for the first time that day. I didn't want him to miss the gorge. "Turn that off," I said with authority in my mind, but a jest in my voice; only the jest could be justified.

"When I die," he said, returning the jest. I wondered if he meant when his character in the video game perished, or was he whimsically saying, "Years down the road, old man . . ."

Kim came by. "Riley, there it is." He sat bolt upright and doffed his headset, instantly mesmerized by what he saw. Waters stormed before us in a gale of activity and threats. I'd rafted through Hell's Gate on a dare with friends years ago. The churning waters spit out rafts and rafters, and make people throw up. Once through, the waters push you toward the one-time boomtown, now tiny community, of Yale, once the northernmost point of navigation for riverboats.

YALE OF THE MID-1800S saw its share of rogues, among them Captain William Irving. Irving was a master mariner and ship owner whose fleet of sternwheelers dominated the lower Fraser River between Yale and New Westminster during gold rushes, frontier settlement, and railway construction. The arrogant "King of the River" owed his life to a younger man's pride.

Twenty-five-year-old Smith Baird Jamieson was captain of the *Fort Yale* steamer, owned by a group of Yale businessmen who had it built to give them relief from the exorbitant rates charged by the British Columbia and Victoria Steam Navigation Company, in which Irving held a controlling interest. The *Fort Yale* launched in 1860 and quickly earned its keep, setting a time record from New Westminster to Yale, fully loaded, in seven and a half hours.

The wooden structure of steamboats made them buoyant. Their paddlewheels could propel them through mere inches of water yet maintain their stability in deeper water. The riverboats' capacity for weight enabled them to carry men, livestock, food supplies, and, eventually, the heavy equipment needed by railway crews. These were flat-bottomed sternwheelers fuelled by one cord of wood per hour. (In nicely stacked cedar or fir, that's a woodpile about 4 feet deep by 8 feet wide by 4 feet high, which is to say about 3 cubic metres of firewood.) Against a current, or facing headwinds, it may take three cords an hour to power one of the boats. They were profitable, and thus the competition between Jamieson and Irving.

Captain Jamieson felt justifiably confident on board the *Fort Yale* near Hope on April 14, 1861, and was a little cocky when he learned Irving needed to hitch a ride with him. When Irving offered to take the helm while Jamieson went downstairs for dinner, Jamieson laughed, "Not bloody likely." Captain Irving withdrew and went downstairs for his dinner.

The *Fort Yale* blew up.

Remains of an over-heated boiler were found over a quarter mile (half a kilometre) inland. Jamieson's body was never recovered; he was one of six brothers—and the third of five to die in steamboat explosions.

Irving survived, shaken but otherwise a healthy man with a thriving business, a wife, and plans for the future. Originally from Scotland, he had met his wife while operating his first riverboat, in Portland, Oregon. Elizabeth Jane Dixon had arrived on the west coast of America by foot and wagon with her family from Indiana. She was eighteen when she married the thirty-five-year-old sea captain, and among her possessions was a blue dress she had worn on the Oregon Trail. Their marriage brought them four daughters and a son, and uprooted Elizabeth to New Westminster to set up a home of stature while her husband created the preeminent steamboat enterprise on the Fraser River.

However, by 1865, the demand for passage and supply shipments on sternwheelers was declining. Gold mines near Fort Hope and Yale and beyond had been mostly worked out. The miners now toiling in them were wage earners who lived close to the sites. The independent gold seekers had headed to the Cariboo Plateau and elsewhere. Freight rates dropped. Then came 1871, and B.C. joined Canada.

The entrepreneurial King of the River undoubtedly anticipated the financial boon to his sternwheelers on the lower Fraser during construction of the promised railway, but he did not live to see it happen. He died at fifty-six from pneumonia in the summer of '72. His son John steered the family business through the era of railway building. In 1878, John won the contract to deliver 5,000 tons of steel rails to Yale. A year later, he ordered a new sternwheeler, which he named the *William Irving*. For years John Irving and *William Irving* fought rate wars and backroom deals for lucrative rail contracts with the same grit his father had for supply contracts during the gold rushes. In 1883, two years before the CPR's last spike was driven, John Irving founded the Canadian Pacific Navigation Company. The transportation industry is driven as much by irony as innovation. Back and forth went the steamers, in profitable service to the railway that would replace it, on the boats' inexorable journey toward redundancy. Why struggle upriver on a sternwheeler in bad weather when you can relax on a train and look out the window? Comfort became a commodity.

I watched Riley look onto the Fraser River from the *Rocky Mountaineer*, lost in his own thoughts on our final leg to Vancouver. I thought of Irving scrambling to shore and safety, exactly where we were passing, as the *Fort Yale* sank. I imagined him waiting stoically for rescue while calculating the advantages of one less competitor on the river.

And the blue dress Elizabeth had worn crossing the Oregon Trail? It's at Irving House Historic Centre in New Westminster, the oldest intact house in Metro Vancouver, once home to the King of the River, Elizabeth, and their family. You'll find it on display in an upstairs bedroom.

# — 10 —

THE FIRST GOLD STRIKE on the Fraser River happened over lunch just 13 miles (22 kilometres) upriver from Fort Hope, in March 1858. A group of prospectors had built a cooking fire and were squatting around it as they ate straight from their cooking pots. One of them, Edward Hill, saw the moss at his feet glittering. Taking his pan out of his pack, he filled it with moss, added a dose of water, and swirled it to separate particles of gold from the gravel. This was the first of $2 million worth (about $63 million in today's dollars) taken off the 145-foot (45-metre) gravel riverbed between spring and the coming winter's snow. Hill and his fellow prospectors were but half a dozen of the 25,000 Americans to hit the Fraser River that year, 400 of whom would make a settlement out of Hill's Bar.

The nearby town was originally given the name Fort Hope in 1848. "In the *hope* it was a good access route for fur trading, though the real *hope* soon became that of gold and eventually the *hope* of trains as it became a railway town," Kim told us. Hope townsite, despite uncertainty about the provenance of its name, became a centre for CNR and CPR traffic coming along the Fraser, and the spot for the Kettle Valley Railway to connect with its parent corporation. Today, Kim said, "the Kettle Valley's railbeds have been converted into bicycle paths and hiking trails as part of the area's recreational activities." Hope, which is nicely nestled by the river and effectively contained in size because of highway borders and abutting mountains, remains a town in want of a master plan for year-round visitors instead of passers-through.

I have panned for gold along these banks of the Fraser and found specks of "colour," that hint of gold. But as our train rolled toward the Fraser Valley, it was a different adventure along the river that came to mind. One morning years ago, my friend Gordon and I pushed our canoe off Hope's riverbank into the mist-shrouded river. We'd driven there in the dark after leaving another car 70 miles (110 kilometres) downstream, where we intended to arrive before dusk. Within two hours of paddling our canoe, we had the shock of a lifetime. Gordon was at the bow, and I had the stern. We were stroking in earnest, when a sturgeon broke above water two feet in front of us. "*Jaws Three!*" yelped Gordon, forecasting a new movie. My mouth gaped. The white sturgeon is an ancient creature, its ugliness belied by a nice demeanour. It lives year-round in the Fraser. Only a fortunate few ever see it leap out of the water like that. The splash covered us with more fear than water.

The largest white sturgeon caught by a fisherman and released in these waters is said to be 1,100 pounds (almost 500 kilograms) and nearly 12 feet long (4 metres). An endangered, prehistoric figure, sturgeon can live to be more than a hundred years old. The one we saw was likely a seventy-five-year-old fish, a few hundred pounds (over 100 kilograms) and 6 or 7 feet (2 metres).

Exhilarated, Gordon and I made our way toward the Fraser's shore, finding ourselves in a swirl of water that tipped our canoe and tossed us into the river. We righted the canoe and swam ashore pulling it, our packs strapped in its swamped belly. We built a fire to dry our clothes and ourselves as best we could, cooked lunch, and got back into our canoe. The unexpected adventure meant we were now in our canoe on the river in the dark, without running lights. That made us even more nervous than had our once-in-a-lifetime encounter.

THE WOMAN IN FRONT OF US on the train—the one who'd peered into our space the day before—knelt on her seat and looked over her chair. She said to Riley, "You're a very good traveller." She sought no response, and may have missed Riley's blush at her compliment as she sat back down.

"Who's she again?" he asked, genuinely curious.

"Someone who sees her younger self in you," I said, feeling the urge to hum Harry Chapin's "All My Life's a Circle."

I WAS LUCKY ENOUGH to meet Wade, a *Rocky Mountaineer* veteran, who was on our trip, one of hundreds he's taken during a twenty-five-year career that's seen him graduate from onboard attendant to train manager. He walked into the group of us who were hanging about on the observation deck. He was easygoing with his greetings, and right away folks jumped in with questions.

"I see smaller coaches toward the back. They have partial domes and only one level. Where'd you get those coaches?" asked a woman from Italy.

"Would you like a tour?" Wade said. "I'll explain as we walk."

We laced single file behind him into the trailing coaches until we reached three cars back and stood at the front of a SilverLeaf Service coach. "We bought twelve coaches from CNR, via VIA, in 1990," he said.

"They must have been old even then," said the catalyst for our tour.

"Rocky Mountaineer had only them in the first years and called it the RedLeaf Service," said Wade. "The company was keen to refurbish them, as soon as they could afford to. RedLeaf was discontinued after the 2015 season."

"What vintage are they?"

"Not what they look," said Wade, with a bigger story to tell.

"Mid-'50s," I whispered. Wade overheard me and said, "They were great then, and they're great again now, but in between times they went wanting for care and attention."

CNR originally ordered them from Canadian Car & Foundry, some seventy years ago. They were maintained but not modernized until Rocky Mountaineer made the investment. "A California company,

Alstom, rebuilt each coach for us, from their gutted frames and bare bogies up," said Wade. "That means only the chassis and wheel carriages remained when they were stripped to their hulks." It sounded like a rather fun challenge for architects to design double the window space with a slight bent-glass curve into the ceiling for a nearly 180-degree view, and to make roomy space for each of the fifty-six guests, integrate a kitchen, and redecorate the entire interior and façade. In essence, they were rendered new and fresh, and became known as the SilverLeaf Service. Wade said, "All meals are served at your seat, which many people prefer."

To me they felt like the true train travel of yesteryear—less a cruise and more a journey, with a nicely adorned heritage.

"All our coaches are 3 metres wide, and at least 26 metres long. For those of you from America, that's, say, 10 feet wide by nearly 80 feet long," said Wade. "Some of the domed GoldLeaf Service coaches, like the one where you're travelling, are a few feet longer. They're also 5.5 metres—nearly 18 feet—high."

Wade led us back to an empty dome car being pulled along with us, as it was needed on the next departure out of Vancouver. It had art deco seat covers and tones and lighting fixtures, and retro-style carpets reminiscent of *The Mountaineer* of the 1920s.

"This was one of our first dome cars," Wade told us.

"Did you pick the colours for our coach?" asked Riley.

"Guests helped design it."

"We get to design one?" Riley asked.

"Guests have given us ideas to make seats even more comfortable and for new items to put on the menus, and for colour schemes. That reminds me—the chefs design the galleys. Every time we get a new coach built, the kitchen is a little better than the last one—dishwashers, stovetops, counter space where they prepare the plates ... We're always learning how to do things better."

Wade sat in one of the seats, his legs in the aisle. I sat across from him. A man from Australia asked, "Your new coaches, American-made? Canadian?"

"The newer domes are Swiss-designed and engineered. German-made," said Wade. "A company named Stadler Rail."

"Never heard of them," said the man. Later I would learn that Stadler Rail makes trains running on inter-country tracks in Italy, Austria, Germany, and Switzerland.

Wade said the GoldLeaf Service coaches were currently being built in Berlin. "They ship across the Atlantic and through the Panama Canal. Then head up to the Port of Tacoma in Washington State. There they put the coach on the rails, and here we are."

"How much does a dome coach like ours weigh?" asked the Aussie.

"Sixty-eight tonnes," said Wade.

Wade said that Stadler's design and material improvements means they are "almost ten tonnes lighter than the Rader-from-Colorado units we bought a dozen years ago." A man standing with us said he knew that a single-level Amtrak car weighs 65 tons. "An engine of ours can weigh over 130 tonnes," said Wade. Tons/tonnes? I jotted a note to clarify: In America, 2,000 pounds equals a "ton"; Canada measures in "metric tonnes," or roughly 2,200 pounds.

"How much do they cost?" asked Riley. "A million dollars each?"

"That would be a very good price if true."

AFTER WE'D CROSSED the Fraser River on the bridge from Mission over to Abbotsford, leaving the CPR tracks for those of CNR, Kim said the *Rocky Mountaineer* was rolling through some of the richest agricultural land in the world. Metropolitan Vancouver has an ocean to its west, mountains to its north, the U.S. border to its south, and this breadbasket, the Fraser Valley, as its eastern backyard.

Our tracks ran alongside Sumas Prairie, with the river nearby on our north side. Government regulations protect this land as a food resource for current and future generations. However, regulations could not protect it against nature's wrath in June 1948, when two rail lines—including our train tracks—and 54,000 acres (22,000 hectares) of farmland were underwater. It was called the "fifty-year flood" due to its rarity and severity, and because of its predicted return every fifty to seventy years. (Two years after Riley and I made this trip, Sumas Dike was breached mid-November 2021 with catastrophic results; I write more about this in my Author's Note.) The flood of '48 cut access to the area by rail and road, and the only way in or out was by boat.

That year an unusually heavy snowpack had built up in the mountains during the winter. It melted unexpectedly quickly because a cold spring had delayed the traditional start of the melt. This was followed by sudden and steep rises in temperature at the end of May. Beating rain came next. Tributaries the length of the Fraser River flowed into it at record levels. The river swelled with runoff, picked up speed and debris, and went wherever it pleased. At the same time, the water table rose under the Fraser Valley farmlands, giving the floodwaters nowhere to drain. The rising ocean tide was another factor, as it pushed back daily against the river current's attempt to empty out into the ocean, making the river waters even higher. Because the river backs up all the way to Mission at high tide, that's where the famous river depth gauge is located. That spring it reached a high-water mark of 25 feet (7.5 metres) at the gauge in a matter of days.

The Army and the Red Cross were called in. People living in the Valley prepared their homes and communities as best they could, moving materials and animals to higher ground, while readying to evacuate. Preliminary lines of defence were already in place: an intricate system of dikes, dams, and drainage canals had been built in the 1920s. That's when engineers were tasked with draining the Fraser Valley's wide, shallow, windswept Sumas Lake, which would have been right beside our train had it not been emptied. One goal of that 1920s project was to better protect existing farmland from regular Sumas Lake flooding, as well as to reduce the annual scourge of mosquitoes. More pointedly, it was an initiative of the newcomers—settlers—who craved the rich farmland they knew lay in the fertile soil of the lakebed that after the draining was named the Sumas Prairie.

TRAIN BEYOND THE MOUNTAINS

The defences in the flood of '48 were overcome by the volume and reach of the rising river waters. Dike after dike was breached. The event forced more than 16,000 people from their homes as 22,000 hectares (equivalent to 84 square miles) flooded. Throughout it all, an estimated 30,000 volunteers sandbagged perimeters, checked on remote homes, and rescued livestock. Others provided meals and coffee. Everyone watched in horror as Sumas Prairie reverted to Sumas Lake, and then some.

For the Sumas First Nation, whose ancestors had lived near Sumas Lake for centuries, the draining of the lake in the 1920s was a disappointment. It had been a sustaining ecosystem of plants, fish, birds, reptiles, and mammals, rising and falling with nature's rhythm. The farmers and real-estate agents said the land had been "reclaimed" by the 1920s project, although the Sumas questioned the very notion of reclaiming what had never existed.

TWENTY MILES (30 KILOMETRES) farther on, our train moved alongside the fields of a large farm bordered by trees. To my disappointment, there was no trace left of a townsite called Derby. In the mid-1800s there was talk of Derby becoming the capital of the new Colony of British Columbia. The site was surveyed for the construction of barracks for the Royal Engineers but they were never built. Proper fortification was established at the trading site mere miles away, and the whole setup was relocated to there. Troops and traders moved into HBC's Fort Langley, where a quaint town sits today. Fort Langley, which was never a military fort and whose walls were built to protect food supplies and provisions from predators, both the animal and human kind, is called the birthplace of B.C., with wilful disregard for Derby's flirtation with that designation.

It came about in this way. James Douglas was the chief factor of Columbia, HBC's west coast lands. Fort Vancouver (on the Columbia River, in today's Washington State; that name had not yet been appropriated for Canada's west coast city) was Douglas's base until the

U.S.–Canada border was drawn at the 49th parallel in 1846. Douglas moved his capital out of territory he no longer oversaw to Fort Victoria on Vancouver Island, setting the British-occupied island to become the Colony of Vancouver Island three years later.

After gold was discovered on the Fraser River in 1858, a tent city sprang up around Fort Langley. Thirty thousand hardscrabble miners, most of them from the United States, passed through the transient town around the fort. With the major influx of Americans, it was determined that the British settlers on the mainland needed protection. So it was that the Colony of British Columbia was created, separate from the Colony of Vancouver Island. Douglas, who oversaw both, was inaugurated as the Colony of British Columbia's first governor at Fort Langley.

The Royal Engineers soon dismissed Fort Langley as a suitable capital for the new colony since the flat lands around it would offer no protection should American forces attack to take control of the territory. The British remembered the War of 1812 when the U.S. unsuccessfully invaded Canada though successfully stormed Fort York, now Toronto. It left everyone leery of a further American invasion, this time possibly in the west. (There were also rumours of a possible Russian invasion from their Alaska territory.) Colonel Richard Clement Moody, commander of the Royal Engineers, favoured a place for the capital farther west and on the north side of the Fraser River. "Background of Superb Mountains—Swiss in outline, dark in woods, grandly towering into the clouds there is a sublimity that deeply impresses you," he wrote to the colonial office, making his recommendation.

"Queen Victoria granted Moody use of the name New Westminster," Kim told us onboard. The site where once the Qw'ontl'en (pronounced Kwont-len) First Nation fished and trapped has ever since called itself "the Royal City."

By 1866 it had been decided to merge the Colony of Vancouver Island with the Colony of British Columbia to form a single colony under the name British Columbia. New Westminster became the combined colonies' capital, a decision that rankled Victoria. Victoria called its mainland sister "a miserable one-horse town." New Westminster referred to Victoria as a "former penal colony." Debate rose again in 1871 about which town was more suitable to become the capital of Canada's newest province. One of the people chosen to explain New Westminster's case appeared in front of the legislative committee drunk and unable to read his notes. Victoria was chosen, and remains the capital of B.C.

AS WE PASSED the wooden walls of Fort Langley, I pointed to them and asked Riley, "When you were in Hawaii with your family, did anyone tell you that one of the Hawaiian dishes you ate originated right here?"

"Not a chance," he countered.

But it was true. From our position on the train, the Fraser River was to our north (right side) and the fort was to our south (left side). Nearby were the flat lands where the Qw'ontl'en and Katzie grew crops and dried salmon when the new fort was thriving around the mid-1800s.

Hawaiians also lived at Fort Langley then, fishing and working on farms. They'd been forced here from Oregon Territory where they'd first settled in search of opportunities. However, non-whites in the Oregon Territory did not conform to the vision of Manifest Destiny held by subsequent newcomers when Americans from the eastern U.S. pushed toward the west coast. White settlers enacted laws against the Indigenous Peoples, African Americans, Chinese, and Hawaiians who had already settled there. As a result, many of the newly disenfranchised left Oregon, and of those, some came to the Derby and Fort Langley area where they found the Hudson's Bay Company's laws to be more equitable.

That the Hawaiians were welcomed above the 49th parallel had to do with the HBC's evolving attitudes toward anyone who helped their company succeed, regardless of race. When first establishing their enterprise, the HBC discouraged white settlers from occupying its lands because of the disruptions they caused the fur trade. But it soon realized that intermarriage was one of the best ways to solidify alliances with the Indigenous people, who knew the land best, and to maintain peace. Not only was a trader's marriage with an Indigenous woman good for business, a married man was more likely to remain working in the remote outposts. Where it occurred, interracial harmony proved beneficial. The arriving Hawaiians therefore had a good chance of assimilating with the existing community and ways of commerce.

As a result, a Hawaiian community was thriving around Derby and Fort Langley in the late 1840s. The HBC acknowledged the local Hawaiians to be hardworking: they helped build the barrels that were filled with salted salmon, of which the Indigenous people provided plenty for export. Hawaii was a big market for Fort Langley's cedar shingles as well as for its fish. Without adequate ways to keep the exported salmon cold and fresh on the long ocean voyage, it often arrived in Hawaii "a little off." The solution to this problem came from the Hawaiians at Fort Langley: to cover up any bad taste, they mixed tomato, onion, and hot red chilli peppers in with the fish.

"They called it *lomi-lomi* salmon," I told Riley, "and it's still served at luaus in the Hawaiian Islands today. You probably ate some there. Many visitors do."

"You'd ask for yours without onion," Riley pointed out.

Derby is a forgotten crossroads, little cared about except in stories like this one. Its spot is not marked. The only reminder of its aspirations as a community is the Church of St. John the Divine, which was moved across the river to Maple Ridge. As for those enterprising Hawaiian settlers, among the naming tributes in honour of their settlement is Kanaka Creek, which flows from a low mountain north of the Fraser River to where it joins the river on the shore opposite Fort Langley.

PART OF THE VISUAL THRILL of being in the Fraser Valley is that the mountains leave you in no doubt that you're in a bona fide valley. The east–west flow of the river and the railroad tracks pretty much align with the mountains on the north and south. One of these is Mount

Baker in Washington State, a signature peak in the Cascade Range that Riley and I saw out the south side of the train. This year-round-snow-capped volcano last erupted in 1880, to the shock and surprise of settlers living around the young Fraser Valley communities of Mission, Port Haney, and Langley. From the other side of our train we looked across the Fraser River, where two peaks overlook a shadowy story of lost gold ... But I'm getting ahead of myself.

I pointed to those peaks. "There are the Golden Ears." Riley nodded. They're not far from where he lives and they have lent their name to a bridge across the river.

"Why golden?" he asked. A teacher likes such questions, and I waited to respond thinking maybe I'd next hear: "Why ears?"

Talk about he who hesitates ... Before I could answer, someone said, "Because there's gold at the foot of them. Legend says a Native man found nuggets in a creek. Now the mine is lost. There's a curse." Would only a local know that? I wondered. No, the man was from the U.S., and the story he referenced is one of North America's best-known lost gold legends.

But he was wrong about how the Golden Ears got their name. I set about setting him right. "Winter's setting sun turns the snow-covered sides of the peaks golden. When you're looking at them from Fort Langley, their angle gives the impression of perked wolf ears, alert to danger."

"Grampa," huffed Riley.

"It's true. Two mountains. One angle. Lots of imagination. It was too wordy to call them Two Golden Perked Wolf Ears Mountains."

"Golden Ears," said Riley, as if cued.

"Yes. And the legend of Pitt Lake's lost gold began in the shadow of those mountains."

"Why do you say legend?" This time the question was posed by our fellow traveller, who evidently thought the lost gold mine story was true.

"A legend is something that makes people do crazy things trying to figure out what parts of the story are true," I offered. "People like my grandfather."

"You've got a grandfather?" Riley's smile implied he didn't see me ever having been his age.

"My dad's dad."

"I get that," he said.

Ariel moved into our conversation a little late, a quizzical look on her face. "Your grandfather's a legend?"

"No, but he knew of one." I started at the beginning: "When my grandfather was nineteen, he came to Canada from Norway. Sigurd was his name. He lived in Saskatchewan. He met my grandmother there; she was from North Dakota. They had four sons, and the youngest became my father. In the summer of 1930, my grandfather took the train through the Rockies to the coast to look at land, and bought an acre near Port Moody before taking the train home again to the Prairies. The next summer they all drove out west to start a new life. He had land to farm, millwork on the side, and was soon building houses for other people."

I turned to Riley. "Money was tight, and the chance of finding a creek of gold nuggets was pretty tempting. When I was your age, my grampa told me he'd gone gold prospecting. When I got older Sigurd told me that he and my great-uncle Torval traipsed about the Pitt Lake area, near the Golden Ears, hoping to stumble upon the lost gold."

"Who lost the gold?" asked Riley.

I TOLD RILEY one version of the Lost Gold of Pitt Lake legend, a story that's been making the rounds with embellishments for over a century. For treasure hunters, it ranks alongside the Lost Dutchman Mine of Arizona, or the fictionalized Treasure of Sierra Madre of Mexico, or the Oak Island mystery of Captain Kidd's buried treasure in Nova Scotia. There's a bit of fact and a lot of hearsay—a proper enigma. The origin of the story is a haunting scene on the morning of January 16, 1891. It's partly truth and partly fiction. A gaunt elderly man climbed a set of wooden stairs to the top of the gallows in the New Westminster Provincial Gaol. His name was Slumach and he was a member of what is today called the Katzie First Nation. A few weeks earlier, a judge had sentenced him to hang for a murder committed 10 miles (16 kilometres) northeast of the city, near Pitt River. That part is recorded history. Just before he was hanged, the legend takes over. It says Slumach looked out from the gallows with cold, dark eyes. "Nika memloose, mine memloose," he intoned, seconds before the hangman sprang open the trapdoor and Slumach dropped to his death. Those gathered to watch the hanging shivered. "Slumach's curse," as it became known, was emphatic: "When I die, mine dies," a promise that the location of his gold would follow him to the grave. And it was also a threat that anyone who tried to find his mine would die in the pursuit.

Legend has it that years before, Slumach had stumbled upon a creek littered with gold nuggets while hunting in the Pitt Lake area. According to the tale, sometime around 1889 or 1890 he periodically appeared in New Westminster and spent wildly, paying with gold nuggets the size of walnuts, which he rolled across the counter. Then he'd disappear again. Anyone who followed him in hopes of discovering the whereabouts of his gold disappeared as well. Only Slumach was seen again.

Slumach's water commute between his cabin on Pitt River and New Westminster would take hours of paddling. He'd canoe down Pitt River and approach the five-year-old CPR railway bridge, perhaps enjoying the rumble of a steam locomotive and its passenger cars travelling overhead as he paddled under the log beams and wooden trestle supporting the bridge's rails over the 1,600-foot-wide (500-metre) river crossing. Port Moody–bound passengers would have waved at him, not knowing the dishevelled man staring from the canoe had nuggets of gold in his satchel.

About the only part of this known to be true is that there was a man named Slumach and he was hanged for murder. The man he shot was Louis Bee, and it could have very well been in self-defence. In a rush to justice that I hope would be questioned in today's legal system, Slumach was convicted and sentenced to hang. Accounts of his curse emerged only years later coincident with reports of him having a secret stash of gold. There are no contemporary newspaper accounts indicating that Slumach ever brought gold to town, let alone that he sprinkled nuggets along the top of a tavern bar, or uttered a curse seconds before he was hanged.

And yet, countless people and television crews (including from Germany and the U.S.) have tried to find his hidden gold. Some adventurers have died in the area, feeding a sense of the curse. One had to cut off his toes because of frostbite suffered in the frigid mountains after following the directions of the man who may have started this whole legend. W. Jackson apparently deposited $8,500 in pure gold in a San Francisco bank in 1901, claiming it was from the lost creek. Any proof of that was destroyed in the San Francisco earthquake of 1906 when the bank tumbled and burned. Jackson died around that time, but not before writing a letter that described how he found the nuggets. There was too much gold to carry, so on his way out he cached some of it at the foot of a tent-shaped rock.

"Now, if Jackson's letter is real..." I said to Riley and the American man hovering beside us. "And I've seen a copy..."

Riley gazed toward the mountains, unconcerned the train was moving away from the story. "Let's go looking for the lost gold, Grampa. OK?"

There it was again, my hesitation around a commitment to a risky adventure with Riley. The mountainous terrain is indeed dangerous, and fog drops in unannounced. Trails end abruptly, dropping off the cliff. The lake is subject to sudden winds. I wondered what might have happened if my grandfather had taken me hunting for the lost gold. Had time reduced my appetite for escapes into danger? Or was I fearful of the responsibility of looking after a grandson in such circumstances? Regardless, Michiko's wisdom had taken the delay tactic term "one day" out of my vocabulary.

THE PITT RIVER, the mouth of which was now across the river from us, is a worthy tributary of the Fraser River, feeding it sturgeon and snowmelt. At this point the Fraser is the product of more than 120 named tributaries that flow into it directly or indirectly through major systems such as the Thompson or the Quesnel, or through lesser networks that comprise more than eighty named creeks, and others not named, in the dozen mountain ranges where waters trickle before expanding and ending up in the Fraser. Countless lakes play a role as water sources or holding ponds along those creeks. (For example, Pinchi Lake flows to Pinchi Creek that flows to the Stuart River, and those waters go into the Nechako River that flows into the Fraser.) Despite the crystal blue of some contributing waters, the Fraser River is brown, dominated by muddy silt.

I WAS ABOUT TO ASK Riley to teach me Fortnite when Wade asked if he'd like to meet the "smoothie chef."

We followed Wade to the front of the coach where stairs delivered us straight into a kitchen. It was at most the size of the outside observation deck, and yet it was the source of meals of a five-star standard. It had been cleaned of activity, but I could envision it with vegetables being chopped, fish on the grills, potatoes on the boil, and desserts topped with fresh fruit in the fridge. Wade explained: "Each GoldLeaf coach has one of these, designed by chefs, for use by chefs, and managed by chefs."

"It's true," smiled Jeff. "I'm the chef and this is my kitchen. Welcome."

"You make my smoothies?" asked Riley.

"Not me," said Chef Jeff, turning to a colleague also dressed in kitchen whites. "Kieran does."

In a gesture that surprised me, Riley reached out his hand. "You're good," he said, shaking with a confident grip.

"Is Vancouver the end of your trip?" asked Kieran.

Riley said, "We get back on the *Rocky Mountaineer* in two days. We leave Sunday for Whistler and Quesnel. We're going to Jasper."

"Oh," said Kieran. "My best friend is sous-chef on that route. His name is Francisco. I'll tell him you'll be on board. He'll make you all the smoothies you want."

"Is he as good as you?" asked Riley.

"No, he's not," said Kieran. "But he's OK."

*Rocky Mountaineer* staff don't have many reasons to be modest.

Riley, Wade, and I strolled through the empty dining room and outside to the observation deck, which was also empty, except for Michiko. The train passed over the Fraser River on a railway bridge 3,000 feet (1,000 metres) long. It would later come up as one of Riley's favourite moments, heading into territory at once familiar yet strange give the viewpoint. Once on the river's north side we entered New Westminster less than half a mile from Irving House, home of the King of the River and Elizabeth. It was a similar distance at level ground to the remnants of Front Street, where legend says Slumach tossed about nuggets of Pitt Lake gold. We curved away from those attractions on trackage that Kim told us was owned by Burlington Northern Santa Fe Railway. We travelled in a half loop that tracked into Burnaby, and moved west toward Vancouver. Our train's location was a few miles from Port Moody, whose once-upon-a-time status as the CPR's western terminus is celebrated in an annual festival called Golden Spike Days.

"Let's stay here till the train comes into Vancouver," said Riley, taking up his favourite spot. Wade said he'd be back in a minute, and asked if Riley would help him with something when we got to the station.

"Sure," Riley said. He turned to me and said, "Today was more fun than yesterday." He paused, then asked, "Why isn't funner a word?"

Michiko remained motionless against her post. The mood around her remained circumspect, and it was not my place to intrude. By giving Riley his solitude during the final minute on the train, I inadvertently stood closer to her. I wanted this solitary woman to say something to which I could respond (quickly this time) before we got off the train. Was she a recluse? Or a hunter of peace? Or...? Given half a chance, I'd ask for her stories, even one. Would it be about a missed chance to journey with a loved one? Perchance a dream she had for tomorrow? The train slowed into the Vancouver station. Michiko spoke with Buddha-like brevity: "The mistake we make," she said, "is we think we have time."

WADE SUDDENLY REAPPEARED. "Ready, Riley?"

Other passengers came onto the observation deck, eager to detrain. First lined up were the couples I'd heard bantering on the Banff station platform two days earlier, and later jibing one another over the term "private varnish." I'd not noticed them since that first morning. They were hushed now, in a nice way. One of the women said to the other, "I've never seen my husband so thoughtful as in these past two days. Well... last day and a half." The man she referred to looked happy hearing this, so she continued. "He took to listening. He put his attention to the world alongside the train. I don't think he knew what to say. I think I'll take him on another train trip."

The train stopped. Wade unchained the safety bar. He had arranged for Riley to take on a role usually reserved for the train manager. Wade made sure Riley was the first person he let off the train. Riley stood on the station platform looking up and down the train. He saw *Rocky Mountaineer* staff watching from each coach, awaiting an "all clear" signal. At Wade's call, Riley wound his left hand in a baseball pitcher's motion, throwing an age-old signal to let crew know it's safe for their passengers to disembark. Riley's face was serious, and he relished the responsibility. Wade joined him on the station's platform, similarly declaring we'd arrived at our destination. Riley continued to wave passengers off the train with a "Welcome to Vancouver," as though his message was personal for each and every one.

Our arrival was like the closing vignette of a satisfying movie when each character's role resolves. Some struggled with leaving behind two days of new friendships, uncertain if there'd be re-encounters. The bonhomie was expressed through hugs and a few tears, and the last-minute jotting down of addresses, postal or email. As far as I'd heard, only the couple on their honeymoon were going to be on the train Riley and I would board heading north on the next leg of our journey. "See you in two days," they waved. The Aussies walked by us as a group, some tapping Riley on the head or inviting him to Australia to meet their grandkids. Getting off a train simply continues one's journey, as it introduces the telling of stories, the sampling of memories captured in photographs, and the recalling a new friend. Ray lifted his hat as he walked by us, and it bent under the weight of the railway pins stuck into it. He twisted it with his wrist to signal goodbye. He walked toward the train engine; he'd earlier said that the efficient hotel–train transfers meant he never had time to stroll along and meet those who were driving the train. Now he would.

A family with little kids met the stylish woman who reminded me of my nana. (I like to think the youngsters were her grandkids.) The rest of the passengers—the family with two teenagers from New York State, Brenda and her husband—all of them were as salmon in a stream, flowing around the luggage waiting on the floor inside the station.

Only when Riley tugged at my sleeve did I realize I'd been staring at the scene while he'd been a part of it. "I found our luggage," he said. "I want to go home and see my brother." He and I would meet up in the morning and spend the day together, starting at the recast CPR Roundhouse in Vancouver's Yaletown, but he had two nights at home in his own bed before we'd be off again on the train. A reprieve? He was jubilant, bouncing about.

"You need a washroom?" I asked.

"No. I'm just happy. It's been a great trip, Grampa."

I liked hearing that. Then came his inevitable qualifier. Fighting to control his lower lip so he didn't laugh, he said, "So far..."

Outside the *Rocky Mountaineer* station was a line of taxis. At the front, and a little to the side, was a nicer car still wet from a recent washing and with a man standing beside its open door waiting for his passenger. I held the door of a taxi behind it for Riley to pop in while the driver loaded our luggage into the trunk. Just before we got in, Michiko walked to the car ahead. She stopped at its open door and looked at Riley, then at me. She smiled, showing lovely teeth, and nodded a classic Japanese bow without putting her shoulders into it. Not for the first time, I understood what a train does to the human heart.

# — III —

# ROUNDHOUSE

"Our national railway is the basic
institution of our history, the thread that stitched
the provinces together and made Canada possible.
It is the elemental symbol of Canadian unity."
**GEORGE RADWANSKI AND JULIA LUTTRELL,**
*The Will of a Nation: Awakening the Canadian Spirit*

# — 11 —

MID-MORNING AT THE ROUNDHOUSE in Vancouver, Riley fended off my encouragement to climb aboard an old train locomotive. We were in the Engine 374 Pavilion, standing beside a beautiful piece of machinery.

In the late 1800s, the CPR moved its machine shops and sorting tracks here from Yale, bringing with it an appellation claimed by the relocated workers: Yale Town. The name was later contracted to Yaletown, and it is now a restaurant-laden trendy neighbourhood on the north side of False Creek, with renovated warehouses housing small tech firms and live-where-you-play millennials.

A roundhouse is commonly the heart of rail yards. The function of the near-circular building is to take steam (later diesel) engines onto a choice of short tracks arrayed atop a turntable and rotate them to where tracks await the engine's redeployment into the yard, and to house locomotives during maintenance, providing below-ground access to undercarriages. Yaletown's roundhouse originally had ten such tracks. Work sheds were clustered conveniently close by.

By the middle of the last century, the Yaletown Roundhouse had become redundant, the surrounding structures dilapidated. My older brother Brian and I had traipsed about the machinery graveyard as teenagers in the early 1970s; it was off limits but we'd found our way in. A steam locomotive rested in the abandoned grounds. We clambered aboard.

"This is a *Royal Hudson*," said Brian, running his hand over its identifier: 2860. We played at being the American train engineer of television fame, Casey Jones, "steamin' and a-rollin'." We went back a couple of times, perhaps drawn as much by the teenager's thrill of trespassing as by the actual relic. By the 1980s the roundhouse was targeted for demolition. Railway buffs rallied, claiming it represented a social lynchpin for heritage and education, and the historic face should not be dismantled. A more practical impetus for preservation came with Expo 86 when a refurbished roundhouse became one of the fair's pavilions. The industrial area was revived, and turned condo-chic. The repurposed roundhouse became a community centre when Expo ended. The *Royal Hudson* my brother and I had played on was moved to better surroundings, refit in the mid-'70s, enjoyed popularity again through the 2000s in promotional segments, and now sits idle at the railway museum at Squamish, 35 miles (60 kilometres) north of Vancouver.

For Riley it was a tag-along day with Grampa, one he was indifferent about, though he was happy to help me fill in the blanks of a story. "All right," he'd said. "If that's what you want to do. I'll go. Can we have sushi for lunch?"

"Authentic Chinese food," I countered, and we had a deal.

Adjacent to the post-Expo roundhouse is a glass atrium housing another steam engine in the Engine 374 Pavilion, and that's where Riley perked up. How could his eyes not widen beside that monster of steel, imagining steam curled into giant grey puffs. The steel numerical badge that reads "374," at the front of the engine, right above the cow-catcher, draws a passerby's attention.

"Lean against that," I urged Riley. I wanted to take his photograph.

"You're not supposed to touch," he said.

"Trust me. It's steel. You won't break it."

"Can I help?" asked the custodian, George. He looked the type of man to have fed wood into the burner, or shovelled coal to fire an engine like this, or worked as a stationmaster.

"Umm ... I was wondering if it's OK to prop my grandson against the train."

"Trust me. It's steel," he said. "You won't break it ..."

George continued unprompted. "This is one of eight passenger locomotives, all of them 4-4-0 wheel arrangements, one of which was Number 371, which brought dignitaries to the driving of the Last Spike, after which it terminated in Port Moody. It's gone; scrapped. This one, Number 374, pulled the first transcontinental train with 150 passengers into Vancouver in spring of 1887, after the original terminal moved here, 12 miles from Port Moody. That meant Canada had a spine of steel, coast to coast."

HUNGER CALLED FOR RILEY. It was only 11:00, and we decided (my prompting; his acquiescing) to have lunch in Chinatown. We drove less than a mile from Yaletown to a handful of streets that harken back to the gold rush and railway construction days; many storefronts are originals from well over a century ago. The neighbourhood served as a segregated portion of the geo-political landscape of the late 1800s and for decades afterward. Its land values and building façades struggle in today's battle between character preservation versus profitable land use. It's a place I wanted to be with Riley more than he wanted to be with me, but when a grandparent is on an educational mission, nothing can stop them. We parked near one of my favourite restaurants.

Vancouver's racist nickname, "Hongcouver," was reported on by *Time* magazine in 1989. The ethnic diversity of Vancouver is one of society's great experiments. As a result, the city reaps dynamics, distractions, and bragging rights, such as the forty-three different first languages spoken among students and staff at the average Vancouver school. But it was not always so, and the brunt of not-being-wanted-other-than-as-cheap-labour was the reality borne by early Chinese Canadians.

My father was born in Canada of immigrant parents of Norwegian origin, making me a *second-generation* Canadian. When we were growing up, Dad would remind us that some of our Chinese or East

Indian friends at school were *fourth-generation* Canadians. "*We* are the newcomers... not them," Dad would say whenever he felt such a perspective important. However, being of European descent, we were treated better socially in the 1950s and 1960s than some of our more established immigrant friends for no other reason than we were of said European descent. Canada eventually sorted out the benefits of multiculturalism, using the term "Canadian mosaic" to describe its fabric of ethnicities woven together for strength, conveying a different perspective than "melting pot" used in the U.S.

Chinese miners had followed the gold trail around the world, from Australia to California and northward. Every bustling B.C. community on the gold trails or railways had a "Chinatown": Quesnel, Lillooet, Kamloops, Vernon, Salmon Arm, Revelstoke, Cranbrook. Chinese citizens referred to the west coast of North America as Gāmsāan (Gum Shan), the "Gold Mountain" (or the Golden Mountain). It was supposed to be a land where a man could make his fortune and return to China wealthy, admired by his friends, and a hero to his family—though few returned. Those were not favourable prospects in the view of the women left behind, as lines from a translated poem of the time pondered:

> *Husband says he's going to Golden Mountain*
> *[...]*
> *What man doesn't treasure a lover's bond?*
> *Youth, once gone, will never return;*
> *We may become rich, but wealth is really nothing!*

One miner recorded a lament of isolation for loved ones back home:

> *O sojourn in Canada:*
> *[...]*
> *Ambitions are unfulfilled, sorrows unresolved.*
> *In debt up to my neck.*

Or for the few that were fortunate:

*I am red hot under the Wealth Star.*
*[ ... ]*
*My savings, kept in a vault, are all yellow gold.*

European and American miners were mystified by the Chinese culture and thus mistrustful and often cruel. But the unflappable diligence of the Chinese miners allowed them to work and live socially distanced. Unlike other miners, they were rarely seen "intoxicated or quarrelsome in the streets."

Another quality aided the Chinese miners in their quest for riches. European and American prospectors frequently gave up on slow-producing claims to hunt for greater riches they speculated were around the river bend. As those prospectors moved literally upstream, the Chinese prospectors patiently withdrew a moderate fortune by working the rejected spots. The Chinese miners preferred to labour at a sure thing than gamble on a long shot.

Mortgage and mining records in the Cariboo show property deeds, mining licences, water rights, and claims freely exchanged with the Chinese from early on. Research by the Friends of Barkerville shows that more than 800 Chinese men acquired mining licences between 1861 and 1868. Chew Nam Sing was one of the earliest gold rushers on the Fraser River, making his way to the mouth of the Quesnel River. When mining was not possible he tended a garden. Within a few years he was selling produce from one of the largest gardens in the area near the site where Quesnel airport now sits. He brought his eighteen-year-old wife, Noey Sing, from China in 1880, and the pair extended his farm. In the ensuing fifty-two years, Noey was away from her farm for only two days. Nam Sing hauled produce with their team and wagon to Barkerville, where he had a store. He also did commerce with local First Nations people. Lily Chow, researcher and writer of historical non-fictions, more recently said, "Nam Sing's narrative was emblematic of the 'Cedar-Bamboo' relationship between the early Chinese pioneers and the Indigenous Peoples that played an important role in the founding of modern British Columbia."

Before the Chinese workers who left mining began working on railway construction, many worked on building roads. When Walter Moberly was a Cariboo Road contractor, he noted Caucasian labourers frequently ignored their debts and headed for the goldfields as soon as he paid them. "Their bad faith and unscrupulous con of the white labourers was the cause of the employment of Chinese labour in constructing the road," wrote Moberly. "I found all the Chinese employed worked most industriously and faithfully and gave me no trouble."

Some of the railway workers from China lived in boxcars that moved up the new railway line to where the next rails were being laid. Each day was spent bent over with work that was in equal parts demanding, dangerous, and endless. There was no time to sightsee. One railway labourer's descendant said, "My father didn't appreciate the beauty of the country until four years later when he was a passenger travelling from Vancouver to Calgary."

Because of all this, I'd wanted to have lunch with Riley in Chinatown, once home to many of those who built the railway he and I were enjoying at leisure. Those men blasted mountainsides to make them hospitable for bridges of track: more hospitable than the country that begged them to come over, and then tried to ignore them. It is a blessing for Canada that many stayed and built new bridges between our two countries. Therein lay truths Riley needed to know, and I needed to remember.

WHEN WE STEPPED OUT of the bustle of the restaurant and into the sunlight, it was spot-on noon hour. We heard the sound that marks that time of day in downtown Vancouver, every day of the week: O-Can-A-Da. The national anthem's opening four notes blared in what sounded suspiciously as if a train horn was tuned to deliver the opening phrase. The sound emanated from atop Canada Place on the harbour. Five horns face north to the mountains; another five face east, more toward where we stood. (Or were they aimed at the former CPR terminus, Port Moody, farther up the inlet?) The notes seeped through Vancouver's Gastown and reached us in Chinatown.

As we stood, I was reminded of the origins of this daily ritual. Trains signalling an upcoming tunnel or level crossing or logistical points along the tracks had been a soothing part of our two-day journey on the train beyond the mountains. The aura of rail travel is partially drawn from two things that are no longer part of most train travel: the steam whistle's outbound call, and the clickety-clack of wheels over the track joints. Neither exists now, their distinctiveness replaced by the diesel horn and continuous welded rail, respectively.

The transition from steam locomotive whistles to diesel engine horns in North America took place during the 1930s to 1960s, as one style of locomotive went out of use and another came in to fashion. The new horn had different tones according to region, and often replicated the tones of existing equipment such as logging trucks.

But the refrain Riley and I heard that day sounded like a train horn, because that's what it is. Now. Train horn sounds heard all over North America today originated about half an hour's floatplane flight from Vancouver, in Nanaimo on Vancouver Island. And they came about because of B.C.'s primary industry, forestry. Decades ago, a logging truck driver in a remote setting misinterpreted a train's diesel horn sound as that of another logging truck. He ended up crossing a railway track, encountering the oncoming train. The train's engineer, of course, thought his horn had given ample warning. That accident led Nanaimo resident Robert Swanson to develop the railway horns that are now the standard (though not the only) train signal sound heard throughout the United States and Canada.

Working on his "horn farm," Swanson developed unique diesel train horns that would never be mistaken for anything else. He replicated a steam engine's musical notes. Those "chords" or "chimes" now deliver information in keeping with time-honoured traditions of railways, such as when a train approaches a crossing: two long blasts and one short followed by a long expression as the train moves through the crossing.

Swanson was commissioned to create the "O Canada" horns for Expo 67 in Montreal, where they became known as the Heritage Horns. They were later moved to Vancouver. Today, the ten horns "sound off" to signal noon, this in a city where a nine o'clock gun is also fired every evening.

# — 12 —

CHINESE WORKERS ON THE RAILWAY came to my mind that evening. Many of them were ancestors of my friends. Two days previously, our train had passed over a vertigo-inducing trestle bridge, which had made Marsha, a fellow passenger and retired policewoman, nervous. Like all of us, she tried to imagine the "climbers who dangled from ropes to drill holes" and then prime them with explosives to blast away rock for the path of the tracks. Unsurprisingly, they didn't all make it to safety before the explosions. "Imagine the Chinese men straddling the bridge beams without a safety harness," she said. "Companies didn't offer much worker protection in those days." She then turned to a few of us and added, "You know, I almost wasn't born because of a fight over how train companies treated their employees."

The looks on our faces encouraged her to continue.

"My mother's father was a staunch socialist from Newfoundland, and my dad was a conservative from Ontario," Marsha told us. "When my parents got engaged, Mom's dad hosted a party for them at his house. Over the celebration dinner, he got into a huge argument with his future son-in-law.

"It was 1949, with trains in the transition from coal-fired engines to diesel. As part of those changes, it took fewer people to keep the train running. My grandfather-to-be believed the train company owed it to the men who had stoked the engines to find them other jobs and keep them on the payroll. My father-to-be believed the job loss was simply part of progress, and it was too bad for the workers who lost their jobs. My mother took her father's side in the disagreement. She got so angry with my dad that she slapped him across the face. He stomped out of the party! Luckily for me, they found a way to reconcile. I was born a year later."

Marsha had then turned to Riley. "At bedtime, when I was your age, instead of reading us a story from a book, my dad would sit on the end of our bed and sing his kids to sleep with a song. One of his favourites was 'Working on the Railroad.' Do you know it?"

Riley nodded his head. Marsha sang. "I've been working on the railroad, all my live long days. I've been working on the railroad, just to pass the time away."

Brenda and her husband joined in. "Can't you hear the whistle blowing...?"

Workers were the lifeblood of the railway. They were as much a part of its success as the financiers or surveyors. The new province of British Columbia had only 35,000 white settlers (many of them women and children) when the railway's construction began. Though some labourers were drawn from the Indigenous population, 10,000 workers were needed to keep the work on schedule. The American responsible for the west to east portion, Andrew Onderdonk, contracted with Chinese firms for labourers direct from China. In the winter of 1881–82, he chartered two ships to bring Chinese men from Hong Kong—1,000 on each ship.

Onderdonk's treatment of these workers was often questionable, reflecting poorly on the railway that contracted him, since its reputation, not his, was very much in the public domain. He charged each worker $40 for the voyage and made them pay for their gear and supplies necessary to do the jobs he'd hired them for—all for $1 a day in pay. It's easy to judge in hindsight, but even by the standards of the day, those were ethically dubious labour practices. While workers voiced grievances, the response was insufficient. Eventually, any infraction was magnified. The first railway "strike" by these workers occurred when the company accountant mistakenly shorted them a penny per day on their paycheque.

After that was rectified, Chinese workers continued to fight for their rights. When they were denied permission to build fires to heat their teapots, they refused to work until the decision was reversed. On another occasion, after a flying rock decapitated a worker, they pelted a foreman with stones to draw attention to unsatisfactory working conditions.

It has been said that one man died from accident, sickness, or exposure for every mile of transcontinental track laid in B.C. One estimate is that 600 of those men were Chinese, and when those workers died near the tracks, they were expediently buried nearby. The marking of such graves was haphazard. Markers could be washed away by weather, rendering the graves nameless and later making it difficult to identify the remains they held. On occasion, the remains from these graves were interred in a nearby community and more respectfully designated.

After Onderdonk's contract was complete, Caucasian policymakers felt the immigrants' job was done. The welcome mat was rolled up and tucked away. The B.C. government signed an agreement with the CPR, including a clause that read, "No Chinese shall be employed in the construction of the extension of the main line from Port Moody to English Bay." Premier Amor De Cosmos turned his back on those who'd helped the new land prosper, introducing a head tax to discourage further Chinese immigration. Their descendants had to wait until 2006 to get a formal apology from De Cosmos's successor.

It was not only Indigenous and Chinese people who were exploited. General labourers of any description faced difficult circumstances, but jobs were scarce, and this was gainful employment. Despite the demands and hardships, working on the railroad had merits, such as near-term job security with reliable paycheques. Alas, it took a long time for railway wages and working conditions to improve. Retired engineer Harry Home's father, whose railway career began in 1913, had been a "hoghead." "He worked for 13 cents an hour, 12 hours a day, 7 days a week," recalled Harry. He vividly remembered his own early working days on those coal-fed locomotives. His lungs have paid the price for breathing in the smoke. "When we went through a tunnel you closed your eyes, covered your nose with a piece of wet cloth, and tried to breathe."

FRAUGHT LABOUR RELATIONS have been a part of most every railway company's story. For most years of its operation, GCRC's main labour worry was potential unrest between CNR and CPR management and the workers who kept the tracks open; GCRC had no influence over such disruptions. However, in 2011, Rocky Mountaineer had a 444-day labour dispute all its own. It is still the cause of rumination and regret among employees and management, and the lessons learned underpin a stronger company today.

"Working on the *Rocky Mountaineer* in the early years felt like family facing challenges together," captures a common employee observation. "There were lots of difficulties, starting with the second-hand train coaches. Transfer to Kamloops hotels was in old school buses that sometimes broke down. If something could go wrong, it did. But we got through it together."

From onboard hosts to financiers, from suppliers to engineers, everyone breathed a sigh of relief when Rocky Mountaineer started making money. Compensation increased. Cash flow enabled orders for state-of-the-art coaches. The future looked prosperous. Then came the economic tossed salad of 2008. Taking a vacation is a want, not a need; when the economy slows, people postpone discretionary consumer spending like travel.

In 2011, the company was recovering from a more than 40 percent drop in business as the result of the economic slowdown. Though its wages were higher than most in the hospitality industry, the new union that had taken over the representation of the onboard staff, the Teamsters, wanted a significant increase.

"Our relationship with employees went wrong," said company owner Peter Armstrong, looking back on that troubling time.

"We felt ignored," is a fair representation of one long-term employee's comment. "Many workers had given years of their life to a company we saw as doing well financially, despite the turndown. The union said it would be an easy win for us."

Armstrong observes, "We weren't trusted the way we thought we should be. The union evolved the situation into a confrontation." That put employees and their jobs at risk, which put the company's viability at risk. After six months of negotiations, the company and union were unable to reach agreement. Uncertainty entered the equation, including for passengers who had booked, or were thinking of booking, their trip of a lifetime.

The company's onboard staff voted in favour of a strike, with no set strike date. The union then issued the company seventy-two hours' strike notice. Worried that staff could legitimately strike half an hour before a train was scheduled to depart a station or engage in unpredictable, partial job action, the management team reciprocated by issuing seventy-two hours' lockout notice to the union. The company then initiated the lockout. This meant that unionized employees were not allowed access to the trains. But the trains could still operate and depart with passengers aboard. Because the *Rocky Mountaineer* falls under federal jurisdiction rather than provincial, the company invoked its right to hire replacement workers and deploy managers and other non-union employees to perform the onboard service. That added hurt and anxiety, and a sense of betrayal, to the talks between company and union. It frustrated long-term employees, who in turn decided to picket the departure terminals and vocalize their views, as they were entitled to do.

Both sides thought the other was mean-spirited. Passengers felt compromised—and embarrassed—having to cross picket lines.

"We believed a strike or lockout could not last more than a week, maybe three or four departures," was the sentiment of a striking employee, long after the confrontation started. "No one's proud of the behaviour of either side." One-hundred-and-twenty staff members were affected by the lockout. Only a dozen of them would return to working with Rocky Mountaineer when the conflict was resolved in September 2012. Fewer remained the following year.

Aside from thinking the discord could have been avoided, Armstrong is still haunted by "the ugliness of it all, how employees who had been such kind people would be yelling and screaming at replacement workers and management." He tried to understand how management's decisions exacerbated the drama. "There were no winners in this. It harmed each employee and the company. [ ... ] It doesn't matter what job they have, every employee has to be important if a company like ours is to thrive. That sense of belonging had lapsed after the Teamsters issued strike notice and caused the company to have to react in order to fulfill its contractual obligations to its guests and protect the business."

As railroader Mac Norris had advised Armstrong from the start, "It's all in the recovery." Armstrong takes that philosophy to heart: "We work harder today to build mutual respect into our culture. We never take it for granted." And offers a lament: "But there was that time it slipped away from us. We didn't see it coming. We didn't understand it. That's one of the biggest regrets for me."

VANCOUVER SERVED AS a roundhouse for the journey Riley and I were on, taking us in off westbound tracks, holding us for a while, and in the morning sending us off on northbound tracks.

**ABOVE:**

A signature of train travel in North America, Morant's Curve is defined by mountains, the Bow River and, today, the *Rocky Mountaineer*. Morant's Curve is named after Nicholas Morant, a Canadian Pacific Railway photographer of the 1930s.

**LEFT:**

The Yankees' centre fielder Joe DiMaggio (Joltin' Joe) repeatedly declined to pose with his soon-to-be wife Marilyn Monroe, yet here, at the Banff Springs Hotel in 1953, he looks rather cooperative.

ABOVE:

Mary Vaux photographing wildflowers while camping in the Canadian Rockies in 1907. In her memoir, she wrote, "A camera is a very delightful adjunct, for it is pleasant to have some tangible results to show, on your return home."

LEFT:

Mighty engines pull coaches, drawing travellers into mountain vistas. The term "train" may have originated with *trahiner*, "to pull" in Old French, also meaning "to draw."

**LEFT:**

The Smoothie Kid

**BELOW:**

A canopy of glass appears to bring mountain-high wilderness within touching distance of train travellers.

ROCKY MOUNTAINEER RAILTOURS®

**ROCKY MOUNTAINEER®**

ABOVE:

Stoney Creek Bridge was once claimed to be the "highest railway bridge in the world." Its deck is over 270 feet (82 metres) above the waters it crosses.

LEFT:

The name "Mountaineer" and the Rocky Mountains have long been synonymous for train travellers, reflected in iconic graphics: "The Mountaineer," under the Soo Line (1923–1960) with Canadian Pacific; "Rocky Mountaineer Railtours," a.k.a. the Great Canadian Railtour Company (1990–2006); and "Rocky Mountaineer," formally under the Armstrong Group (2006–present).

LEFT:

Riley bent into the train's breeze, history, and geography.

BELOW:

Nicknamed the Craigellachie Kid, Edward Mallandaine nudged himself into what is now Canada's most famous railway photograph, by Alexander Ross, portraying Donald Smith driving the Last Spike, November 7, 1885.

TOP:

This child's spike-driving escapade contrasts with Alexander
Ross's formal rendition of the Last Spike, taken the same
day, November 7, 1885. The boy is likely Johnny, the son of
Canadian Pacific construction manager James Ross, since
the women on the train are said to be from the Ross family.
However, identification of the same photograph elsewhere
claims the boy is Benny, son of William Van Horne.

BOTTOM:

Imported as reliably hard workers to build Canada's national
railway, Chinese immigrant workers were often given the
most dangerous and difficult work.

153

Barren land, rocky lands, grass-lands, ranchlands, and farms mark the *Rocky Mountaineer*'s journeys as surely as mountains and forests do.

British Columbia has an extensive coastline, numerous rivers, and over 20,000 lakes, and the *Rocky Mountaineer* journeys near beautiful displays of each.

Of the many mountains of note along the train
route, Mount Robson is often the most notable
to travellers from afar.

# — IV —
# NORTH BY NORTHEAST

"Yet there isn't a train I wouldn't take,
No matter where it's going."
**EDNA ST. VINCENT MILLAY,** "Travel"

# — 13 —

WITH A ONE-TRACK MIND, our train rolled out of GCRC's North Vancouver station as the *Rocky Mountaineer* headed north to Whistler. The rails glistened in the sun, boding well for the coming days. It was at once a new trip and a continuation of the one Riley and I had begun in Banff. We would travel for three days on CNR trackage, patches of which were once owned by other railways. The new batch of curious travellers were without names, as yet. There was pent-up anticipation like that first day in the Rockies—or a first day at school. Expectations were as varied as the scenery we'd see, the history we'd encounter, and the new friends we'd make. As I'd expected, the two young men from Atlanta were the only ones I recognized from our Banff to Vancouver train.

One of the Pacific Ocean's most sophisticated harbours (complete with natural scenery comparable to that of Sydney and Hong Kong harbours) was on our south side. Across from us stretched the seawall and forests of fir and cedar trees that define Stanley Park. We fell under the gaze of the Coast Mountains' twin granite peaks, The Lions, that watch over North Vancouver. They have lent their name to the Lions Gate Bridge that emerges from Stanley Park, crosses the ocean's Burrard Inlet, and anchors right next to where our train moved.

We were travelling on the traditional lands of the Coast Salish people, and over three days would venture through the traditional territories of many Indigenous Peoples. These ancestral territories remain unceded land as they have never been legally transferred by agreement of the First Nations and government of Canada. The original place names, once all but disappeared, are being acknowledged again in a respected and informative way. I wondered if traditional names may again take root in everyday references, and if they do, how that might affect well-known names such as Lions Gate Bridge, given that "Lions" replaced a centuries-old, legend-born Indigenous designation for those mountains.

I first encountered the legend when I got off a train in California, of all places, many years ago. Janice and I had taken the *Napa Valley Wine Train*, lunching during the two-hour round trip in hundred-year-old coaches and travelling on trackage that remains in periodic use a century and a half after the first rails were put in place. We stepped off the train and walked straight into a second-hand bookstore. There I found a leather-bound copy of *Legends of Vancouver*, by E. Pauline Johnson (Tekahionwake, in the Mohawk language of her father; her mother was a British immigrant). In the book, published in 1911, Johnson writes of the mountain peaks we know as The Lions as "where the dream-hills swim into the sky."

Johnson shares a story told to her by Chief Joe Capilano, recounting that long ago, an earlier Chief of the Capilano planned a feast for his daughters. What, the Chief asked the two sisters, would they like as a gift?

"Will you invite the great northern hostile tribe?" they asked, meaning those from Haida Gwaii. Upon invitation, the Haida filled their war canoes with salmon and gifts of beads and woven blankets and arrived, as guests, on the forested shores of the Squamish Nation for a feast in the name of peace.

The Tyee (here meaning a god) watched the good that happened through the two sisters' initiative. "I will make these young-eyed maidens immortal," he said. And so it happened that he lifted the Chief's daughters and set them forever as mountaintops. Chief Capilano knew the peaks as The Two Sisters, Ch'ich'iyúy Elxwíkn, "wrapped in the suns, the snows, the stars of all seasons." Capilano is the name of a river that flows with their snowmelt.

In the late 1800s, John Hamilton Gray, having moved to Vancouver from Atlantic Canada, saw the mountain peaks and was reminded of sculptures of African lions in Trafalgar Square in London, England. History both condemns and recognizes Gray, one of the Fathers of Confederation, for colonial appropriation when giving the twin peaks a British ancestry, renaming them The Lions.

Another important figure in the story of The Lions was Alfred Taylor, an engineer who stood on the Stanley Park hillside and looked longingly at Capilano's mountains. There was real-estate gold in those hills below—if only a bridge could join them to Vancouver. The CPR adamantly opposed such a scheme, as it had landholdings in downtown Vancouver and in the swanky neighbourhood of Shaughnessy, named after its former president. Fearing that its land would be worth less if the north shore were developed, the CPR fought Taylor's bridge proposal, which was eventually defeated in a 1927 plebiscite, not least because Vancouverites did not want a road through their beloved Stanley Park.

Deflated, Taylor decamped to London, where he met with members of the wealthy Guinness family. Intrigued by his description of the mountainside land to be developed, they funded the bridge's construction, which included giving $75,000 to the Depression-strapped municipality of West Vancouver for 4,700 acres (1,900 hectares) of prime real estate that would become the British Properties. The need for work made Vancouverites more amenable to the project—especially with the Guinness family picking up the tab—and they now voted 2–1 in favour of the bridge. Thus, the Lions Gate Bridge opened in 1938. However, consolidating the new "lions" imagery on the landscape was not yet complete.

The tough economy of the 1930s affected everyone from labourers to business owners to artisans. The times had reduced Italian-born sculptor Charles Marega to crafting garden gnomes for the lawns of Shaughnessy mansions. Then he was retained to sculpt two art deco lions

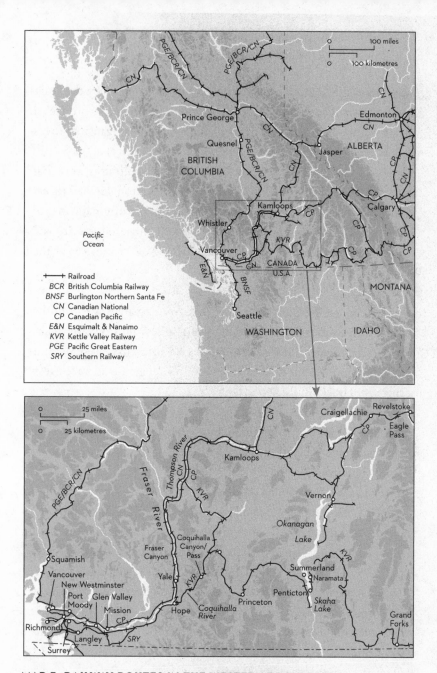

## MAP 5: RAILWAY ROUTES IN THE WESTERN PROVINCES

Railroads have moved passengers and freight throughout Canada's western provinces for over 135 years now, developing, going bankrupt, expanding or contracting, appearing and disappearing. Many B.C.-based railway names are mentioned throughout this book, and most are captured here for ease of reference.

as sentries at the south entrance to the new bridge built by the Guinness family. "I would have preferred the lions to be in bronze or stone—but it has to be cheap, which annoys me," Marega wrote to his family. "However, I have to content myself to get work at all."

It is almost a hundred years since Marega's sculptures were first put in place, but it seems finally the colonial anachronism they reflect may be reversed. There is a move to repatriate the original name to the mountain peaks, Ch'ich'iyúy Elxwíkn. If those efforts are successful, perhaps that will also bring a renaming of the crossing as the Ch'ich'iyúy Elxwíkn Bridge.

THE TRACKS WE TRAVELLED ALONG that morning are not part of the "National Dream" exploits of nation builders. Still, they are tracks dreamed into being by those who envisioned access to raw goods, minerals, and lumber, and the movement of passengers—as were every other set of tracks in these parts.

Acquisitions and mergers have seen all but one of the various rail companies operating along these tracks disappear from common reference, remembered only by bloggers and anecdotes. CNR is custodian of these rails from North Vancouver to Jasper. HS&NR, PGE, BCR, and GTPR are among the initials that used to garnish conductors' badges, engineers' hats, and stations on the route. They were important designators in their day. All those railway initials and names reflected relevant geographic tie-ins, except the incongruous Pacific Great Eastern (PGE), which came about because someone knew someone who funded someone who... Well, there was the Great Eastern Railway that connected Norwich to Liverpool Street in London, England. It had been around for fifty years when transatlantic investor affectations transported the name here in 1912, with the clarification that the shirt-tail relation was to be called "Pacific."

When I was a kid, my dad used to call the PGE "Please Go Easy." I'm guessing that had to do with the railway's start–stop–start approach to building out its ambitions to connect Vancouver with Prince George.

In 1912, when the PGE set out to link Squamish and Clinton in the Cariboo, tracks had already been laid northbound out of Squamish under the Howe Sound & Northern Railway (HS&NR). The goal of the PGE's company, but not its working capital, was to lay more tracks and attract more passengers and more freight. What they got in return was more aggravation, more government subsidy, and more endearments coined to reflect the delay of progress, "Prince George Eventually" being the most telling.

Enter Mac Norris, a former RCAF pilot who left CPR to join PGE just before its name changed to BC Rail in 1972. Norris was president and CEO of the railway from 1978 to 1990, a period of stability, growth, and the realization of those earlier goals, and more. Retiring from those accomplishments, he then became instrumental in starting up GCRC in the early 1990s.

CNR's name has covered the complete railway line in this part of B.C. since 2004, bringing the legacy of HS&NR, PGE, and BC Rail into its fold. Ironically, in the early 1870s, the sprawling and successful Grand Trunk Railway (GTR) of eastern North America was the first railway company to attract government suitors who wanted to wed it to the Rocky Mountains in order to lure British Columbia into confederation. Declining the initial overture, GTR went on to other endeavours, including an eventual Western Canada line—Grand Trunk Pacific Railway (GTPR) through Yellowhead Pass and to Prince Rupert on the Pacific coast, which in 1920, after initial successes, segued into CNR's care.

RILEY, CONVERSANT WITH the protocols, did not wait in our new seats for the hot towels and morning treats. When he met Kyla and Robyn, who would be our coach attendants on the upper level, he announced to me, "I'm going downstairs to find us someone to have breakfast with." And he was gone. I surmised there'd be no one else there yet for him to meet, as all the passengers were settling in up top to receive their morning's orientation.

Ten minutes later Riley reappeared by my side, motioning me to join him downstairs. "Come on, Grampa. I've got your coffee waiting."

When we arrived below, a man and woman were seated on one side of the first table in the dining room. Across from them on the table was a steaming cup of coffee for me, as promised by Riley, and a recently refilled smoothie. Clearly, he'd been visiting with them. "Grampa, this is Mack. Mr. Mack. And she's Mack, too." They were from Indiana or Illinois, or maybe it was Idaho.

"Your grandson told us that you're a lot of work to travel with."

I looked at Riley.

He gave me his limited-edition grandson smile.

"We've travelled with our grandchildren," said Mrs. Mack. "It's like having an extra passport. People lean into conversations with kids. And kids' eyes walk along lower, seeing things we miss."

"I'm as tall as Grampa when we're sitting down," said Riley.

"We've made a point of taking each of our three grandchildren on a journey—not just a holiday," said Mr. Mack. "We call it our legacy travel." There were two words I should contemplate together... *Legacy. Travel.*

I said it out loud. "Legacy travel. I've another grandson, Riley's younger brother, Declan. If I've time this summer, I'd like Declan and me to go camping and sit around a campfire he's helped me build, while he roasts hotdogs and I sip whisky. And we'll sleep with the rain pounding down on the tarp we've strung above our tent. We'll wake up to the freshest air imaginable, with no one else around."

"'If I've time,'" quoted Mr. Mack back at me, "is a flimsy excuse."

"Don't put it off," said Mrs. Mack. "Procrastination is the thief of time."

A SINGLE STRING of railway tracks clings to the very edge of the coastline up Howe Sound, the southernmost fjord in North America. In some places, only a few feet separate iron rails from blue sea on the left and the highway on the right. Islands pop up to the left, with names such as Gambier, Keats, and Anvil. Mountains soar to the right of the tracks and highway, thousands of feet up from the water.

"The best railway stories used to be about tracks. Now they're about trains," Ray had told me when I last saw him. As we settled in for breakfast on our new journey, I was missing his banter about train lore and the conversations he sparked about international trains, travels, and routes. He'd said, "There are wonderful railway journeys all over the world." Although he'd not been on as many of them as he wished, he was well read and wanted to be well travelled, so knew whereof he spoke. "Of them all, only a handful, including the *Rocky Mountaineer*, qualify among 'the most spectacular train trips in the world.'" He said a train only claims a mantle like that by virtue of scenery, history, fame, lore, service, or a blend of those blessings.

Ray had been particularly clear on one point: "The most famous train in the world is the *Orient Express*." It's entrenched in an air of intrigue and an era of mystique. Alfred Hitchcock's *The Lady Vanishes* was filmed with the train as a star. Carol Reed directed Rex Harrison aboard it in *Night Train to Munich*. The train has a roll-on part in *From Russia With Love*, when James Bond (Sean Connery) boards it at Istanbul's Sirkeci Terminal. Graham Greene's novel *Stamboul Train* is set on a variant, the *Ostend-Vienna-Orient Express*. When it was published in 1932, Greene's U.S. edition was titled *Orient Express*. Agatha Christie's *Murder on the Orient Express*, published in Britain in 1934, was titled *Murder in the Calais Coach* for its U.S. edition, to avoid confusion with Greene's already popular book. When her book came out, Agatha Christie admitted, "All my life I had wanted to go on the *Orient Express*. When I had travelled to France or Spain or Italy, the *Orient Express* had been standing at Calais, and I had longed to climb up into it." When she eventually did travel on it, the train ended up stranded for twenty-four hours. Fellow passengers told Christie of longer delays they'd experienced. One was for six days in a snowstorm. This was her inspiration for the novel, which is actually set on the great train in Croatia, the *Simplon-Orient-Express* line, which passes through a 12-mile (19-kilometre) tunnel called Simplon that opened in 1906. That line was separate from the main *Orient Express*' traditional run: Paris Gare de l'Est via Munich, Vienna, and Budapest to Constantinople. It's a coincidence that both Christie's hero, Hercule Poirot, and the creator of the *Orient Express* line, Georges Nagelmackers, were Belgian.

Nagelmackers's *Express d'Orient* (today better known by its English name, *Orient Express*) was inspired by his travels while in his twenties in the United States. Railways there impressed him as efficient and prosperous. One, the Union Pacific Railroad, was adding miles a day to its trackage westbound to join the Central Pacific Railroad line in Utah Territory. Nagelmackers returned to Belgium to start a new train venture in 1869, the year the first transcontinental railroad in North America was completed. The Pullman coaches had particularly fascinated Nagelmackers. Sleeping cars were beginning to appear in Europe but there was nothing comparable to the cogent design embodied in George Pullman's work. Nagelmackers approached Pullman about forming a partnership to build such carriages (wagon-lits) in Europe, but Pullman declined.

Rebuffed by Pullman, by 1874 Nagelmackers had built an enviable reputation for his own company, soon to be named the Compagnie Internationale des Wagons-Lits (he extended the name ten years later by adding "et des Grands Express Européens"). His focus was on elegant, long-distance travel for affluent clients. While he owned the coaches, he relied on a variety of train companies to haul them. It would take years of diplomatic negotiations before he had a train of his own.

Nagelmackers's *Express d'Orient* debuted at the Gare de l'Est in Paris in June 1883, on a promotional test run for thirty adventurous travellers.[6] However, it would be another six years before passengers boarding in Paris rode all the way to Constantinople (Istanbul) without needing to change carriage or train, and they would do so in sixty-seven hours and thirty-five minutes. This was a train suited to Europe's *belle époque*. Of their dining cars, one guest wrote: "The bright-white tablecloths and napkins, artistically and coquettishly folded by the sommeliers, the glittering glasses, the ruby red and topaz white wine, the crystal-clear water decanters and the silver capsules of the champagne bottles—they blind the eyes of the public both inside and outside."

The name *Orient Express* has been appended to various excursions in the one-hundred-plus years since Nagelmackers established the brand, and not always accurately. There has been a somewhat bewildering use of "Orient Express" to define a train or part of a train or a short route within a longer route, or to reference the initial train or an offshoot, and of course for the splendid revival of the original. In the 1970s, on one train trip I took in Europe, my ticket had *Orient Express* printed on it. It was a poached use of the name. The final passage for a faded rendition of the *Orient Express* from Paris to Istanbul was in May 1977, and after that the opportunity to ride aboard the fabled train was unavailable for a while.

Revival of the elegant *Orient Express* experience began under American-born businessman James Sherwood, who had a long-term vision—and the patience and resources to pursue it. In 1977, he set about to methodically create what the author Jean-Paul Caracalla called "nostalgia on rails."[7] His train is the *Venice Simplon-Orient-Express*, known as the VSOE. The similarity of its initials to VSOP, Very Superior Old Pale amber cognac, is a happy coincidence for Sherwood. He'd chosen the name for his refurbished train from Paris to Venice in 1983, and kept the shorthand form even after it no longer routed through the Simplon Tunnel featured in the Agatha Christie novel.

Sherwood was a successful entrepreneur in the shipping container business turned train aficionado whose investment in tourism began in 1976 with the purchase of a hotel in Venice. He wondered about acquiring the *Orient Express* train as part of an overall travel experience involving his hotel and his favourite city. The train he sought no longer existed as a consist (or a "rake," as the British call a sequence of coaches and engine). There was no original *Orient Express* for Sherwood to acquire, let alone reintroduce. And if he wanted to restore something, he'd have to find former first-class *Orient Express* coaches wherever they'd ended up around Europe. None of those he initially found was rail-worthy. Thus began a journey of tracking down discarded coaches, finding train paraphernalia, and creating a sense of the past for people to experience in the present. Sherwood's first purchase was two carriages built between the world wars and featured in the 1974 movie *Murder on the Orient Express*, acquired at a Sotheby's auction.

As he acquired more hardware, he encountered more problems. Refurbishment involved adherence to strict safety codes and expensive redesigns. Had he wished to place them stationary in museums, restoration costs would have been modest and volunteers would have provided help. But he wanted the coaches to carry paying passengers. That meant the best craftsmen were needed, and all current standards met or exceeded. The result was an extraordinary set of coaches, simultaneously thoroughly modern and in every way historic, with a rare sense of authenticity.

Sherwood determined that the best market for travellers from Paris to Venice was in Britain, which meant the journey best begin in London. But the British width gauge is different from that in France, which meant a need for two trains: British Pullman coaches in England and the reconfigured *Orient Express* wagon-lits on European soil. A ferry ride would connect passengers from one train to the other. The expense of providing a consistent high-quality passenger experience linking train, ferry, and train was significant but not to be shied away from. It became a marketing tool, and travellers would always have an unparalleled sense of bespoke travel.

Sherwood's publicly traded company, Sea Containers, was profitable. That enabled his train empire to go through a sextupling of its original U.S. $5 million budget before getting to the point where paying passengers could ride the train. Then, in keeping with the way Nagelmackers had created a subsidiary of his railway company to operate Grands Hôtels, James Sherwood formalized Orient Express Hotels as part of his railway enterprise. He adored the reputation his company quickly acquired, noting, "We have restored the art of travel."

RILEY WAS DETERMINED that we'd pass most of the four hours from North Vancouver to Whistler standing outside on the observation deck. A dozen passengers were enjoying the fresh air, and it took some effort for him to wiggle his way into his favoured corner. He got there with a few minutes of smile-and-push. Adults had no qualms relinquishing their spot to a smiling kid prodding them while saying, "'Scuse me."

Often the train rode pleasingly close to where the shoreline dipped into the ocean. On the other side of the tracks, the highway came in and out of view from the train, or could be seen filtered through the buffering forest. In the late 1970s, the Sea-to-Sky Highway was so named in a local tourism contest to create a more alluring image than "the road from Vancouver to Whistler."

From the train we could see some of the highway signs showing transliterations of original place names juxtaposed with the designations imposed by the Europeans. The original names can appear overwhelming for English speakers. The Indigenous languages were not originally written language systems and most have a wider range of phonetics than the Roman alphabet can accommodate, so you'll see symbols used in some names. For example, "7" indicates an exhaling sound. The bilingual signs are part of a program begun in 2003 to restore place names that were displaced by the arrogance of (and for the convenience of) colonial settlers who overtook the land. Thus, Squamish, the English name, is seen alongside Sḵwx̱wú7mesh . Whistler's traditional name is Sḵwiḵw.

By way of making such names relevant to our journey, Kyla told us to keep our eyes right "to see a granite massif that is 700 metres high— that'll be 2,300 feet." There it loomed: The Stawamus Chief. Its name is derived from Sta7mes (meaning "sheltered"). The designation "Chief" was added as colonial cosmetics.

"Some days you can see climbers on the mountain's side," said Kyla. "Keep in mind it can be a two-day climb. That means those you see up there today may bivouac overnight in sleeping bags pinned to the rock."

A friend who climbs told me of having to sleep on the Stawamus. When he woke in the morning his first thought was, "I know where I am but what am I doing here?" I've hiked up the back trail to the top of the Stawamus, which was challenging enough, but overall does not require any particular skills beyond determination and fitness. From the top I remember being able to see forever, and we watched what in those days was a PGE train hauling logs southbound along the tracks we now rode.

SQUAMISH IS HOME to the Railway Museum of British Columbia (formerly the West Coast Railway Heritage Park), a sprawling collection of refurbished train coaches and engines in an early-nineteenth-century-style village with assorted train parts strewn in studied disarray—a petting zoo for train buffs. How many hands have reached out to stroke the human-sized wheels of the museum's prized possession, the *Royal Hudson #2860*?

That train's tie to royalty comes from the cross-Canada journey, in 1939, of the British king and queen, whose official duties included cutting the ribbon on the newly built Lions Gate Bridge. The engine's durability made such an impression on George VI (who frequently rode in the cab with the engineer) that a year later he bestowed the "Royal" designation on this group of Montreal-built engines. This is the same engine my older brother and I saw in disrepair in the desolate rail yard where the Yaletown Roundhouse now sits. A team of craftsmen devotedly restored the engineering beast, but after making trips to the United States during the late 1970s and 1980s to market B.C., it again fell victim to the cost of maintenance and insurance, and now rests at the heritage park.

Two years prior at Christmas, Riley and I had visited the *Royal Hudson*. (It is one of four still alive in captivity.) I hadn't found the words to explain the connecting themes of endurance and perseverance, but I thought Riley picked up on them. Under the same roof at the railway museum is the 1890s CPR business car that I'd clambered aboard years earlier at the Vancouver station, when I learned the term "private varnish."

AN EAGLE SOARED high above, its course traced by the passengers pointing at it through the glass ceiling. Like all birds of prey, eagles hunt with patience, knowing eventually their next meal will come out of hiding, whether from trees, tall grass, or the water's camouflage.

"Near here is where you can see one of the greatest gatherings of bald eagles," said Kyla. "There's an annual weekend count each autumn in the community of Brackendale on the Squamish River, and in past years they've tallied as many as 3,700 eagles."

I looked about the coach and saw every passenger alert, looking in every direction for signs of wildlife or landmarks. Some were anxious for a chance sighting of an obelisk in the mountains, which Kyla called the Black Tusk. It is more readily seen in good weather from the highway. The descriptive is apt for the tooth-shaped shaft. This volcanic protuberance reminds us that here was smoke and fire and the explosive tossing of giant boulders. We glided on rails, ignoring such dangers of the past and hoping they did not return, as volcanic surprises do happen.

Rounding a curve, we saw a line of towering peaks ahead. The Tantalus Range to the west evoked sufficient memories of Greek mythology to have been named after a character from those epics— one whose name is the genesis of the word "tantalize." (This is an apt descriptor, yet so too would seem the original Squamish name for the range: Tsewílx', though I was unable to find a literal translation.)

Mount Garibaldi's geometric profile vaults almost 8,850 feet (2,700 metres) high. To its right, "just out of glimpse," as one passenger said, is the volcanic projection, the Black Tusk, that thrusts toward the heavens, south of Whistler. Riley pointed at where he thought he'd glimpsed it.

The Tusk soars over 7,550 feet (2,300 metres) high, and bears the reference "Landing Place of the Thunderbird" in Squamish. It is the core of an ancient volcano, which formed over a million years ago. Perhaps 170,000 years ago, the summit around it was formed with further volcanic action. In some parts, the Tusk's chimneys (cracks or fissures) allow climbers to put their back on one side of the cleavage and their feet on the other. They shuffle up ever so slowly, ever so surely, until they reach the top, and inhale one of the most magnificent views in a land abundant in magnificent views.

Along with Garibaldi Mountain and other local volcanic sites, the Tusk is part of the Pacific Ring of Fire, which encircles the Pacific Ocean from the tip of South America, up the continent's west side (including where we travelled), along the Aleutian Islands in Alaska, across the Bering Strait to Russia, and down the western side of the ocean through Japan, the Philippines, Southeast Asia, and into Indonesia. Every year, volcanic action along the Ring of Fire produces no end of geological events: earthquakes, tsunamis, and related disasters. The last volcanic activity in Canada was in northwestern British Columbia, before either the country or the province had those names, around 1780; the Tseax eruption killed 2,000 people living in two Nisga'a villages that were destroyed.

The Black Tusk is but one such Ring of Fire–related feature on the west coast of North America. Farther south, in Washington, Oregon, and California, a string of volcanoes breaks the skyline, with names such as Mount Baker (which Riley and I had seen when we rode through the Fraser Valley), Mount Rainier, Mount St. Helens, Mount Hood, and Mount Shasta, from a list of peaks (including what was once Lassen Peak, now a crater) formed by fire and brimstone in the Cascade Range.

In the case of the area plied by the *Rocky Mountaineer*, no such current activity is seen. Famously, though, Mount St. Helens, 330 miles (530 kilometres) to the south of where our train travelled, erupted in 1980 with a massive explosion that wiped 1,300 feet (400 metres) of its elevation off the map, spreading ash over a huge swath of Washington State and plugging rivers at the base of the mountain. Weather patterns were affected in B.C. and Alberta. Fifty-seven people died in the catastrophe, and decades later few who lived through it have forgotten the lesson taught on a quiet Sunday morning: Mother Nature is in charge!

THE CHEAKAMUS RIVER is never more beautiful to a traveller as when crossing its canyon over a bridge that is underpinned by a trestle structure. Below are crags, mid-river boulders, and the white furls of water. One trestle bridge over the Cheakamus River will forever remind me of a scene in the movie *Stand by Me*: kids playing on the railway tracks are caught mid-bridge by an approaching train, and run for their lives. As a youngster a little older than Riley, I once camped in the woods near here with my brother Brian, a friend named Harrison, and a handful of other boys. One morning we went for a hike and ended up walking on the tracks. When we came to what I now recall as a 200-foot (60-metre) bridge, we were frightened by how unbelievably high it was above the roaring water but dared one another to cross it. We had no business being there; it is private property owned by the train company. I double-dared Harrison, and he started to go across the trestle. Not wanting to be left alone, Brian and I joined him and the others trailed along behind us. Mid-span the ties started to vibrate. Harrison put his ear to the track, listened, and whimpered, "There's a train coming," though none was in sight. We ran toward the other end of the bridge, making sure to place our fox-trotting feet on each tie for fear of tripping and falling off the tracks into the canyon far below. As we neared the other side, Harrison shouted, "TRAIN!" Frantically, we ran the remaining stretch to the end of the bridge, jumped to the side of the tracks, and lay in frightened lumps. A small, open-air "speeder" went by with two railway maintenance men aboard, checking the tracks. They scowled a reprimand our way. After they left, we all piled on Harrison for his false alarm.

ON A DIFFERENT TRIP, I'd first travelled here by train nearly sixty years ago as a Boy Scout when the station stop was called Garibaldi. The day we'd arrived, a grader was smoothing gravel alongside the tracks, improving a road to accommodate the increased number of skiers heading for Garibaldi and London Mountain. A dozen of us Boy Scouts were let off at Garibaldi Station to make our way through creeks and up to Packer Meadows and onward to the Black Tusk Meadows. Things have changed since then: the hike to the Tusk now begins in a parking lot about 2 miles (3 kilometres) in.

As the *Rocky Mountaineer* neared the former Garibaldi Station, our route passed along the west bank of the Cheakamus River. Kyla told us, "A few kilometres east, a huge lava flow formed a solid barrier of rock 9,000 years ago, a natural dam that backs up the outflow from Barrier Lake, Lesser Garibaldi Lake, and the beautiful glacial green waters of Garibaldi Lake, nestled between the Black Tusk and Mount Garibaldi."

In the mid-1800s, much of the face of this barrier collapsed over the course of two years and crumbled into the valley, its rubble distributed down toward the locations of today's highway and rail right-of-way. Here, water draining from Barrier Lake cascades 800 feet (243 metres) underground and emerges at the bottom to form Rubble Creek, which flows through the boulder field until it connects with the Cheakamus River.

"Aptly named 'The Barrier,' the bare rock face greets hikers today as they climb up steep switchback trails heading to Garibaldi Park," said Kyla. Rock continues to fall down the face and wary hikers can stand on outcrops and listen to its crumbling ways. Development of a potential recreation site has been restricted by government policy due to the inherent danger of building in an area that could be affected by future collapses and the flooding that might result.

LEAVING THE GROWLING Cheakamus behind us, the train slowed into the storybook village of Whistler. The railway station in Whistler is of modern construction with a gingerbread motif found throughout the town. Some relish how the station evokes the glamour of train travel from past eras. We were soon outside of it, bus-bound for our hotels. Checked in, we now had the rest of the afternoon plus the evening to ourselves, which is to say I'd be haggling with Riley over how he relaxed and if that involved electronics.

Riley knows Whistler well and had been there only weeks before with his brother and parents. Making this a novel visit for him was a challenge. There's the Peak 2 Peak gondola, zip-lines, or mountain bike rentals. All of those required organization and transfer times and, anyway, Riley was hungry. What interrupted our quest for food was a huge joy ride. "We should do that," suggested Riley when he saw the slide-of-sorts elevated slightly above the ground. It offered us (for he'd not be going alone) something that neither of us had ever done. The gadget took us one at a time in our carts up a few hundred yards where the cart curved out of its incline and tore down a sluice (if you let go of the hand-brake) to the fun's exit, all within a few minutes, most of which was spent on the ascent. It was like riding an enlarged can-opener around the rim of a giant sardine can, and proved about as satisfying in our opinions.

Back on our lookout for food, Riley pestered me with, "Let's go to the Old Spaghetti Factory."

"I'd like to find a place with more of a story," I said. "And the Old Spaghetti Factory is not about this place." With that pronouncement I was wrong on two fronts. The more important was my overlooking the need to keep a travel mate fuelled, especially a kid. As we wandered right by his chosen place, and with disagreement clouding the air and my judgment, I screwed up the timing. It was almost an hour before we retraced our steps to the restaurant's front door. Stepping in made me realize my second mistake. Though the Old Spaghetti Factory originated in Portland, Oregon, in 1969, it opened in Gastown in 1970 and has been a part of the local fare ever since, leading to the common belief of locals that it was created here. Close enough. What counted to Riley was proving to me his claim that "they have the best Caesar salad in all of Whistler."

"YOU KNOW, RILEY," I began, once we'd both ordered his recommended Caesar salad for lunch, "I heard a story about a young guy not much older than you being the first person to ski down Whistler Mountain the day it opened in 1966."

Even though there'd been skiing on Vancouver's North Shore mountains since the 1930s, the terrain wasn't challenging enough for a group of local ski enthusiasts who had enjoyed a ski holiday in Switzerland in 1963. They returned amazed by the Alps' steep slopes and proffered adventure. As they flew home to Vancouver, the plane curved over the peaks of Garibaldi Mountain, and the slopes they saw out the window matched the best they'd seen in Europe. The passengers dreamed of descending one of those mountains on skis and, then and there, they vowed to help make it happen. Two of those passengers were Vancouver radiologist Ernst Frinton and his twelve-year-old son, Peter.

They were not alone in their quest. A transplanted Norwegian named Franz Willhemsen led the search for a new ski resort that would meet the growing interest of like-minded skiers. His venture to Garibaldi followed in the footsteps of Alex and Myrtle Philip, an American couple who opened a fishing lodge on Alta Lake in 1914. To get there you had to travel on a steamship from Vancouver to Squamish and hike for two days along an old fur-trading trail. PGE opened part of their railway in the 1930s, encouraging other fishing lodges, as well as lumber mills, mines, and a mink farm. Awareness of the opportunities in the area grew, and skiing was a big one.

Electricity and running water didn't exist in the area when the Frintons jumped in a rickety Land Rover and took the all-day journey to scope out sites for a ski hill. "It was unbelievably rough," Peter remembers of the forest service road that was their route past Squamish. "We often had to get out of the car and coax it forward."

Willhemsen and his Austrian sidekick, Stefan Ples, met the Frintons at the base of Black Tusk Mountain in 1963, one of Willhemsen's choices for a ski site. Ples encouraged them to look at nearby London Mountain, which lords over Alta Lake. They liked the mountain but not its name. Even then they dreamed of hosting the Winter Olympics there. Not only did the name London conjure images of rain instead of snow, but also, if they attained their dream, they wouldn't want to host the London Olympics, would they? The mountain's name needed to be changed. A few years later, it was formally changed to the name the locals used, Whistler Mountain, in honour of the hoary marmot (a large ground squirrel), referred to as the "whistler" for its distinctive call.

Their resort was eventually ready with its first chair lift and run. Opening day was scheduled for February 1966. By then, Peter Frinton was into his early teens and, having lied about his age, was a volunteer with the ski patrol. He spent most of his Christmas holiday helping with the final preparations. On a stormy day in early January, he was asked to deliver lunch to people working at the top of the mountain. It was a lonely journey up, and the ski lift's landing area was not finished, so he had to jump 3 feet (1 metre) to the ground. He looked around him. No one was there. He heard the wind blowing down Singing Pass.

Other than waiting for someone to restart the lift, there was only one way for Frinton to get down the mountain—on skis. The view from the mountaintop to Alta Lake was tempting. It's possible a few people had gone down from the top between Christmas and New Year's Day, but even rumours of such bravado were rare. Though the trail was not yet properly marked, Frinton couldn't resist.

The wind howled through the mountains, whipping up the snow as Frinton set off. "I was scared out of my wits," he remembers.

Swoosh.

It's quite possible Peter Frinton was the first skier to do the full run, a story he's since recounted in the 2005 documentary *First to Go Down*. Forty-four years after his 1966 run, Frinton watched the Olympic Torch being carried along a roadway near his home as part of the 2010 torch relay to light the Vancouver/Whistler Olympic and Paralympic Games cauldron. His thought: "My father would have been very proud."

IT WAS MY IDEA to go for a walkabout after lunch. It was Riley's idea that our walk be around Lost Lake. The nature trail started fifteen minutes from our hotel. As we wound closer to the lake thumbnail-sized creatures forced a change in route. A teenaged volunteer pointed with her right hand to a detour, and with her left hand beckoned us over. She was hunched, watching the ground.

"I saw something hop," said Riley. "There's another."

"Frogs?" I asked.

"Miniatures," said the woman. "We call them toadlets. They breed in the lake. It's migration time." Her role was to ensure cyclists and hikers kept away and let the wee critters hop along. Their little lurches meant it would take them hours to cover open ground and reach the relative safety of the forest. Predators would harvest the unlucky ones.

"How many of them live?" asked Riley.

"I know the answer and will AirDrop it to your mind," I said. With that I stood and scrunched my face as though teleporting the information.

He thought me silly, and walked on. Whether he intended for us to walk for hours, talking along the trail and its offshoots, or it simply happened, I'm unsure. The walk informed my notion that the world will be fine in the hands of the coming generation.

"I'd like to make more movies," said Riley, when I asked about a recent course he'd taken. The week before we left for Banff, he'd been at a young filmmakers' program at Simon Fraser University. "I came up with a plot. We wrote the story. Tutors helped us make the script. Then we filmed it. My film was three minutes long."

He talked about his idea for a series of linked film vignettes. He identified the characters, their roles, and the narrative. When I asked a question, he had a ready answer. This was not a kid's casual "I want to be a firefighter" banter. His characterizations and plotting were easy to follow. Then I spoiled it all by saying, "That's quite clever. I think I'll write about it."

"Don't you dare," he said. "I'm just telling you 'cuz you're Grampa."

It was cool to realize a new generation of storytellers was emerging.

WE TOOK DINNER at a restaurant adorned with ski poles and memorabilia celebrating the early days on the mountains. Riley likes grazing on appetizers, so he ordered a bunch, deciding for me what I should have. A couple sat down next to us as my draft beer arrived, and we recognized one another. "You're from the train," said the man. "I'm Donovan. She's Dara. We've walked miles today. We're knackered."

They'd been travelling in Western Canada for several weeks and were now headed to Jasper and from there to Edmonton and a flight home to Dublin. "We've never had travels like this," said Dara. "I thought our country was gorgeous."

"It is," I said.

Donovan asked, "Did you get to the museum this afternoon?"

"Missed it," I said.

"It's a stunning display," Dara said of the gallery. Then she held up her glass of wine in a show of respect, saying, "This place is as old as Ireland. I never knew that."

The cultural centre had been closed when we walked by, but we'd looked in the windows. The Squamish (Coast Salish) and Lil'wat (Interior Salish) Nations built it, as this is their traditional territory. Many of the windows stretch three storeys high to capture the magnificence of tall totem poles. Their signage looks like this:

*Sḵwx̱wú7mesh Úxwumixw and Líl'wat7ul*

Raising his Guinness beer toward Dara and us, Donavan said, "Sláinte."

I raised my Kokanee beer, and Riley his soda. "Cheers."

RILEY AND I sauntered to the hotel beneath a canopy of stars.

BACK IN OUR hotel room Riley gravitated to headset seclusion and I to television news. Which did more brain damage, I wondered. I tossed a pillow at Riley and it bounced off him and onto the floor. I tossed another (one of my measures of a top-tier hotel is the number of pillows they provide for you to throw). He deflected it. Another. And then another.

"Enough," he said, sounding like the adult in the room.

# — 14 —

A MORNING MOUNTAIN DEW GLITTERED. The smell of cinnamon scones greeted our arrival at the train coach, complemented by an almond aroma of coffee wafting our way. It made you forget crawling out of bed early, showering away the sleep, and busing to the station. We weren't the only ones to notice the delicious smell. A bear cub was cavorting near the train when we boarded, shushed out of the way by crew to ensure passenger safety (and for the justifiable fear a Momma Bear might be close by). The cub moved into the bushes. There was a snort.

"What did he want most," Riley wondered, "coffee or cinnamon scones?"

"A wild berry smoothie and the kid holding it," I said.

Anna and Kristi welcomed everyone aboard as they were setting up the lower level for the first sitting of breakfast, which was not ours. We climbed the stairs to the upper level, where Kyla was placing cloth napkins on our tabletops, followed by Robyn with the cinnamon treats.

I played with my scruffy beard. Riley played with the buttons that adjusted his seat. Not because it needed adjusting but because they were buttons. Playful but unproductive activity is something one hopes follows kids into adulthood, but it's usually pestered out of them in the guise of encouraging better behaviour. I was learning not to do that. He leaned over and pressed away at my chair's buttons, his curiosity pleasing me.

"I'll see you on the deck," he announced, speaking through his hand as his fingers wiggled his loosening tooth.

"Let me have a coffee and then we'll go." Grampas are best when they're pliable; kids are best when they know you're pliable.

"Fine," he said, with a theatrical shrug.

Leaving Whistler in a northerly direction is a pleasant experience. You have the satisfaction of putting the population bulge behind you. Each home you pass is stage-worthy, its design slightly over the top (given neighbourly competition), begging to be noticed. You're rolling beside a beauty pageant. Green Lake's serenity gives way to the upper Cheakamus. Rivers here have argued their way through rock, and had their way with geography, and pay you no notice. They are low in the mountains and rush where they wish.

At Nairn Falls the water plunges 120 feet (40 metres). Steve, who had a Boston accent and was seated across the aisle from us, said, "Can you imagine being the first to flow down that river without the benefit of an advance scout?"

"You'd hear the roar long before you got there. You'd reconnoitre. You'd portage," was the calm appraisal from Michael of Kansas.

"One would hope," countered Joy, whose arm looped under Steve's, "but Steve doesn't always think that far ahead." Things went quiet.

An Aussie was in the aisle, standing away from his seat in anticipation of a view of the falls; he broke the newly formed conversational ice. "All up, we've been travelling five weeks in Canada," he said to no one in particular. "Today is what I've been waiting for."

RILEY AND I had an hour outside on the coach's deck, as our breakfast seating was in second place. The rural crawl around Pemberton, a semi-affordable alternative to costly Whistler, particularly for resort workers, was peaceful. The train tracks headed out on their own, having carved their preferred route here long before the paved road came along. We headed toward the few streets and few homes that make up D'Arcy, marking the south end of Anderson Lake. By the time we got there Riley and I were seated across from Bruce and Maggi of Missouri, and all four of us had ordered breakfast. Our views were unobstructed for the 13 miles (21 kilometres) we spent travelling beside the lake.

Maggi said, "I see a dozen cabins across the lake and no road access."

"You can only get there by boat," Bruce said. "Think of all the work that means when you build your cabin, tugging in all your supplies. The nice thing is that everyone who lives there wants to live there."

When Anna came by to refill our coffees, Bruce's was only filled halfway by prior agreement. When he raised it to his lips, his hands shook but nothing spilled. "You know, two years ago our travels were different. We went anywhere. Now, I'm slowing. And shaking." He said it matter-of-factly. "We always dreamed of a train trip together, the comfort and the commotion, the countryside. Trains prattle along, they sway, and passengers get jostled. With my shakes it makes me feel at home." His laugh was subdued, as was Maggi's. We weren't the first to hear this self-deprecating jibe at his Parkinson's disease.

"You OK?" Riley asked him.

"I'm OK, son. Never take your good health for granted. We've watched you and your grandfather. We'd like our family to know what it's like to travel by train together. Never thought about it until being here. Now, we're going to make it happen after we get home." He had excitement in his voice. "There are more than 200 places Amtrak can get to out of St. Louis. I'm going to book one of those as a start, and invite them along, and I'll take a megabyte of photographs to remember it all."

Whenever Riley and I had talked about my possibly writing a book about our travels, I'd explained that it changed your encounters with other people if they thought you might portray them in a story. I told him the old adage from the psychology lab: "Watching an experiment changes the experiment." We'd therefore not mentioned it to anyone. During a lull in the conversation with Bruce and Maggi, though, Riley piped up, "My grampa might write a book about this trip."

Bruce sat back in his chair and looked at me. "Will you write about us in your book?"

"Sure," said Riley, blithely changing the experiment.

Riley had spent time with my earlier travel books, liking "the one about Route 66 that Dad reads to me so I fall asleep" (not what a writer wishes to hear...). When we were planning our getaway it seemed reasonable that he would ask, "Will you write about our trip, Grampa?" Like most people, I've had exciting trips that would never merit being documented in a full-length book; perhaps a blog or magazine piece, but it's difficult to sustain a longer narrative. That requires incidents and anecdotes, mistakes and missteps. No reader wishes to hear that the writer is a smart traveller; they'd prefer to read about flubs and floundering. Having explained that to Riley, his suggestion was, "You should produce a beta version of your book. I can help you post it online and ask for reviews so people can make it better. Video game makers do that all the time."

AT LILLOOET WE were again beside the Fraser River, which we'd last seen when approaching its mouth in Metro Vancouver at the end of our other trip, but it would remain close for only the next 30 miles (50 kilometres). I was pleased we had a map to show us the flow of the Fraser. Thankfully, a map eases confusion, highlights the geographic markers, and helps explain the interrelated exploration. We were less than 40 miles (about 60 kilometres) from where the Fraser flows southeast, toward Lytton and the confluence of the Thompson and Fraser Rivers that, a few days ago, our train overlooked. As our train was heading north, it would be easy to overlook that proximity. Not long after a place called Pavilion, the Fraser River disappeared from our view where it courses across the Fraser Plateau and we routed away from it. We'd not see it again until after Williams Lake, much later in the day.

Indigenous Peoples are prominent in this vicinity, notably the St'át'imc Nation. Suffice it to say they are the original inhabitants. Among the St'át'imc the notion of an Elder is important. Elders are respected as "repositories of cultural and philosophical knowledge," responsible for conveying that to future generations. What might I learn from their practices? I knew their Elders shared traditional teachings with the young in part through cultural ceremonies. Would this train trip qualify as such for my role? I wondered if Riley saw me as Elder-Rick, or was it Older-Rick? I decided not to ask, as I knew my approach would guide his answer.

Fishing shacks we saw along the river were those of Indigenous Peoples who have specific harvesting rights. Anna explained, "Fishing and hunting rights are entrenched in treaties signed by leaders of the Indigenous Peoples on behalf of their people, and the leaders of government on behalf of all Canadians." I would later learn that this was not embedded in Canada's constitution until the early 1980s. I share a responsibility with Indigenous Elders to ensure that all our grandchildren understand such rights.

ANNA HAD EARLIER pointed out the "jade-green colour" of Seton Lake as the train snaked along its shore. She was quick to add that the lake's colour came from glaciers feeding it, not from the semi-precious jade stone found nearby: "The jade was overlooked by the American and European miners who came seeking gold. The 'large black rocks' identified by government assayers along the banks of the Fraser River from Hope to Lillooet were in their way."

Then, in the mid-1880s, Chinese miners arrived to rework the tailings of those earlier miners. They did well with their collaborative sifting, finding overlooked gold. In their spare time, they cleaned and piled the "large black rocks," recognizing them as China's "Imperial gem"—jade. The Chinese miners called it Yu, the "Stone of Heaven." Its characteristics personified virtues: *Courage* for its ability to not bend; *charity* for the warmth of its lustre; *rectitude* for its translucence, which revealed its inner markings; *justice* for its sharp angles; and *wisdom* for the clarity of the bell-like tone it made when struck.

"There is a price for gold but no price for jade," asserts a Chinese proverb. Commercially, not philosophically, there was a very good price for this nephrite jade—if the miners could get it to China without a costly tax being levied. Fortunately for them, they realized no one taxed rocks.

A miner named Foster found a spectacular "Stone of Heaven" resting on his claim at Hell Creek around Bridge River near Lillooet. The boulder became beautiful when polished. The one-ton block of "Lillooet jade" came to rest in the reflecting pond at the Academic Quadrangle on the Burnaby Mountain campus, designated Simon Fraser University's "founding stone." When the university opened in 1965, Haida artist Bill Reid placed pieces of jade, cut from this boulder, into the university's mace that he created.

"We should come back to Lillooet," Riley said to me, when I told him about the miners who left gold behind and overlooked the gemstones. "Maybe they missed something." It seemed fitting to me that the "Stone of Heaven" was understated in its natural form and took time for its value to be revealed, kind of like that of a grandson—hiding in plain sight.

AFTER OUR HOST Anna explained that we were travelling alongside part of the old Cariboo Road, an American passenger in his late thirties raised his scholarly eyebrows and asked her, "Which Cariboo Road are you talking about?"

All travellers have encountered a road with a name used by locals that's not the same as the name on the map you hold. Sometimes a road takes a new name when it makes a curve, or when it crosses municipal boundaries, or when two independent roads merge. The Cariboo was called the Gold Colony, and transportation of goods and police required the building of reliable roads, coincidentally carving the way for portions of the future railroads, like the one we were travelling on.

Here's a patter that may bring eye fatigue, but it speaks to the man's question: Lillooet's Main Street marks Mile 0 for the Old Cariboo Trail, which was rebranded Old Cariboo Road, just because. In 1861, when wagons could travel over it, it became the Cariboo Wagon Trail. It headed northward to the town of Clinton, and on to Williams Lake,

Quesnel, and east to Barkerville. The name of the Harrison Trail of 1862 (an old HBC route), which came up this way from Vancouver via Harrison Lake to Lillooet en route to Clinton, eventually blended with Northern Cariboo Road to differentiate it from the southern branch, the Yale Cariboo Road. The latter was also referred to as the Second Cariboo Road or Southern Cariboo Road. It was built in 1865 from Yale through Hell's Gate and on to Clinton, joining the Cariboo Wagon Road proper at Mile 47. The result was sometimes called the Great North Road. Portions constructed by the Royal Engineers earned it the honorific Queen's Highway. When the CPR came through the Fraser Canyon they built over or destroyed much of the road. Thus, after 1885, Ashcroft replaced Yale as the south end of the south road. Ashcroft to Clinton was colloquially called the Third Cariboo Road. Roadhouses along the way were identified in terms of their distance north from Lillooet; hence names such as 70 Mile House and 100 Mile House. Many towns retain those names today, though the road beside them is gazetted Highway 97, while locals call it the Cariboo Highway.

Got that?

OVER THE PUBLIC ADDRESS SYSTEM, Kyla said, "There were camels on that plateau." A few passengers glanced out the train windows in hope of seeing what was not to be seen. Once called the Dromedary Express or Cariboo Camels, a group of camels was introduced in 1862, but the animals proved of questionable use despite being able to carry twice the load of mules or horses. They'd been transferred north from Nevada where their use in gold rushes and along mail routes was no longer viable. What didn't get transferred was word that they struck fear into mules and horses. Camels sent stagecoach drivers and miners alike into a frenzy as they tried to protect their animals. They smelled so badly that horses would not pass them on the trail, and mules would jump off a cliff to avoid them. Eventually, the unwanted pack animals were set free and left to roam, until the last among them died circa 1900.

"We had those in Australia," said one of the more boisterous Aussies. His booming voice commanded everyone's attention. "They helped us build a railway. So we named the train after them. It's *The Afghan Express*. Well, we call it *The Ghan*."

*The Ghan* is a three-day run in the Outback, from Adelaide through Alice Springs to Darwin in the Northern Territory. Camels were already in Australia when construction of the railway began toward the end of the nineteenth century. Workers from Afghanistan had brought the camels to Australia. One use was to transport travellers. When the train was first established, it needed to route where water was in sufficient supply to maintain power in the steam locomotives. Such facilities did not extend all the way to Alice Springs. Passengers wanting to go beyond the tracks had the option of dromedary transport, hence *The Ghan*'s logo: a rider atop a one-humped camel. *The Ghan*'s name references the earliest camel drivers, not the beasts of burden.

"Coaches aren't as nice as what we're on here," said the Aussie, "but there aren't any mountains to get in the way of the view."

WE WERE SEATED at lunch with a South African couple, Friedrich and Barbara. I was ready for the seared tuna and veggies that Kristi had recommended. I've a good relationship with white wine, but daytime drinking makes me sleepy despite the gratification it bestows. An elderly friend of mine has a way of encouraging mid-day libation, asking those around her, "Would you like a little sensation?" As I had a relaxing seat waiting for my reclining self after lunch, I accepted such enjoyment in the spirit of Woody Guthrie, who said, "I never drink unless I'm alone or with someone else."

As lunch service began, we pulled onto a siding to let a southbound CNR freight train slip by, laden with milled lumber and woodchips. The woodchips were en route to Asia, where they would be processed into premium paper products before returning to Canada. Barbara said into the noise of the passing train, "The economy here would stand still without rail transport."

She paused, and went on. "Well, I guess they had gold rushes without the trains."

Friedrich said, "We also come from a land of gold rushes. We had ours in the Transvaal. That's really Johannesburg. And, like here in Canada, the gold rush brought a boom in railroad construction, not the other way around."

"What you'll want to do in South Africa is ride Rovos Rail," said Barbara. "Its trains are the real thing. Steam locomotive. Restored coaches. There's nothing like it in North America. And, for style, Rovos Rail's trains sit alone."

THE *PRIDE OF AFRICA* TRAVELS several routings offered by Rovos Rail. For example, you can be aboard their trains from Cape Town to Victoria Falls. Pretoria-based, the company's trains operate in South Africa, Namibia, Zimbabwe, and Tanzania, with special runs elsewhere on the continent. The train is a stretched-out museum. They do not have televisions, and cellphone use is restricted to one's room.

"You'll not have more than seventy fellow travellers," said Friedrich. "Waiters, porters, butlers—all the staff are in retro-style uniforms. Dining is formal, too." He made it clear this was not a train for the scruffy: "When dinner is served, plan on cocktail dresses for ladies and jackets for gentlemen."

Owner Rohan Vos (thus Rovos) said of his initial idea in 1986, "I remember the occasion very clearly. On a wintry evening I was subsiding into a hot bath with my Red Heart rum and Coke close at hand. There'd been a power cut, so [I was] musing by candlelight about the consequences of turning a hobby into a business."

They don't teach that at Harvard.

And so began what he unabashedly calls his "delusions of grandeur." As he put it, "It was an uncharted course and I had little idea where to start, let alone where to aim . . . During the next few years or so, I had many agonising thoughts regretting the move. I could never have imagined how all-consuming the business was to become both financially and emotionally."

Vos had once accepted an invitation on a train ride with no thought of it becoming his life's passion—a train to the one-time Afrikaners settlement of Magaliesberg in South Africa's Western Cape, and it inspired his interest in heritage train travel.

Fixing things, restoring things, that's what Vos liked. The coaches were bought at auction or rescued from retirement and subsequently restored. Initially, he wanted to have the careworn carriages hitched behind existing South African Railways trains for private family excursions. But he considered the coupling costs prohibitive. What might it cost to run them privately, he wondered, other than acquiring a 1938 steam engine and rebuilding it? That's how it became a business rather than a family hobby, as he needed to recoup the costs.

Vos's first consist for his initial trip in 1989 included seven coaches and the locomotive. "Per kilometre and per carriage fees to the railways had to be paid in advance," he said. And a proper season of train trips that could be booked in advance required his commitment to an advertised schedule, to "project consistency and reliability to agents and passengers." While an announced schedule is common in transportation enterprises, it's a daunting prospect for a start-up operation. "By printing the schedule, you have to run," he said. If the passenger numbers did not materialize, he was still obligated to honour the train's departure. "One can lose considerably more money establishing a reputation than it might cost to buy or construct the hardware," said Vos.

He recalled 1993 when he thought, "I'm going broke. It's the end of the line for me." Then, his positive nature took over: "That's not a problem, we'll sell more tickets." Getting Rovos Rail to the break-even point financially, not to mention to the point of profitability, took Vos into his sixth season. "Bankruptcy was avoided by a nose," he said. His financiers were "by turns sympathetic and skeptical." Looking back today, Vos said of the unfathomable risk he faced in the beginning, "It was the best bad decision I ever took." Rovos Rail is still family-owned and now also operates hotels where their guests can stay.

Vos recounted, "It was guests who first called our train the *Pride of Africa*." Such reputations need to be earned, not claimed. The age of the coaches and the sense of an elusive past create a timelessness that enhances the landscape's primordial beauty. The *Pride of Africa* shares a hidden truth of most train travel; it's not a step back in time, it's a step away from the times that consume us. Vos admits to passengers as they depart, "We're never on time. But meals will be." That's fine with everyone, especially when they next hear his philosophy: "I like to think we bring a lot of happiness to people."

# — 15 —

ONE OF THE DELIGHTS of train travel in the Cariboo is that you enjoy everyone's backyards—the open range and seldom-fenced vistas where wildlife roams unfettered.

"Bear!" shouted Riley, his second sighting of our trip. "There! Bear!" The black bear ran beside the train. "A bear behind!" shouted a woman pointing to a cub chasing its mother.

This is the Cariboo. Though there are a hundred countries I've never been to, travels in the others have shown me only three places where I personally "feel centred," if I may use that term. Since my first trip here as a teenager, one such place has been the Cariboo, for reasons I can't identify but probably include a sky without borders, people as real as dirt, and creek stones that tumble underfoot of wildlife; all that and the fellowship of pine trees. Richard Thomas Wright told me the unexplainable emotion is *topophilia*, which he termed "a strong love of place."

KYLA REMINDED US, "It was not always this comfortable to travel here. Even though thousands of people came to the Cariboo, it was a difficult journey. Many thought the gold rush town of Barkerville would last forever, and had that turned out to be true, surely a railway would've been built there from Quesnel. Perhaps our routing today would've followed those tracks. But they don't exist." Barkerville, 50 miles (80 kilometres) to the east, was named after lucky striker Billy Barker,

a boatman from Cambridgeshire, England. He was not the first prospector in the area—indeed, he was a veritable latecomer, not arriving
until 1862—but he was the luckiest.

Placer mining at its simplest is gold panning, swirling dirt in the
hope it sheds shining "colour" and reveals gold. Its next mode is rush-
ing water over gravel shovelled into a sluice box, to speedier effect.
Barker watched others panning and sluicing small flakes profitably. He
wondered what might be down deeper where larger, heavier pieces
of gold may have settled. He dug a shaft and discovered a rich vein
more than 50 feet (16 metres) down. The Barkerville boom was such
a success that anyone dreaming of railways would envision one ending at this sure-to-be metropolis. Alas... Barkerville is no longer the
bustling town it was briefly in the 1860s, when one newspaper confi-
dently stated that "Barkerville is fast becoming the largest town west of
Chicago and north of San Francisco," a status it never actually achieved.
Today it's a provincial heritage site of renown, with more than one hundred of its once nearly condemned buildings resuscitated, along with
their stories.

BILLY BARKER'S STORY is not unlike that of the town named after him.
Success came only temporarily to both. He had left his wife and daughter in Britain when new railroads put the canal men out of work, and
he headed for the California Gold Rush. From there, he struck out for
the Cariboo. It's often left unsaid that his wife, Jane, went to the work-
house (most probably with her daughter), where she died a horrible
death from syphilis. His daughter survived his abandonment, but they
never reunited. Barker amassed enormous wealth from his Cariboo
gold strike in 1862; his wife and daughter saw none of it, even before
bad investments and high living left him to die a pauper in Victoria.

Barker's story is oft told, but what about the other people who
gave Barkerville the charisma and character of its reputation? I'd never
heard the term "bonepicker" until I found it used for a series of doc-
umentaries about little-known personalities who played a part in the

Cariboo Gold Rush. The creators of *The Bonepicker* series are historians Amy Newman and Richard Thomas Wright. Newman told me, "We borrowed the name from the Chinese people who travelled to the interior of British Columbia, searching for the graves of Chinese workers who had died from the hardships of working on the railroad and mines. They dug up the graves and placed the bones in large pottery jars. They collected more than 300 unidentified individuals in this way, to be returned home to China for proper burial. The person who did this became known as a bonepicker—someone who captures the essence of a little-known individual." Newman said, "And that's what we hope to achieve with our storytelling."

The Chinese bonepickers were being honoured when Newman and Wright adopted the appellation to define their work today. In that light, it is thanks to the work of bonepickers past and present we know stories that, like those related to bones in a jar, might otherwise have disappeared completely. Even well-intentioned writers push truths under the blanket of time, and it takes patient work to find and share them.

The video series by Newman and Wright reminded me of how American radio broadcaster Paul Harvey delved into little-known aspects of history whose truths had been distorted by common beliefs or a lack of information, an early version of Snopes.com. For more than thirty years, beginning in 1976, Harvey introduced a storyline at the start of an episode, and then his sonorous voice would urge program listeners to wait for "the *rest* of the story," which he'd soon reveal (after a commercial).

The gold rush to the Cariboo was a potpourri of hopes and hazards, secrets and scenarios, and men and women chasing difficult dreams. Harvey described his own enthusiasm for finding such tales as "can't wait to get out of bed every morning and rush down to the teletypes and pan for gold..." Here's how I think Harvey might have introduced two colourful Barkerville residents and their individual stories.

"Doc Keithley was an American miner who found gold on a creek running into Quesnel Lake in 1860.

"Now wait for the *rest* of the story... Doc Keithley was *not* a doctor, as The Bonepickers divulge. The actual truth is that he was given the name Doc because he was an educated man, a solicitor in the early days of the California rush of '49. He hightailed it north in search of gold on the Fraser and Quesnel Rivers, where a creek still bears his name. But he skedaddled south again, slightly ahead of his debts. He appears a few years later in South Dakota's 'town with no law, no law at all,' where he was a judge known as 'Old Necessity.' He ran for mayor of Deadwood and lost (against E. B. Farnum, of later TV *Deadwood* fame)."

Again I hear Paul Harvey's voice: "Florence Wilson arrived in North America aboard a bride-ship; the enigma of Barkerville started a saloon and remained single, then disappeared in 1874...

"Now wait for the *rest* of the story... Florence Wilson is remembered as the esteemed librarian of Barkerville, a much-reviewed actress of the Cariboo Amateur Dramatic Association at the Theatre Royal, and the celebrated nun-like Bride of Barkerville who never dallied with miners and who built a saloon. She disappeared in 1874. Ah, but wait, Dear Florence. Research by *The Bonepicker* series and friends on four continents tells her story differently.

"Florence Margaret Baron Wilson was born upper-middle class: landed gentry from Wales on one side and a solicitor father on the other. Her mother, Margaret, was, as Wright puts it, 'known to Queen Victoria and the Duchess of Kent' and was asked to write a song for Victoria's eighteenth birthday. Margaret was a friend and neighbour of Charles Dickens in Bloomsbury; both Florence and her mother wrote for Dickens's magazines. When her father died the family fell on hard times and Florence became governess for an English family. The Crimean War put an end to that employment and she eventually boarded a ship for North America. After a stop in Victoria, Florence headed for the Cariboo. Unmarried, she was not cloistered. The first crack in *that* story was a contemporaneous diarist's note, discovered in 2015, telling that she was 'living with Samuel Tompkins, blacksmith.' In 2019, research for *The Bonepicker* showed that in 1864 a Presbyterian minister travelling through the area conducted a marriage service for Florence and Tompkins in Barkerville. The couple and their child, Alice, moved to San Francisco. Samuel died of the long-term results of typhoid, which he'd contracted on Williams Creek, and which caused a 'softening of the brain,' or dementia. Florence then married a James Hopkins, may have had more children or step-children, was widowed, married again, and finally died in 1902 in Napa, California, of heart disease. She was a more complete person than Barkerville residents or visitors ever knew, as it was easier for locals and historians to say she disappeared."

As Harvey would say, "And now you know the *rest* of the story…"

DINNER WAS NOT part of our day's itinerary. Yet as the day wore on, track delays and our time on sidings resulted in dinnertime arriving while we were several hours from our destination. Soon Anna and Kristi were walking the aisle serving a delightfully presented meal of bow tie pasta with creamy pesto and chicken, sun dried tomatoes and spinach, belying its last-minute preparation. One could imagine the same happening in each coach of the train, as unexpected circumstances met solution.

Twilight overcame the landscape—and our conversations. The crew slowed then stopped their storytelling. Foxes and songbirds, snowshoe hares and grouse in the woods alongside the tracks scurried to their sleeping quarters; in their predator-prone world, not all would survive the night.

OUR TRAIN PASSED through Williams Lake without slowing, and without incident. Not that we were expecting anything. This was once Canada's "wild west," but today it's pretty tame, at least when darkness has fallen and you're on a train.

There's a perception that Canada's West in the 1800s was less wild than that of its U.S. neighbour. True, there were fewer guns, a smaller population, and respected law enforcement. But what happened in Canada's West was every bit as difficult, unpredictable, vile, and coarse as anything unfolding in California or Oregon absent the promotion of revisionist history for a tantalized television audience—it's simply that Canada West's shenanigans never caught the attention of Hollywood in the same way. For example, bad guys easily crossed the unguarded border. Like Boone Helm.

As The Bonepickers rustled through dusty files and archived newspapers, they pieced together a sketch of the once infamous, now forgotten scoundrel. Born in Kentucky, Helm's ne'er-do-well antics brought the thirty-three-year-old to Quesnel around 1861. Helm played the real-life parts of an unwelcome interloper: bandit, outlaw, horse rustler, killer, and cannibal.

I see Helm as tallish with a face that is jaggedly unattractive. His hair is unkempt and in need of a wash. His clothes are second-hand and scruffy. He's got scars from more than one bullet wound and maybe a cut on his cheek that never healed. That kind. The roustabout's life was mayhem after he renounced his wife, stabbed his cousin, was judged insane, escaped custody, and headed west in time for the California Gold Rush of 1848 to 1855. From there he would make his way to Oregon, then Utah, and eventually the Cariboo in British Columbia.

In 1858 his plot to steal thousands of horses from the Pend d'Oreille tribe in Oregon went awry. Pursued by the affronted Indigenous people, Helm's band of thieves fled into a blizzard. Trapped by snow, they quarrelled. Lost, the weak and wounded died. Eventually, a starving Helm stumbled alone into a camp on the Snake River. He carried the well-chewed leg of a fellow gang member.

Accounts have Helm surfacing in Salt Lake and being hired out to Mormon vigilantes, the Danites ("Destroying Angels"). Leaving this questionable employment, he stole U.S. Army horses, shot the herders, and killed a soldier before gum-booting his way north, stopping to work in the Salmon River mines near Florence, Idaho. After putting a bullet in gambler Dutch Fred (you may think these names are made up, but they've been fact-checked), Helm headed for B.C., chased by a posse of Fred's friends and revenge-seeking miners.

Helm rode, walked, and hitched rides to the Cariboo goldfields. In late winter 1861, a sixteen-year-old cowboy named Andrew Splawn was winter-herding a rancher's cattle near Cache Creek. A departing April chinook wind swept snow across the grass, and Splawn went in search of more accessible pasture. He trailed the cattle north on the Cariboo Trail, recently carved for cattlemen and gold rushers. While Splawn made camp one evening, a rambler appeared fireside and befriended him. "My name is Boone Helm," the man said. "Did you ever hear of me?"

"Who had not heard of Helm?" Splawn later wrote. "The very name spelled blood and crime." Splawn's recollections placed Helm in the Cariboo where gold strikes made prospectors rich, fuelled legends, and tempted thieves.

Helm tried to convince Splawn to join up. "We'll make one big haul, then skip," offered the man wanted by authorities in five U.S. states. Splawn rejected the overture, but Helm found other willing acolytes. During that summer of '62, two outlaw groups worked along the Cariboo Trail, threatening passersby and robbing the defenceless.

That July a packer named Charles Bouchier left Barkerville with merchants Harris Lewis and David Sokolowski. Reportedly, they carried $18,000 in gold and cash. Wishing to make headway in the summer heat, the three branched off from the protective comfort of a larger party and were later found murdered beside the trail, pack animals missing, riches gone. A coroner's jury hastily raised $700 to fund a hunt for the suspects.

Helm was arrested in Victoria three months later, on the unrelated charge of not paying his bill at the Adelphi Saloon after threatening the barkeeper with "Don't you know I'm a desperate character?" An extradition request was received from Florence, Idaho. But Helm had already been released from prison. He continued to wreak havoc in Yale and in the Thompson country before leaving B.C. and venturing on to Virginia City and Bannack in Montana. There he joined the notorious Plummer gang. Their robberies went uncounted; their murders numbered more than a hundred. Homesteaders and communities formed a Committee of Vigilance in 1864 to end the rampage by banishing most every outlaw. They drove many away through harassment, rounded up others for jail, and kept a few for hanging. Boone Helm was on the gallows within hours of his capture and confessions. As vigilantes cinched the rope around the man ahead of him on the gallows, Helm shouted, "Kick away, old fella! I'll be in hell with you in a minute."

OUR TRAIN WAS again travelling alongside the Fraser River, our night's destination of Quesnel still 60 miles (100 kilometres) ahead. We were having a rare late arrival. Eight or ten hours make a terrific train day for most people. Twelve hours breeds novel ways to pass the time.

Trees, the forest floor, and rangeland, each in its way provided me with a form of relaxation I've enjoyed since childhood. I see faces in their midst. It is more than observing a cloud that looks like a lobster. The phenomenon even has a name: *pareidolia*. I think of it as a fancy rather than a condition, a perception rather than reality. It happens to certain people when things like overlapping leaves, crossing branches, or hillside rock formations appear to form random images; to me, faces. Particularly intriguing are cedar bows with their droopy moustaches, and pine bark with knotty noses. For example, alongside our train at dusk, I watched blemished fence posts wherein nicks and notches formed eyes below which rain had eroded elongated noses, above mouths eaten away in the wood (by squirrels, woodpeckers, or beetles?) in what together formed a gallery of sharp-jawed women and squinting men—Cariboo pioneers. You may snicker at how I relaxed in this way as the train moved slowly enough for me to witness a dozen smirking faces. But I'll bet you can see the man in the moon...

By this point Steve and Joy were sleeping soundly across from me. Snores punctuated the sound of the train's wheels on the tracks. Both sounds were soothing in their way. Riley dozed, perhaps the only one in the coach asleep but not snoring.

It was, for me, the nicest time on the train—the world slowly coming your way as the train takes on the ambience of night-time travel.

Trains heading into dark make few demands on their passengers. There's little to say or point to. We travelled under curved glass. I could see stars.

In this contemplative setting, I recalled my friend Jess, who hailed from this part of the province and was an early advocate for establishing the Alexander Mackenzie Heritage Trail between Quesnel and Bella Coola. His work in 1987 aligned with that of the Nature Conservancy of Canada, a lead agency aiming to bring this about in time for the bicentennial of Mackenzie's 1793 trek. Jess convened a meeting in Quesnel for all the stakeholders along the trail. After most of those present had offered their views, the lone representative of the Nuxälk Nation stood and said, "I want to remind you that when your man Mackenzie was lost, it was my people who showed him the way to the Coast... on *our* trail." The trail of which he spoke was the same one, also called the Nuxälk-Carrier Grease Trail, named after the oil of the oolichan fish that came from the ocean on this trading path, exchanged for tools and produce. As Mackenzie likely saw, you can actually get the fish itself to burn like a candle, though a more practical application is to consider it a butter spread.

Whatever appeal Quesnel held for our arrival this night was masked in shadows, and the limited traffic of a Sunday in small-town B.C. Motor coaches waited at the train station, their yawning drivers standing in front of them. Our fellow travellers detrained. Those walking by me smiled at the sleeping Riley. We were the last off, and when I woke him to move, we went straight onto the bus.

The low-rise hotel was ready for our arrival. Management had been alerted of our lateness and had sent staff aboard the buses to hand out room keys as we made our way to the hotel. Those at the property realized there'd be little need for bar service (yet it was open, just in case) or meals (they'd kept staff around, though no one had left the train hungry), and that most of us just wanted to get to our rooms. They thoughtfully opened fire escape doors to accommodate those wanting to walk up instead of waiting for the elevators.

Riley slumped along the hallway, critiquing the hotel's age and décor. I opened the door to our room where our luggage waited for us. I turned down the sheets on Riley's bed, expecting him to wash up. Instead, he crawled into bed fully clothed, wrapped his arms around the pillow, and fell asleep immediately. I pulled the covers over him in a gesture that comforted us both.

# — 16 —

W HISTLE POSTS (SIGNED WITH A "W") are reminders to train engineers to blow their horns for a level crossing ahead. I should have anticipated the one about to appear in our journey.

"Shower?" I said to a sleepy, fully dressed Riley who was staring at the clock. It was 5:30 in the morning. "It's the only way you'll wake up." The transfer to the train was in twenty minutes.

"You shower," he said through a yawn.

"I did. Now you."

Riley washed off the previous day's travel and brushed up a smile. I wished he were old enough to drink coffee, as I thought he could use one.

"We're first sitting for breakfast this morning," he said. "I'm starving."

Once on board, Riley—tuckered out of conversation—dove into the front two seats in the lower level dining room. They were the loners, with no seats across from them.

When I was his age, our family couldn't afford to dine out often or go to fancy places. If I asked my mom to leave something off my dinner plate (like onions) or put something different on it, she'd say, "I'm not running a restaurant here..." Riley leads a more charmed life. He was aboard a train that offered one of the country's finest restaurants experiences—and he realized it. When Anna greeted us, he asked, "I'd like one pancake please, and the kind of potatoes you served yesterday at lunch, and strawberries. That's all, thank you." I put coarse pepper on Riley's strawberries telling him it would give his mouth the taste contrast he needed to wake up. Ever game, he tried them. Often, the best parts of life are not on the menu.

Ground mist informed the passenger mood as we rode into the low hills. "Breath of God," a traveller called it, an analogy I'd never heard and immediately liked.

Later, in our seats on the upper level, I asked Riley if he'd like to hear a story about the geography or how these rail tracks were built.

"I think, Grampa, I'd like some quiet. I'll just look out the window and think."

Wise man.

EARLIER IN THIS BOOK, I mused about explorers Mackenzie, Thompson, and Fraser, asking, "What was it about three teenagers in the late 1700s that set them in motion to become Western Canada's most important explorers?" The answer was a desire for independence. Such a trait holds true today. When the future owner of the *Rocky Mountaineer* was a teenager, a 1972 Toyota symbolized independence for him. It wasn't the coolest of cars but relying on his parents for transportation wasn't cool, either. Peter Armstrong worked summers and after school, and, at seventeen, walked into a dealership and plopped down his entire savings of $1,600, expecting to drive away with the car. However, he didn't realize that the price of admission to adulthood would cost an additional $500 for insurance and licensing. He took a bus home.

That night, he shared his disappointment with his father. David Armstrong had grown up in New Brunswick during the Depression. After serving in the Second World War, he took advantage of the free university education offered to those who agreed to military service for five years after graduation. Eventually he sold stocks and bonds for a national firm, doing well enough to become a regional vice-president. Vancouver became the family's home.

Instead of offering to finance the $500 Peter needed for the car, David turned to his favourite parenting trick: transforming adversity into a life lesson. "Meet me downtown tomorrow," David told Peter.

Peter recalls, "My father introduced me to my first bank manager, who startled me by asking, 'Have you had a loan before?'" *No* was the truthful answer but was it the right one when you're being asked if you can be trusted with someone else's money? By the time the bank manager granted the loan, one message was received loud and clear: "You gotta pay this back."

Peter signed up for every shift at his part-time job. A month later, he was back in the manager's office with the $500. Having squeezed every last cent into the loan repayment, he was surprised to hear: "Plus five dollars for interest, please."

A year later, Peter's father died of pancreatic cancer. Although he felt like the ground beneath him had crumbled, he realized his father had provided a solid foundation for adulthood.

As he worked to ensure the *Rocky Mountaineer*'s success, there were extended periods when Peter got vertigo walking on the thin edge of financial ruin, a slip away from bankruptcy. He'd borrowed every penny he could and came just short of pawning the bedroom curtains. He knew his stubborn focus on the train's survival cost him in family ways as well; being an often absent, always preoccupied dad would take a toll. Yet the echo of his father's wisdom would prove to be his stabilizing factor.

"I'm a little tenacious," said Peter with a smile, half in wry amusement. "Being tenacious is like walking a tightrope knowing you can't go back, and you have to get to the other side. You don't look down because you don't want to focus on failure. If you focus on that, you *will* fail. You need to keep your eye on what success looks like."

It was Peter's older brother, Bev, who took on their father's role of trusted mentor and door opener, particularly when the *Rocky Mountaineer* business was developing. In terms of business success, Bev was a Bentley to Peter's Toyota. Peter was the dreamer, caught up in running a railway, which Bev found more exciting than putting together land deals or feeding people at the restaurant chain he co-owned. Bev adopted Peter's dream, and loved to invite friends on the train, sharing his favourite wines and holding court in the corner of a railway coach.

Peter suffered his most profound loss when Bev died unexpectedly in 2002. Grappling with Bev's death consumed Peter. His passion for business deflated. His drive returned slowly, though, and today Peter is doing for his three adult children what their paternal grandfather taught him: lead by example. And he shares Bev's advice like a mantra: "Think of the long term. Plan for the unexpected. Enjoy your moment."

Yet Peter's philosophy about the *Rocky Mountaineer* is not about his moment but rather the ongoing moment of train travel that each passenger experiences: "Something magical happens when people get on the train. Their behaviour changes in ways they never expected. They become retrospective—or maybe the word is introspective. They dream a little. They tell their life stories to total strangers. They listen intently to people they don't know. Such are the hidden truths of train travel."

I'D ASKED ROBIN, the train manager, if he had time for coffee. I was curious how someone ended up managing a train with responsibility for nearly a thousand passengers. We sat in the dining car with no one around except Anna and Kristie, who were preparing for the next meal service. While we talked, the train bypassed the city of Prince George, near the geographical centre of B.C., and turned east toward Jasper.

Robin said, "Everyone wants a connection to train travel. Some guests are young, though not usually as young as Riley. Some are old, older than you. There's a magic, a sense of history and of what might be."

He shifted the story to his onboard colleagues. "The staff members are as excited getting on the train as the guests. Many guests are reliving a childhood train trip loaded with feelings of surprise that they'd like to recapture. On a recent train trip, an older man from the Netherlands told me when he looked around the world, he decided there were two highlights he wanted to experience. This was one. Next, he was determined to see the pyramids in Egypt. Imagine that—his final travel dreams were the pyramids and the *Rocky Mountaineer*."

Robin was from a railway family out of Alberta. One of his grandfathers was elected union leader with the Order of Railroad Telegraphers.

His uncle, David McLean, the former chair of CNR, spent his first two years living above a CN station house. An advertisement from Rocky Mountaineer caught Robin's eye and soon he was serving meals aboard the train. Ten years later, he's seen loads of changes and expects many more.

"Riley's an unusual guest for us," he said. "We don't have a lot of kids aboard." He told me it's becoming more common because parents worry train travel may disappear before their kids experience the slower glide through time. He said, "From what I've seen, though, it's hard to tell who benefits more from a train ride: the grandkids or the grandparents."

I liked that.

We talked about kids missing school to take an off-season train trip. "You should never let school interfere with your child's education," I said, paraphrasing Mark Twain's paraphrasing of Grant Allen.

I asked him about recycling. "How do you deal with all the waste?"

"You should talk with Zeb," he said. "He heads up the company-wide team overseeing all those programs." Robin got on his walkie-talkie before he wandered off, and asked Zeb to join me.

Zeb is a born storyteller, as I knew from his earlier story about working with *National Geographic*.

"Talk to me about garbage," I said.

"You realize environmental responsibility isn't always about legislation, though that influences corporate and personal behaviour. Mostly, environmental ethics is about attitude and individuals or companies accepting responsibility to deal with the waste they create."

I nodded, remembering all the news stories about politicians and municipal staff ignoring reports of highly contaminated drinking water in poorer neighbourhoods.

"I was a sous-chef on the *Rocky Mountaineer*," he said. "I came out of the restaurant business. My grandfather was a train conductor, that's how I came by my railway chops."

"And the garbage?"

"We travel through a lot of towns, with different facilities to cope with refuse. We had to set our own standards and lead some of those communities to introduce better practices."

There was a Green Team in place already and Zeb joined it. "Every time—and I mean every time—someone comes up with a good idea or finds best practices somewhere else, that gets implemented."

"Every time?" I chided.

"It can't be otherwise. Not for us. Each trip we'll have—count 'em—dozens of guests asking, 'What do you do with this?,' holding up meal trays or handing back souvenir packaging. It gave us a corporate vision: we want to recycle 100 percent of all recyclable materials, and get everything else into proper facilities."

An example from the early years: Rocky Mountaineer inherited coaches with toilets that discarded sewage from the moving train onto the tracks. (Stop: think of the outside work crews replacing ties or rails.) Within a few seasons, it was among the first trains in North America with state-of-the-art onboard sewage facilities for each coach.

Zeb said, "Consider ninety thousand guests a season. Maybe a million plates of food served. We looked at how we could divert products from the waste stream and at what suppliers deliver, so we could reduce our waste by avoiding unnecessary packaging or using biodegradable packaging. Did I say our goal is *zero* waste?"

Zeb nodded a commitment to Riley, who was sitting patiently listening—perhaps because he and his generation expect Zeb's and mine to get it right.

IAN AND LYNN sat across from us at lunch. They were heading home to Edmonton, a four-hour drive east of our final stop, so they'd spend the night in Jasper. "We think this route is more impressive—in some ways more important—than the southern route, Rogers Pass, Banff, and all that. That route might be more famous. But it shouldn't be. Here, through the Yellowhead, the pioneers had real tough sledding."

Lynn said, "What makes this route different is how it was discovered. It was considered earlier than it was developed, because it made more sense. But the southern route got built first by CPR because it was closer to the U.S. border. The Yellowhead was a site of a significant exodus west long before the railroads came. Edmonton is where the Overlanders of '62 marshalled their group, and then moved on into the B.C. wilderness before it was a province. They were the bravest of the pioneers. And they had a pregnant woman with them."

EVEN IN SUNSHINE, the rugged land outside our train windows was an intimidating wilderness. It looked to be impassable except by bulldozer or chainsaw, or maybe on foot, if you went slowly along game trails, ducking branches. I asked myself, what would possess a woman to come from Ireland via Massachusetts, Minnesota, and eventually the Canadian Prairies, to land here at the Yellowhead Pass in the middle-of-nowhere-1862? What gave her the daring to bring along three children—six-year-old Gus, named after his father, Augustus; Mary Jane, only four; and Charles, celebrating his first birthday—and with a baby on the way? Was it the lure of recently discovered Cariboo gold-fields? Was it the fear of losing her husband to the thrills and dangers of exploration? Was it because of her husband's expectation that she'd stick by her man and accompany him? Whatever the reason, Catherine O'Hare Schubert was the only woman to travel with the Overlanders.

*Stop right there.* "That's legend, not fact," Richard Thomas Wright told me. "A number of women joined with the Overlanders. Since they were Métis, however, their presence was not acknowledged by most writers of the day."

It is fair to say that no one else has researched or written about the Overlanders as extensively as Wright. He's read every diary left behind, sussed out dozens of daily reports from the era, spoken with relatives, found tattered letters in attics, and delved into musty archives piecing together lost narratives. The more elusive a story, the harder he works to determine its truths. A strong believer in the concept of "place" and its ramifications in storytelling, Wright has travelled the entire Overlanders route on foot, canoe, and raft. I'll tell the Overlanders' story succinctly here, but it's what Richard told me about the twenty-seven-year-old Catherine that caught my attention as a traveller.

THE OVERLANDERS OF 1862 included more than a dozen individual groups given that designation by history books. The group with the Schuberts was not the first; a total of 352 individuals in overland parties had taken this and similar westbound routes across the Prairies and the Rockies since 1858. Then, in 1862, approximately 230 men and an undetermined number of women formed three main parties and headed for the Cariboo, an area "alive with men and mines." Wright calls it "Canada's largest immigration from east to west before the railroads."

"Catherine seems to have been born a determined woman," said Wright, eschewing any suggestion that her decisions were guided by her husband's wishes. I can see that in later photographs of her: hair parted down the middle and pulled tight to the sides, not the back, revealing eyes with more than a glint of self-reliance. She would not be ignored. Neither would she be left behind when her husband signed on with ambitious gold seekers for an overland crossing of 3,500 miles (5,600 kilometres) from Fort Garry (today's Winnipeg) to the Cariboo. Tales of harsh circumstances that undoubtedly encouraged other women to stay at home did not deter Catherine. "No one was going to leave her behind," said Wright. She must have heard all the warnings. Still, she stared down deprivation and danger, accepting the possibility of having to eat skunk and unsalted horsemeat when supplies ran out. She was prepared to ford raging waters. Male Overlanders were spurred on by the prospect of riches; those who catch gold fever often become blind to common sense. Catherine, however, "was not naïve," claims Wright. "Her commitment was to keeping the family together. And," he smiled, "she clearly had a penchant for adventure."

In June 1862 the Overlanders left Fort Garry on foot or with carts designed for hauling bison carcasses. The two-wheeled, all-wood Red

River carts cost $40; double that if you want an ox to pull it. Named after the famed local river, the carts became symbolic of Overlander transport and troubles.

Journalist Bruce Hutchison paints an evocative image: "Thus with mighty creaking of wooden wheels, with bellow of oxen and crack of whip, with men singing as they marched and dreaming at night of gold, with the sound of fiddle around the campfire and the murmur of Sunday prayer, with three babies and a woman far gone in pregnancy, the Overlanders moved west."

The strewn-out trekkers made their way to Fort Edmonton. Some decided to stay, and some travelled south. Some struggled on through muskeg and mosquitoes, mud and misery before getting to Jasper House in the lodgepole pine foothills of the Rockies. Onward they went over the Yellowhead Pass.

The Overlanders faced two options. One was to follow the Fraser River to Fort George (today's Prince George) and then downriver to Quesnel and gold, which a group of nearly 200 attempted. The other option, which a group of 36 chose, was to work their way down the Thompson River to Fort Kamloops and use it as a staging point in their quest for gold. Both choices were fraught with peril. With Catherine's pregnancy in mind, the Schubert family determined the Thompson River route safer and easier.

The Schuberts and their group moved on foot through the cedars. Many trees had fallen to block what little trail could be found when a portage was necessary. "They would make maybe five miles a day," said Wright. Every day that passed with delays made it less likely Catherine would arrive at Thompson River Post, by then the HBC's Fort Kamloops, on time to give birth, as they'd planned. "Put yourself in her boots," Wright said to me. "Think what must have been going through her mind." Despite my image of her as a force of great strength, I can imagine Catherine wondering to herself, if not aloud: "My God, what am I doing here? What if I give birth prematurely? Do they really expect I'll climb over that six-foot log? Where's my daughter? Who has my little boy by the hand? Really, we're on another raft? I'm not dry from the last time. Why do I always have to carry the one-year-old?"

Their rafts were made of roped-together logs. Makeshift canvas tents were erected on the larger ones, flapping in the wind and sideways-driving rains. Men made Y-shaped wedges from trimmed branches to prop their oars. The river flowed gently at times. More often the waters gnawed at the shoreline, the current pulled, and the raft tossed about. Catherine's raft took on great splashes of water. It swirled toward eddies. Men plied their oars with back-aching pulls to avoid whirlpools, their arms growing stiff. Rocking and rolling on the river, Catherine went into labour. It may have been the look on her face that made the men nervous. She may have shouted a stern "N-O-W!" An Indigenous woman appeared in the distance. Anxious men pulled hard for shore. The raft beached with a jar. The two women moved away for privacy. The midwife soon reappeared, displaying the child to onlookers while shouting a version of the nearby place name, "It's Kumloops! It's Kumloops!" It might have been "Tk'emlúps." Either way, the Schuberts resisted their initial temptation to call their daughter a version of the name the Tk'emlúpsemc gave to the "meeting of the waters." Instead of starting a new baby-naming trend, a bright-eyed and healthy Rose Anna joined the growing number of babies born to European mothers in the yet-to-be-christened province of British Columbia, the first so-recorded baby girl in the colony's interior.

The nursing mother and newborn boarded the raft, and the men pushed away from shore, Fort Kamloops bound.

THE IRREGULARLY SHAPED ROUTE Riley and I were travelling had brought us near the headwaters of the Fraser River, a long way from where we'd followed the river waters a week before. Since then, we'd travelled alongside portions of its 855-mile (1,375-kilometre) flow, from a brook not far from here to its mouth-of-river finish at the Pacific Ocean. We were in Tête Jaune country. Wright said that in the spring of 1820 a party of HBC men crossed the Rockies via the Smoky River

Pass and ventured down the Robson River to the Grand Forks of the Fraser River. They were not the first Europeans to traverse the area, but as Wright noted, most of those earlier stories were lost due to "the scanty records of the North West Company." The brigade's mission was to conduct business with the Indigenous People of the west side of the mountains, the Shuswap (derived from Secwépemc), and capture some of the fur trade going to the North West Company's Fort George and Jasper House.

The leader was an Iroquois-Métis man named Pierre Hatsination (or Bostonais, a derivative of Boston-men, as trappers of American origin were sometimes tagged). The blond streaks in the guide's hair gained him the nicknamed Tête Jaune, or Yellow Head.[8]

The trappers carried heavy packs, clutched hunting rifles, and wore clothing that dissembled with weather, much as once clean-shaven faces grew bearded and scruffy, yellow-tinged or not. A cleansing swim in lakes or rivers was a summer-only option; death by freezing was winter's constant threat.

Earlier that year, Hatsination made a supply stash, or *cache*, near where two rivers met. The site was in constant use and earned geographical recognition as Tête Jaune's Cache. In later years this storage of furs and camping supplies was moved downstream to the western side of the pass near the mouth of the McLennan River, taking the destination's designation with it to where today's town of Tête Jaune Cache is located. The 3,711-foot (1,131-metre) mountain pass that Tête Jaune had entered from the north also took on his name, becoming the Yellowhead Pass.

Hatsination died within a decade of his first exploratory trips into the low, gradual pass. He and his brother Baptiste, along with their wives and children, were killed during a dispute over trespassing with the Dane-zaa Nation in 1828. (Europeans at that time referred to the area's Indigenous People as the Beaver Tribe.) The pass he'd helped develop remained in use by Indigenous traders and occasional hunting parties but few others, until it was singled out and overrun by miners heading to the Cariboo. It came to international prominence in 1862 when the Overlanders passed through. And it was the first proposed railway routing for the national railway line after being surveyed by Sandford Fleming in 1872, a proposal that was declined. When the rival HBC and NWC, the two former employers of Tête Jaune, amalgamated in 1821, they consolidated their efforts and locations, further swinging traffic away from here and southward to more profitable business. By the early 1900s, the town that took on the name Tête Jaune Cache was a construction centre for the Grand Trunk Pacific Railway (which intended to use the Bute Inlet crossing to Vancouver Island). It was also the northern terminus for sternwheelers operating on the Upper Fraser River. For that brief period, Tête Jaune Cache boasted 3,000 residents, transient though they may have been.

History twists; history turns. This place name could as easily have been Hatsination's Cache. With one wrinkle of history, Riley and I could have been on a train travelling through Pierre's Pass. It might even have kept its earlier label of Leather Pass, named for the "leather brigades" of trappers and traders that used it. But instead, Hatsination's nickname appeared on sketched maps and in parlour talk, and eventually entered the cartographer's lexicon where it and the anglicized variation, Yellowhead, beckon travellers two hundred years after his first footprints marked his passage along the trail.

KYLA CAME BY and asked if Riley would accompany her to the front of the coach. He was partway along behind her when her eyes motioned me to follow. Robyn was up there waiting, as was Robin. "We'd like you to have these gifts from us," Kyla said, holding a bag and pulling a t-shirt out of it. Riley's eyes saucered.

Robyn took out a cap that said "Rocky Mountaineer" and placed it on Riley's head. Robin dug deep, as though the bag was bottomless. After an "Ah-hah" he produced a model train coach identical to the one we were travelling on. Even the designated coach number was the same. Riley squinted, laughed an appreciative "Wow," and said, "Thanks."

ROBYN GOT EVERYONE'S ATTENTION with the promise of a clear sighting of Mount Robson. "An unusual day. The clouds have drifted away. Since you can see its peak, you are seeing the highest point in the Canadian Rockies." That news wrapped our minds around the magnificence of its 12,972-foot (3,954-metre) summit. She also called it the "most *prominent* summit in the Rocky Mountains," and I admit having to determine that meaning later. The term "topographic prominence" speaks to the difference between the lowest of the map contour lines around it measured against the mountain's height. Though other mountains in the U.S. Rockies are a higher elevation above sea level, Mount Elbert in Colorado is the only other edifice in the Rockies that exceeds 8,200 feet (2,500 metres) when profiled in that manner, and is therefore slightly less *prominent* in this competition, so it places second.

"I'd like to meet the guy making my drinks," said Riley when Robyn was by our seats. "Is that possible? Please . . ." Robyn took us down the stairs and into the kitchen. The chefs were all in whites, hats on.

"Which one is Francisco?" asked Riley.

"Me," said one. "I'll guess you're the Smoothie Kid." They shook hands.

"Thanks," said Riley. "You're really good."

It's hard to imagine a train experience being any better. Different, yes; better, no.

WE CROSSED THE FRASER RIVER for the last time, near enough to its source to look at the mountains and say hello. A while after we had passed Moose Lake, Robyn informed everyone they were about to "lose an hour from your day, almost without noticing." She said this shift of everyone's clock from Pacific Time Zone to Mountain Time Zone was happening whether we wanted it or not, because of "international standard time." For that, she said, "You can thank a man named Sandford Fleming."

FLEMING, THE CPR'S CHIEF ENGINEER, is rightly remembered for charting rail routes through the Rocky Mountains and for being present at the driving of the Last Spike; a railroader's railway man. Of more renown is his sobriquet, "The Father of Standard Time," which *he was not*. Some have credited him with inventing Standard Time in 1878, which *he did not*. Even when it comes to establishing International Standard Time, Fleming was more a midwife and less a father.

"Standardized time" had been around in Europe since the 1840s, an innovation driven mainly by the railways. Its first iteration was known as "railway time." For centuries before train travel, people moved from one village to another at a relatively slow pace. Adjusting to a locally set town clock (often at a church; often based on noon time) was never an issue. However, train passengers travelled rapidly from one unfamiliar location to another, on a short journey, and time-confusion became an unwelcome travel companion.

It was a worldwide problem, amplified by local intrigues. As recently as the 1860s there were 144 time zones in the U.S. alone. In 1869, Charles Dowd, an innovative thinker and school principal in the state of New York, proposed that U.S. railway executives use four time zones running vertically (longitudinally) to reduce differences. Congress rejected a refinement of Dowd's idea, though they eventually got around to passing legislation on the matter twenty-eight years later. (Hands up, those surprised.)

The world needed consistency. The sequence to establishing it was thus: Three years after he missed a train in Ireland (due to the printed schedule's mistaken "p.m." when it should have been "a.m."), Sandford Fleming recommended the Royal Canadian Institute implement time zones. Four years later, on November 18, 1883, Canada became the first country to adopt this approach. By intention, it was a Sunday, the day on which many (but not all) U.S. railway stations also adjusted their clocks precisely at noon to fall within shared new zones.

Credit also goes to Fleming for having conceived a global solution, then tended to the idea's incubation and nursed the initiative's well-being. He placed the idea before twenty-five nations from North America, Europe, and Asia at the 1884 International Prime Meridian

Conference, in Washington, D.C., which he helped convene. It was there that a version of "international standard time" (also known as "universal time"), similar to what we know today, was endorsed, albeit not formally adopted. The resulting alignment of twenty-four time zones with the already popular twenty-four-hour clock's reliability made for less ambiguity, and has been the international traveller's friend ever since.

Perhaps early talk of Fleming as "father" of the concept reflects the patrimonial lingo of the day, rather than his actual role as enabler. Here's a thought: next time you make a quick, time-certain travel connection through a city longitudinally distant from where you departed, take a moment to thank Sandford Fleming as "the midwife to International Standard Time."

ONE OF THE MOST train travel–savvy people I've met, Jos Beltman, gave me a glimpse at how the future of elegant train travel might evolve. Jos was managing director of Netherlands-based Incento for thirty years. Incento has represented railways operating in dozens of countries, from the *Venice Simplon-Orient-Express* to *The Canadian*, from the *Pride of Africa* to the *Indian Pacific*, and, yes, the *Rocky Mountaineer*. Jos has travelled most of them. As their company name implies, he's led many "incentive" groups—top business performers being treated by their company to a travel bonus—on excursions. He's organized air cruises on private planes around Africa and journeys on private trains in Russia, China, and the Silk Road countries. While I was writing this book, I spent time with Jos in Amsterdam and Frankfurt, and he talked about what lies ahead for glamorous train travel.

"It's here to stay as long as the economy is decent and the tracks safe." He halted, pursed his lips in contemplation, and said, "It really doesn't even need the tracks to be safe. Once, we took the passengers off a train so it could pass over wobbly rails, warped by heat. The weight of the train slowly brought the tracks straight. We bused the passengers around that unsafe patch. Less risky."

He believes part of train travel's future belongs to novelty trains through legendary lands, such as the *Golden Eagle Trans-Siberian Express*. "It's exotic, with the smell of dangerous history all around you. It's as comfortable as a train can be, yet some of what you see outside the windows makes you uncomfortable with its wildness, poverty, and drama. All that and haute cuisine."

We talked about Japan's *Seven Stars*, a train that offers "over-the-top grandeur—and is expensive." You can have an entire coach to yourself as one suite. It makes you feel incredibly special and lightens your pocket all at the same time.

*The Presidential* train in Portugal caught Jos's attention with its one-day stay in the Douro Valley on the way from Porto to Vesúvio, and back again. "We'll see more rebuilt heritage like this," he said. "It was King Louis 1's Royal Train from the 1890s. It seems that travellers like sampling such sparkle."

Amtrak has a range of ideas to improve their reputation in the world of commuter rail transportation. Columnist Fred Frailey mused in *Trains* magazine that Amtrak could bring back the elegance of onboard dining with stitched leather seats, warm lighting, and metal cutlery. This would only work if they moved away from packaged airline-style meals and delivered them from a kitchen instead of a microwave. Travellers once enjoyed such experiences on the *Empire Builder* and the *Coast Starlight*. Food and scheduling are two of the three most important elements to draw passenger loyalty; another is the comfort of seating arrangements. The *Lake Shore Limited* and *Capitol Limited* could be transformed if they replicated seat configurations found in airline business class.

Jos feels bespoke railway excursions—anywhere in the world— will become more popular, though not cheaper. His favourite was a recent excursion with Rovos Rail. "They positioned two locomotives and more than a dozen carriages for a two-week trip you'd never otherwise be able to take." How else would one get from the Indian Ocean to the Atlantic, or vice versa, on the first passenger train ever to follow the old copper trail route all the way? The journey is called the Trail of Two Oceans. Jos travelled eastward and departed Lobito in Angola, a country that hosted six fascinating days of the trip, with a populace recovering from a long civil war and eager to welcome foreign visitors, cheering to see the train. They rolled a total of 2,500 miles (4,000 kilometres) across the African continent, including through the Democratic Republic of Congo and its city of Lubumbashi, where far too few travellers visit these days, and onward. They were unrushed through Zambia and Tanzania, stopping to visit wildlife parks, and enjoyably terminated their journey in Dar es Salaam.

In our conversation about the world of train travel, Jos said of the *Rocky Mountaineer,* "It's now established in every category you can think of. Most memorable train journeys. Most spectacular train journeys. Name a positive adjective, and it's earned it."

Our talking swerved toward the travelling public's fascination with elegance. Said Jos, "In the days of *Downton Abbey,* experiencing material grandeur was the exclusive purview of the rich. The rest of us were standing on the side of the track, so to speak, watching the train go by." Though Jos himself hardly ever experiences busy commuter trains, I could relate to the sense of being a spectator watching fancy trains go by; most of my train travels have involved lugging heavy suitcases into crowded second-class coaches. Today, up-market train travel is more egalitarian, in that more people can afford it. Some do it as a once-in-a-lifetime gift to themselves, a reward for hard work that earned them the opportunity to splurge a little. Others do it simply because the elegance feels good—unpack once and enjoy the attentiveness of staff, the best of views, the satisfaction of all one's needs being anticipated. Travellers know these deluxe trains offer a trip without worries and in maximum safety, especially in exotic destinations or unfrequented locales. There's a communal sense of awe and wonder aboard trains like the *Rocky Mountaineer,* or the *Venice Simplon-Orient-Express,* or the *Pride of Africa.* And, hey, let's admit it, it feels good to experience what *Downton Abbey's* Lord Grantham might have felt like when he left his castle and answered the summons: "All aboard!"

ALL HAIL THE WHISTLE POST. I nudged Riley in his seat, and said, "Come on, man... We're wrapping up our trip and you're playing on your tablet..."

His smile disarmed me. "I'm listening to Coldplay," he said. "Here." He passed me his headset and I listened while he turned it up. The Chainsmokers, a DJ duo, were performing with the British band. The opening lines grabbed me.

*I've been reading books of old*
*The legends and the myths*

And, the chorus:

*I want something just like this.*

Then Riley said, "Listen to this, Grampa," and he put on their song "Yellow."

As he'd been gliding through the Rocky Mountains, he'd been dreaming along with Coldplay, letting the piano and voices give him a sense of being. He'd had an hour of music, composure, and mountains. I envied him. Serenity chooses you through your self-confidence, not your age or job title. I saw that in him. I was thoroughly enjoying listening to his music when he reclaimed the headset. "You shouldn't be on the tablet, Grampa. Come out on the deck for the end of our train trip," he said grinning.

Standing with a handful of other passengers, we watched creek waters play hide-and-seek as the train rolled along through the forest. Riley was as happy and composed as I'd seen him on the trip. He leaned into my left arm, and then he swung it up and over his shoulders.

At the start of our trip Riley's dad had offered the admonition, "Try to be more of a friend and less of a grandparent."

"Last three minutes on the train," I said, melancholy in my voice.

"Deal with it," said Riley. I felt his elbow in my ribs.

Dusk hovered over the mountains as we pulled our way through Jasper National Park. There are too few towns left in North America where one side of the main road belongs to railway tracks and a lone station while the other side belongs to low-rise shops and accommodation and a display of welcome. Jasper is among them.

"Good trip, Kid."

"Good trip, Grampa."

The slowing traction of steel wheels on steel rails can be an annoying sound, but you have to let it be; an option is to think of it as the anthem of a train journey's end. That's how I chose to hear it. When the train stopped, we stepped off the *Rocky Mountaineer* and onto the Jasper station platform.

"Done," said Riley, with a satisfied smile.

Not so fast, I thought. True, our train time was over, but—like finishing an extraordinary long and wonderful meal—it is prudent to take some time to digest the experience. We would do that, savouring more days in the Rocky Mountains.

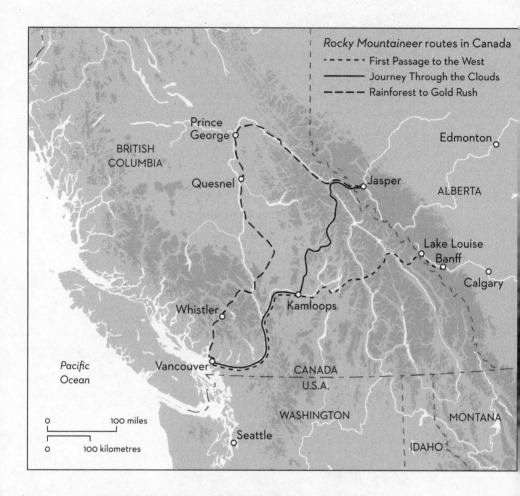

## MAP 6: *ROCKY MOUNTAINEER* ROUTES IN CANADA

As recently as the early 1990s, it was a challenge to profitably carry passengers by train through the Rocky Mountains, let alone on other routes in British Columbia. The success of the brand Rocky Mountaineer has changed that; their trains travel routes named for the heritage of their chosen tracks.

# — V —

# THE NUGGET
# ROUTE

"The mountains themselves will have the last word."
**ANN C. COLLEY**, *Victorians in the Mountains: Sinking the Sublime*

# — 17 —

NOT ALL TRAINS that pass one another do so concurrently. That was certainly true of our train and the one that passed alongside our tracks eighty years earlier when a Hudson locomotive pulled it into the Jasper station. It was the summer of 1939. King George VI and Queen Elizabeth stepped onto this very Jasper platform, greeted by banners, bands, dignitaries, and cheering crowds. Custom painted royal blue and silver, sporting a gold trim, the *Hudson #2850* belched steam, sighed, and expressed its thirst. It was in the process of setting a record for miles travelled by a single steam locomotive without breakdown or replacement. (By the time it reached Vancouver, it would have travelled 3,224 miles, or 5,189 kilometres.) There would be two dozen crew changes along the way, but the Hudson engine itself, thereafter called the *Royal Hudson*, kept going.

I told Riley the story as we disembarked in Jasper, but he was tired of my nods to history. He asked if it was the same king I'd mentioned earlier, and maybe the same *Royal Hudson*? Yes, and yes, but the context had changed, I explained. Maybe he was getting tired of me, too. Possibly he was just tired. "Let's get to that Sawridge place, the hotel," he said.

In the morning we'd be renting a Jeep for our three-day road trip through the Rocky Mountains, ending with a flight home to Vancouver. But on this night, there was no need to stroll about, no need for Grampa-talk time. The setup at the Sawridge Inn was such that I could have dinner, and the non-hungry Riley could have the nearby guestroom all to himself.

I caught last call at the restaurant, asked for a half-carafe of wine, clam chowder (where would they get fresh clams here?), and a steak sandwich. When I got back to the room, Riley was silent, headset askew, Coldplay songs forming the backdrop to his dreams.

THE MORNING IN JASPER was crisp with a hint of snow at the higher levels, even in summer. Riley feigned sleep but I caught him pulling his tablet from under his pillow as I was closing the door on my way out for a walk.

Down the way and across the street, the *Rocky Mountaineer* was leaving the station heading west, full of new faces pressed against the just-washed windows. I did not dwell on the tenfold improvement of meals and décor over the decades it operated, or that the fledgling company I had worked for, when their very first passenger boarded in 1990, had just hosted their two-millionth passenger. What registered as I walked was what had not changed. People loved being on board, they felt released from their daily cares, and they spoke to one another with an awareness of life and living that, for some reason, trains set people free to talk about. As a train company executive, I used to walk the aisles introducing myself to travellers and listening to their friendly critiques and endless suggestions for changes, all pre-empted with comments about the thrill of being in the Rockies on a legendary train.

To think the company almost didn't make it. The year after I left them, GCRC finally started making money. To this day Peter Armstrong will jokingly ask me, "Why didn't you leave a year earlier?"

Peter was not easy to work for in those days. I never properly understood him until I had left the company. He was consumed by the ever-rising tide of potential bankruptcy as he clutched for a safe hold above the financial waterline, only to have it washed over by new circumstances. What he held on to was the dream.

Peter was persistent (read: relentless). My first day on the job in 1990, he gave me a two-foot-high stack of letters and faxes and literature he'd been saving for me. Included were leads on companies he thought should book people on his train. About ten pieces down in the pile I found a note in Peter's handwriting saying, "You should call Thomas Cook in England. They're big sellers of international train travel. Get them to book us for next year." Half an hour further through the pile I came across a piece of paper with the same handwriting: "Did you call Thomas Cook yet?" Another hour, another note: "What did Thomas Cook say?"

When we took over operating the train and marketing it worldwide, the previous owners of the train had not provided us a copy of their contract with tour operators; we had to devise our own. Neither had they shared a list of general sales agents who represented the *Rocky Mountaineer* in thirty countries around the world; we had to scour old brochures and ask other operators in order to compile a list of contact names so we could start selling our second season. In the first month of our first season we did not have a reservation system that assigned seats for passengers; it just assigned them a coach. We had to tell guests, "Find yourself a seat once you've found your coach . . ." The morning of each departure, passengers were held back in the station until the train was ready for boarding. They were excited. They jostled for position. We'd shout, "All aboard!" and stand aside. The rush was on. It was like the Senior Olympics.

We did everything we could to find new sources of passengers in those early years. One morning in our first month, Peter walked into my office and handed me a soggy baggage tag printed with the name of a European tour company. "Where'd you get this, Peter?" I asked. "Oh, I was down at the station this morning after VIA's train left. I found it on the tracks. Must be from a passenger on board. You should call the company and get them to sell our train for next year instead." I could not shake the image of Peter walking along the tracks in the rain behind the VIA train as it departed, looking through their litter for a lead, pushing back the frontier of market research.

The most effective marketing method remains individual recommendations. A company earning those requires everyone's involvement in the tiniest of details, whether it's someone who tightens bolts, garnishes salmon, checks the coach couplings, or mixes a gin and tonic. Few people notice when you do the little things right; everyone notices when you do them wrong. Riley was impressed with what he saw, and said he'd like to work on the *Rocky Mountaineer*: "If I don't work telling people stories aboard the train, I'd be good at making smoothies full-time."

WE WERE NEAR where Mary Schäffer had made her mark in the late 1890s as a storyteller, journal keeper, climber, and explorer, drawing attention to the Rocky Mountains and helping to make Maligne Lake in Jasper National Park famous. She and her fellow naturalist, Mary Vaux, had been brought to my attention on the first leg of our journey when, over breakfast on the train, Colleen and Mom talked about Schäffer leaving behind scrapbooks and hand-coloured slides of astonishing scenery and settings. Mom had explained that Schäffer was one of a trio of women who had visually represented European or American women who had made notable contributions to artistic renditions or writings in—or about—the Rockies. They'd defied gender norms of the era, especially those of the male-dominated mountaineering schools. They dodged parental concerns and went against the grain of their social class, engendering more skepticism than support.

What differentiated Mary Schäffer, Mary Vaux, and Catharine Whyte from the many women who pioneered in the Rockies was simply that they were more widely recognized than the others. How many expeditions or escapades of other remarkable individuals are lost to us because photographs recording them never were developed, or their field notes are stuffed away in a shoebox in an attic somewhere? Think of how close Mattie Gunterman and all her photographic insights and storytelling came to being lost to history. It reminded me of other near-forgotten stories, like that of surveyor Alfred Perry (recounted earlier). Richard Thomas Wright had summed up the man's notable contributions perfectly when he asked: "Now? Who talks of Perry?"

Of Schäffer's many wonderful artistic works, I most admire *The "Rocky Road" in the Yellowhead*, a photograph she took in 1911. Depicting a railway track beside a creek, it is a glass transparency, hand-coloured by the photographer, a separate and equally demanding artistic skill. It shows how nature shifted the ties and forced the rails to curve awkwardly while still staying roughly aligned, and looking about to tip over any train daring to use them.

Schäffer was more at home as part of a pack train, trailing through Tête Jaune's Cache, bothered by the primitive conditions in which the people lived. She wrote, "I wondered how much charity and faith might have been mustered on the spur of the moment to welcome us, and realized that we were probably quite as rough-looking in our travel-worn garments as those we rushed to condemn." Her interest was in what she called "the innocent wilderness." That, and as she put it about her time in these mountains:

> *they like to say "explorer" of me,*
> *no, only a hunter of peace.*
> *I found it.*

I HAD A MAP OPEN over the breakfast table in a café on Connaught Drive, the main street of Jasper. Riley leaned his face into it, pointing a finger at Banff where we'd started our trip. "We end up there again, right?" he asked. He moved his finger westward to Kamloops and onward to Vancouver, then northward to Whistler. His finger got lost. I used mine to indicate the map route on to Quesnel then Prince George where it turned east, heading to Jasper. From there we traced together the route down the Icefields Parkway we were about to drive to Banff. "Circle route," I said. He said, "Doesn't look like a circle." He was correct; it was too rugged of an outline. It offered no sense of smooth contours, which made it all the more intriguing. "Our route outline looks like the shape of a gold nugget," I offered. Riley turned it into a pronouncement: "OK. We say Nugget Route."

226

LEAVING JASPER, Riley and I made an early agreement about driving the Icefields Parkway southbound. No headsets or earbuds, nothing that took one of us out of the in-vehicle conversations and left the other isolated. The trade-off was that Riley got to choose the music. I'd never heard of Marshmello or seen the fun image of the singer's costumes, or listened to the range of songs that instantly fit into my catalogue of great road-trip tunes.

"Wolves" boomed through the speakers, front and back, encompassing the two of us at Riley's chosen volume. I was into the rhythm when something outside struck me as untoward. It had been thirty years since I'd driven this roadway, famed for its view of giant glaciers. My recollection was that the icefields hovered near the road, or at least gave that impression with their immensity. Now, to my dismay, they felt distant.

The defining feature of this drive was disappearing. Sure, they remained monsters of ice, white with snow. But their impact was diminished. Nature's wrath no longer showed on their faces. The glaciers wept rather than calved. Drop by drop they were dripping into history. I missed what they had been, what they'd symbolized, and what it would have been like to share them with Riley. I thought I'd set up a discussion about climate change, on my terms of talk.

"Sometimes we lose things that were once really important to us," I said to Riley, since he lacked the reference point I had for how distinguished these once were.

"Like Gramma," he said, not letting it be a question.

Unsure of myself, and where this might go, I said nothing.

"Gramma's gone. I thought she'd be around forever," said Riley. "She was important to me." He meant Wendy, who for twenty years was my first wife, and mother to Riley's dad, Sean, and our other son, Brent. Riley and his brother, Declan, had been close to her and that closeness favoured the relationship between Wendy and me in very nice ways. Cancer took her, slowly and visibly, depleting someone as delightful as God would be willing to make a person. Grandkids notice that. It etches recognition of loss into their minds even as it is occurring.

The music in the Jeep was soft. Had Riley turned it down? The traffic was light. We cruised along curves in the road, my mind on a disappearing glacier, his on a disappeared grandmother.

I stole a glance at Riley hoping he didn't notice my movement. He looked at me, his eyelids blinking away a tear. He brought me back to the present with a slow smile as if to reassure me. (Him, reassuring me?) He had confidence in his memory. He knew he'd never forget the importance another person's life had had on his. "I miss her," he said. "I really miss her."

The wonder of icefields, I thought.

I LOBBIED FOR RILEY to play my music and got John Denver's ("Who's Denver, Grampa?") "Poems, Prayers & Promises": "How long it's been since yesterday, what about tomorrow... our dreams and all the memories we share?" One tends to sing aloud lyrics we care about sharing, so I did. Riley had sung aloud on the train, wanting me to know his music as much as I now wanted him to know mine. He'd use those lyrics to convey the things he thought I needed to hear, such as, "You shouldn't underestimate me."

In turn, it would have left his soul incomplete (which grandfathers cannot do) if I'd not gotten him to listen to Denver's "Rocky Mountain High" lyrics, with me singing along to underline the sentiments I wished to ingrain into his sense of self.

*He climbed cathedral mountains, he saw silver clouds below*
*He saw everything as far as you can see*

I stopped my singing and left it to Denver:

*Now his life is full of wonder, but his heart still knows some fear*
*Of a simple thing he cannot comprehend*
*Why they try to tear the mountains down to bring in a couple more*
*More people, more scars upon the land*

*Rocky Mountain high*
*Rocky Mountain high*

OVER-TOURISM IS BUT ONE CONCERN for wilderness areas. You can draw a direct line from Canada's national parks' administration being set up in the early 1900s to UNESCO's 1984 consideration of the Canadian Rocky Mountain Parks World Heritage Site. This respect of the environment for future generations pushes against many threats posed for the mountain habitats. Prominent among these would be unregulated land development, though that is under control. We also need awareness of how precious the wildlife is within the safeguarded area. One of the books I'd read on the train was forester and biologist Dave Butler's mystery novel *Full Curl*, the title evoking the majesty of a male mountain sheep's horns (the very image chosen for the initial logo of the *Rocky Mountaineer*, I might add).

The book's plot revolves around park warden Jenny Wilson, who is shocked to find big-game poachers operating covertly in Banff National Park. Whether you're reading a novel about the murder of an innocent bystander set in Paris while you're visiting Paris, or about the murder of bighorn sheep in the mountains you're riding a train through, there is something more real about a drama when you can sense it unfolding right outside your window.

Illegal hunting is an existing threat to wildlife hereabouts, the crime more sinister when it happens in their protected habitat. I wondered how often the real-life storyline ends with the guilty party being apprehended, as happens in Butler's book. I later asked him how much of his story was drawn from his background as a park warden. He acknowledged his situation had loosely inspired the fictionalized accounts. "Poaching in the national parks thirty years ago was largely unexpected and, so thought the parks' bosses, unlikely. If an individual was convicted of poaching, the fine was $250, with no associated jail time."

Even in light of those circumstances, it was disheartening when he told me some hunters "took advantage of the parks as a source of relatively naïve trophies. 'Park animals' such as elk, bighorn sheep, and mountain goats don't view humans as a threat, even during hunting season outside the park boundaries. Trophy animals—with gorgeous horns and antlers a hunter could boastfully display in their home—were easily approached and, easily murdered."

Canada is a country of hunters. Those of us who do not hunt but enjoy steaks and ribs let others do our killing for us; we manage the barbeques. For our providers—hunters and ranchers and supermarket butchers—there are protocols. Those who don't follow those protocols are the trophy poachers. Dave told me, "My sense is that it didn't happen much in the road-accessed areas of the parks. But from time to time, along the boundaries between the parks and adjacent government-owned lands which were open to hunting, it could prove tempting for hunters and guides lacking in ethics to slip into parks to take an elk or sheep or goat. Or," he added, "even black or grizzly bears."

In one situation, which presaged his creation of the fictional Jenny Wilson character, Butler and his law enforcement partner, working with other wardens, B.C. conservation officers, and U.S. Fish and Wildlife agents, broke open a major poaching case.

Dave reckons poaching in the mountain parks today is "dramatically lower than it once was." He attributes that to the awareness and watchfulness of parks staff intent on protecting wildlife. But the biggest deterrent may be higher fines for conviction under the *Canada National Parks Act*. Depending on the wildlife species and the circumstances, they can range from thousands of dollars to near a million dollars, *plus* up to five years in jail.

ROAD TRIPS PROVIDE ANONYMITY. What is inside the vehicle is known: music, company, and atmosphere. Outside is the unexpected. Suddenly, amidst the beauty that is Highway 93, we came upon the aftermath of a forest fire.

"Look," pointed Riley, the first to notice. "The burned trees came right down to that side of the road. Then the fire stopped."

"Or was stopped," I said. "Firefighters would have used the road as a fire-break and tried very hard to keep the fire from jumping over it."

Scarred trees, naked and blackened, stood defying the temptation to tumble over in death. It was haunting.

In July 2014, the Spreading Creek wildfire, described in the media as a "ravenous forest fire," devoured thousands of acres of forest within weeks of the lightning strike that started it. To counter the danger, more than one hundred firefighters were deployed alongside bulldozers and water-tank trucks, and beneath helicopters dropping chemical retardants over the hotspots. The strategy for fighting this particular fire was to establish the perimeter and hold it while the fire above burned itself up and out.

Fire, along with wind and waves, is one of nature's biggest bullies. It doesn't know when to stop, and it orphans its victim lands. Ironically, forest fires can be a healthy part of maintaining the ecosystem, resumption relying on destruction. Over the years, brush, fallen trees, and leaves decompose into helpful fertilizers to grow the trees and sustain foliage. They are also dry, and can carry fires at ground level. Tragedy is always a risk. Rampant fires are nearly impossible to control if winds are at play and the fuel is endless, dry. Yet natural fires are a part of a forest's renewal, clearing ground for a new generation of seedlings to spring forth.

"Climate change?" asked Riley with a contemporary ten-year-old's awareness of environmental issues that I was oblivious to at his age. "Could be a factor," I answered, "but this one was started by lightning." Yet Riley was onto something. A profound change in Alberta's and B.C.'s forest ecology is infestation by the mountain pine beetle, increasing fire risk. The beetles did serious damage to about 18 million hectares (44 million acres) of forestland in B.C. alone during recent years; that's more than 50 percent of the merchantable pine trees in the province. The beetle has been around forever and did its share of work on the bark of trees, but for many years cold Canadian winters killed them off annually before they could spread beyond their usefulness in the cycle of forest renewal. However, winters in recent decades have not brought the necessarily harsh winter temperatures, and the beetle lived through the winters. In the changed climate, they killed more forest than normal, resulting in plenty of desperately dry trees. One lightning strike or a thrown cigarette, and the tinder-making activity of the pine beetle results in fire.

Today, children are exposed to the conundrum regarding climate change risks to our planet. Humankind has contributed pollutants to our air and waters, harming the delicate balance of nature. To what extent do we accept responsibility, and what are we collectively willing to do, or should we be compelled to do, to change our behaviour?

I WAS GLAD Riley and I did not head directly home after detraining. It was good to have time to absorb the meaningfulness of our journey. I was struck by how many people of varying ages wished to have a great train journey in their lives. Their desires were often hitched to the lore of steam trains or the images of dining by candlelight as the scenery passed. Or perhaps they envisioned the social polish evident in the movie *Murder on the Orient Express*. There is more, to be sure. There is the sense that a train journey mirrors life's passage. Boarding is anticipation; the stations are wayside encounters; the vistas reinforce the fleetingness of time and impermanence of how we see things. Strangers aboard a train reveal their life story from career to family to deaths to hesitations and errant relatives, all with candour. Aboard a train, you can expect full disclosure from your fellow travellers, as though there's nothing to lose by being honest with a stranger. The train travels had given me an honest Riley, and I hoped he got something similar in return.

THE NOTION OF our Nugget Route's irregular circle design returned as we neared Moraine Lake, not far from Banff, where we'd first boarded the *Rocky Mountaineer*. A turnoff brought us close to Lake Louise. Our proximity to the trip's beginning suggested a conclusion of sorts. We'd traced the nugget. I didn't want to see somewhere we'd been, such as Banff, however briefly, since that usually means a trip is going to be over. We wished for different. Isn't that what travel is all about? Returning to the familiar is a vacation, and one wants travel to be superior to that. Or I did, and I wanted it for Riley, too. Whether he did or not didn't matter to me. Travellers are selfish.

We would head to Moraine Lake.

As I looked at Riley, the thought struck me that he's lived maybe an eighth of his life. On a comparable scale, I've lived seven-eighths of mine. "I envy you, Riley. You've got almost all your discoveries ahead of you." In my fractional view of time, I saw a kid preoccupied with the present, largely oblivious to the past, and with confident concentration on the future (such as telling me that the petroleum-fuelled vehicle we were driving "will be irrelevant by 2030, illegal by 2040").

It was not yet lunchtime, but park officials had already barricaded the Moraine Lake turnoff. The day's quota for visitors had been reached, or so their arithmetic indicated. The lake's capacity for canoeists and hikers is restricted to ensure that those there have an experience worth the wait, worth the drive, and worth the time. We were eventually allowed past the barrier because our names were on a list of reservations for the lakeside lodge. Other visitors scowled at us from their cars, perplexed about why we were granted passage and they were not. Travel envy is ugly. It was my turn to be perplexed when we pulled up to the lodge and encountered a partially empty parking lot.

THE BALCONY OFF our room at Moraine Lake Lodge overhung a trail bordered by trees, but not too many. The lake gleamed glacial green, a colour that struck me as artificial, but it was nature at its most splendid; as real as real can be. It is unique to lakes fed by the coldest of waters, pushing along rocks that crush one another into glacial flour of small and almost invisible particles, which concoct this shade on the planet's palette. The view helped us settle after the drive.

I'd come to rely on Riley's reassuring presence. We were each pleased in our own way. We had nowhere to be and were happy to be there.

IN THE AFTERNOON, we set out to explore our surroundings. At the northern end of the lake, not far from the lodge, was a hilltop that could be reached up the back way by a responsible pathway, or up the front over broken boulders and their chipped-off rocks, jagged and challenging, the remnants of glacier movement known as moraine. Only a few people dared climb up that alternative access. The lake drew my gaze away, and I wondered about its depth (45 feet; 14 metres). When I again turned to look at the rock filled hillside, Riley was among those half dozen climbers making their way carefully up the dangerous stonework.

To get to the bottom of those rocks making up the hillside's front, a climber had to cross over wobbly logs lying in a shallow stream. The whole trip, I'd tried not to utter the phrase "Riley, you shouldn't do that," as it seemed stupidly predictable from a grandfather. Neverthe-less, the words were almost out of my mouth when I realized it was too late. He had crossed the wobbly logs; his shoes were wet as a result of slipping into the stream, and he was gamely climbing up the jagged hill. It was not mischief, it was adventure; he was choosing his own course.

So I joined him. "Wait up," was all I said. By the time I reached the base of the rocks my shoes, too, were wet. One of my feet wedged between rocks, my ankle twisted.

"There's an easy way up the back," I said.

"Easy?"

"Yes, easy. Interested?"

"No."

We clambered over rocks big enough to try our patience and sharp enough to cut our clothing. Halfway up, Riley sat down and waited for me.

"If you get hurt, your mother will never talk to me again."

"Dad will."

LATER, WE PADDLED across Moraine Lake in a red canoe toward a mountain's cliff face. The dock girl who gave us lifejackets had said, pointing, "That mountain will inspire you, but you need to get close and look up. Way up." Twenty minutes on, we neared where the mountain rose directly out of the lake. Riley shifted slightly in the bow, his paddling strong and steady. He did not rock the boat as he shifted over to paddle on his left. "That's your port side," I said. "You can remember it because left-handed baseball players are called 'port-paws.'" Sometimes I over-explain.

"My mom wanted me to go canoeing with her last summer," he said, ignoring my instruction. "We didn't."

"Why not?" I asked.

"I just said no." He let that linger, then said, "I shouldn't have."

Clearly there'd been a mother's request and a kid's shrug. How often had I done that in life, only to never have a recurring chance for the experience? I sensed Riley was realizing that at a younger age than I had.

The mountainside loomed. We were underneath it, or so it seemed from our vantage point. We felt alone in the wilderness. The beauty reminded me of songwriter Gordon Lightfoot's reverence for such places: "There was a time in this fair land when the railroad did not run / When the wild majestic mountains stood alone against the sun." I expected to hear the mountains breathe, or perhaps moan to discourage us from getting closer. Instead, there was a magnetic welcome, as if a mysterious current was drawing us nearer.

"Awe-some," said Riley as he gave three hard strokes that turned us away.

We aimed the canoe at a distant spot. I squinted all other boaters out of my view, leaving the illusion of us being the sole paddlers, at one with the lake. When we again let others into our field of vision, we noticed two canoes at the mouth of a stream that slammed its way over rocks, smoothing the boulders as it went, feeding the lake. We paddled over to see what it was about.

There was a rush of creek water tumbling down from a roaring waterfall higher up. The flow into the lake pushed our canoe away. We drifted, our paddles resting on the canoe's gunnels. Riley trailed his hand in the water, making a wee wake.

We saw a shore trail. Hikers had taken a pathway half an hour's walk from the lodge. They milled around deadfall logs shoved into a cove. The spot looked to be both a terminus for casual walkers and a set-off point for hikers heading onto a rise and into the mountains. "We should walk there later," I suggested.

"In the morning," said Riley.

My paddle movement curved the boat toward dock. We glided in silence.

"What's your best memory of the trip?" I asked.

"Right now," he said.

"And?"

"Dancing on the train."

He couldn't see me smile.

"Sushi at the Banff Springs Hotel our first night," he added.

It seemed early to be reminiscing, but I liked hearing what registered in a ten-year-old's mind, or was it in his heart? Riley pulled his paddle's shaft out, laying it across his knees contemplatively. Water dripped from the blade. I paddled lazily, a basic J-stroke, keeping the canoe moving forward and straight. We were alone as we crossed the middle of the lake. The sky was turquoise, the wind slight, the smell that of calm water. It could be named Pensive Lake.

Riley shifted as if to look back at me, not able to turn fully around in his seat—knowing our eyes couldn't meet. The canoe tilted slightly starboard in tandem with his words. "I do things with you because I don't know how much longer you'll be around."

MUCH OF WHAT I'd encountered emotionally on this journey left me feeling in uncharted territory. That came as much from Riley's comments as from the sense of wilderness everywhere we looked.

If there were a straight road (there isn't even a winding one) from Banff to the Canada–U.S. border, it would be a drive of 170 miles (270 kilometres). There sits the international boundary agreed to in 1846, the invisible 49th parallel. In 1886 a map was published that informed and identified the border, based on the research and surveying of geologist George Mercer Dawson, the "father of Canadian anthropology."

Charting this international boundary was a surveying task that went beyond finding paths for railways or establishing town sites. Dawson, working for the Geological Survey of Canada, was known as "the little giant." To the Indigenous Peoples he encountered in British Columbia, the diligent Dawson was not just "skookum" in Chinook. He was "skookum tumtum" (said to mean "brave, cheery man"). In Dawson's 1901 obituary, one of his friends fancifully quoted a translation from Chinook that described him as "ready to endure all things and suffer all things, saying nothing, or making a merry jest of what some travellers might call dangerous hardships."

Dawson led the 49th parallel survey, collecting geological specimens that helped convince politicians and settlers that the Prairies were primed to be the country's agricultural breadbasket. He was the first to prove that dinosaurs once roamed Alberta. He mapped a way through the Rocky and Selkirk Mountains, finding possible routes for future CPR passengers. Miners "moiled for gold" in the Yukon town of Dawson named in his honour.

But that's not what made him "skookum tumtum" to the Indigenous Peoples whose cultures he studied and venerated. When George was ten, he'd fallen into an icy stream on the grounds of McGill University in Montreal, where his father was principal. As a result of his ensuing sickness, his spine twisted and his chest barrelled out, causing him to grow no taller than 4 feet, 6 inches (137 centimetres). It also left him with constant headaches. Those physical hardships, however, were no match for his insatiable quest for discoveries.

"As a surveyor," Dawson wrote in 1881, "I had long decided I was really in the business of casting lines around like nets, nets made of imaginary lines thrown down onto a blank map to allow one's country and its citizens to thereafter accurately claim their jurisdictions, be it a farmer's fence or a nation's borders. The progenitors of these demarcation lines were the explorers, and their legacy, in the wake they left, were the lines of subsequent settlement, the trails and the roads and the highways." And the railways, one might add.

BACK IN OUR ROOM, I had a bottle of wine to nurse. Riley had a plug-in. Before we went for dinner, I opened the wine, poured myself a glass, and settled myself in the Adirondack chair on the porch to sip it. I made a few notes in my saddle-stitched booklet. Riley came out and took the chair beside me, something on his mind.

"You really going to write about our trip, Grampa?"

"If I can find the story, yes. And I think I have a start and a middle, so now we must see how it ends."

"When you go places to talk about the book, could I come along?"

"I'd like that," I said. "And you could sign the book if someone asked you to. Do you have a signature?"

"What's a signature?"

"It's how you write your name with style." In digital times there's a return to the illiterate's use of an X or one's printed name, or computer-generated lettering for signing things, and a seeming lack of interest in, or need for, a cursive signature, let alone one with visual impact.

Riley took my pen and notepaper and wrote out his name in a sloppy scrawl. "Like that?"

An idea came to me. "My dad, your great-grampa, had the coolest signature. He's gone now. Maybe you could inherit it . . ." I showed him my imitation of the graphic my father generated thousands of times, which stroked a clever "A" denoting our last name and then darted an unreadable line diagonally from the A's cross-stroke to the level, an inch away.

"Like this?" he mimicked, attempting it a few times.

"Yes. Just like that." Every ten-year-old deserves a signature, I thought.

He practised it, refined it, and made it his, or so I was hoping.

"If you can pull that off, it'd be distinctive," I said.

"What's distinctive mean?"

LIFE ACCENTS TRAVEL as much as travel accents life. When Riley and
I entered the dining room that evening, I saw Nancy Stibbard, the
owner of this lodge and Cathedral Mountain Lodge (as well as Capilano Suspension Bridge Park in North Vancouver). Nancy had been
my board chair when I worked in tourism years ago, and we'd been in
contact before the train journey. She was dining with the property's
general manager, David, and her colleague Julie, whose husband, Jim,
had also come along. Riley and I were invited to join them, and their
table expanded to six.

"How was your drive?" asked Julie.

"Grampa missed the turnoff for Moraine Lake," said Riley.

David took care of it. "Indigenous Peoples have known how to get
here for a thousand years. But the first white man to find it probably got
lost a few times, too. That was a hundred years ago."

"Our lodge had its start around then," said Nancy. "Three single
ladies set a teahouse tent at the end of a trail the CPR built in 1902.
Because people visiting Banff came a long way by train, they stayed
awhile in the area. And the company needed things for them to do.
Moraine Lake became a day trip out of Banff."

I stated the obvious: "There are endless mountain peaks around
the lake to hike."

"It looks like countless mountains, but it's actually called Valley
of the Ten Peaks," David said. He added that explorer Samuel Allen
named them one to ten using Nakoda, which today we'd refer to as
Stoney First Nation, numbers. David wrote them out for Riley and me:
"One is wazhi (try saying heejee), two is nûm (try num), and three is
yamnî (try yamnee)."

"These may not have been what the Nakoda originally called them,"
he continued, "but they became the designations, for a while. Then
they were superseded with white man's labels. Wazhi becoming Mount
Fay, and Shappee—that is the number six in the Stoney language—was
named for Allen himself. There's now a movement to re-establish the
named-by-number approach, using the Indigenous language."

I sipped my wine, wondering why there was so much I hadn't known before this trip.

"Nine and ten have kept their original designations, Neptuak Mountain and Wenkchemna Peak. As has four, Tonsa," said David. In the present, we once again favour using the original names: Heejee, Nom, Yamnee, Tonsa, Sapta, Shappee, Sagowa, Saknowa, Neptuak, and Wenkchemna.

Throughout dinner Julie was attentive to Riley, her own kids at home 530 miles (850 kilometres) away. It was as much a kid-fix for her as a mom-fix for a delighted Riley. Asking Nancy if he may be excused from the table when he'd finished dinner, and getting a nod from her, Riley turned my way before leaving.

Looking me square in the eyes, he said, "I've had enough of you." An unvarnished Riley leaned into me and then gave me a trainman's hug, bear-like in intensity, journey-worthy in duration. "It's all about Grampa," he laughed to everyone's relief, and was gone to our cabin an hour ahead of my follow-on. Yes, he walked there alone in the dark. Yes, I later thought better of letting that happen.

When I got to our room he was barely awake; his eyes opening only long enough to blink good night.

I fell asleep to the sound of little kid snores, remembering a song by The Seekers in the 1960s:

*Train whistle blowin'*
*Makes a sleepy noise*
*Underneath the blankets*
*For all the girls and boys*

*Rockin' rollin' ridin'*
*Out along the bay*
*All bound for Morningtown*
*Many miles away*

# — 18 —

ALL TRAVELS END. I wanted morning trail time with Riley. Riley wanted morning time on his own. The standoff lasted an hour during which I took coffee, read, and pondered. Maybe sulked. Once outside on the path beside the lake, we found it smooth and wide and not at all busy with walkers. I wanted to head to the logjam we'd seen from the canoe. The trail had the potential to be a hike if we stayed on it long enough. Instead, my suggestion led to a protracted negotiation.

"You've had your walk," said Riley fifteen minutes in, turning for home. "And so have I."

We kept walking. Then he stopped, turned, and took one step as if to leave, just to tease me.

"Another ten minutes," I said.

"Five."

A thing I'd learned about Riley was that he enjoyed brokering, with less concern about winning or not. I liked that in him, and took advantage of it. We walked for ten minutes, him as happy as me. Maybe he had simply become Grampa-immune.

When he turned and made a bolt in the return direction, I cut a deal. "Let's go beyond that bridge, then head back for breakfast."

"OK." He was clearly enjoying this as much as me.

As we neared the bridge, I saw another one a hundred yards ahead, and pointed to it. "That's the bridge I meant," I lied.

"No, it's not."

"Is too."

I realized how much I would miss our casual banters, the one-upmanship, and my teaching him the joy of sarcasm while bridling at his mastery of it.

I grabbed his wrist in jest, as though to drag him onward. He was all smiles and broke loose intent on beating me to the bridge in question. He ran. He tripped. He dove into a ditch of branches and rocks. I heard a yelp. He rolled over and I saw the pain of a knee scraped deep, bleeding dirt and blood.

His smile turned to a grimace. The grimace turned to anger. "This is your fault. I'm only here because my dad made me come."

What followed was an hour of absolute quiet between us. It was filled with unseen lessons. I've read that "God's first language is silence."

I cleaned the wound in our room, bloodying towels I did not own. I packed ice on his sore.

Something had to break the tension. I wasn't up to the task. Riley was. Eventually he looked me in the eye as an equal and said plainly, "I only said that 'cuz I was mad. I didn't mean it."

Blue sky came our way courtesy of a ten-year-old's sense of self.

WHEN RILEY AND I were aboard the train on our early days as travel companions, which seemed quite some time ago by this stage, we'd nodded at our final destination as the train wove toward Cathedral Mountain's spiral tunnel, and then to Mount Ogden's. Off and away from our train's window that day, I'd pointed toward Cathedral Mountain Lodge. "It would be a great place to wrap up our trip," I'd said. Today, we left Moraine Lake and drove less than an hour for a night's stay at that very lodge. I missed a turnoff. Instead, we landed at a roadside stop in Field. The Kicking Horse River flowed beside the highway. A helpful man penciled out a map and gave it to me with his assurance that even a fool (he was thinking of me; Riley nodded affirmation) could not get lost heading back up the highway, taking the only turnoff available, and simply following along. Privately owned enterprises in national parks receive little formal signage, but lovely lodges are difficult to hide.

Our Jeep looked at home alongside the log cabins and creek. The spruce and fir trees, warmed by the afternoon's sun, locked in our welcome. We were tucked well away from the railway tracks Riley and I had passed along almost two weeks earlier, though we could determine where they were over the way and up higher. The lodge felt remote and singular.

Before checking in and finding our log cabin, Riley wanted a walkabout, hearing the coursing roar of the river. It swirled murky with glacier dust, foamed over rocks, and gushed noisily. We found an incongruous sand beach, and small tuffs of islands midstream. Riley said, "We could walk out there."

In spring runoff, all those patches of land would disappear underwater, which—not surprisingly—was what I feared would happen to my grandson and me if I took him wading into the inviting rush of water. One misstep and the creek would wash us downstream like human logs. A maxim of grandparent-as-custodian with grandchild-on-travels is, "First, do no harm."

Above and across from us, the massive presence of Cathedral Mountain's thousand-foot slope gaped with intimidation. It was unto its own among the jags and pillars and downslopes and overhangs and peaks. Its rock face brought to mind the wall of a fourteenth-century cathedral, though its magnitude outdid the believability of any manmade edifice. I think most observers benefit from someone else's description before they'll say, "Ya, that's a cathedral all right."

It feels poetic that the Spiral Tunnels move through and within Cathedral Mountain, as they are a tribute to visionary design. Looking up, I recalled once riding in the cab of a train with the engineer while the train snaked through the Spiral Tunnels. That was thirty years ago, when I had a role with the train company that gave me such privileged security clearance, and the train's mechanic took me with him to the locomotive.

Around noon, Riley and I formally checked in for the final night of our trip. I picked up the cabin keys at the reception desk in the lobby, and turned to find Riley holding two cups of hot chocolate. "I met the chef," he said. "This one's for you."

Instead of unpacking, we headed to our cabin's porch with the drinks in hand. The two of us slid our bums along the flat slats of Adirondack chairs. We leaned back as though we owned them and over the years had worn their shape to the contours of our bodies. "It is good," I said, of the setting.

"It is good," Riley said, of the hot chocolate.

Then, "I don't think it looks like a cathedral," he said of the mountain.

"Well," I postured, "how would you know?" It was patronizing, but it slipped out.

He'd have none of that. "Not like the Vatican," he said. Brat, I thought, having forgotten his family travels in Italy. "Or that Saint Mary's place in Edinburgh. It was big. Squarer. Longer."

"Listen," I said. "A famous painter I know about, Arthur Lismer, called it 'a great gothic structure,' and that's good enough for me."

"Gothic? Kids who wear black?"

I shut up. Posing a Group of Seven painter versus modern-day Goths wasn't a debate I'd win. I held no hope that I could manage my way along the word trail from Cathedral to Gothic to Goth to, inevitably, Vampires.

My hot chocolate had turned cold sitting on the chair's armrest while I talked instead of drank.

"I'll get our gear," I said, heading for the Jeep.

Riley took the keys from where I'd put them next to his mug, and made for the cabin door. "I'll find a plug-in and charge our music."

THE ROOM WAS made from logs that were cut and hewn within feet of where they now formed a timbered tribute to the lodge's namesake. Local craftsmen built the furniture. The place rang true to an earlier era. Last night at dinner Nancy said they'd be here this evening and we decided to meet up for drinks and stories. Five of us settled over wines, one of us over a smoothie.

In such situations, Riley's a born listener. I'm an interrupter. I'd begun this trip taking for granted that Riley would learn much, and by now had realized how much I'd learned on the trip by listening to him, and others. It was happening again.

David, referencing the previous evening's conversation about newcomers bringing new place names, said, "The town of Field is named after a Chicago industrialist lured here in hopes he'd invest in the fledgling railway. To influence his decision, the railway executives named a mountain and the village after him. Cyrus West Field accepted the honours but declined to support the railway's well-being."

"Why didn't they drop his name in favour of someone else?" I asked.

"The railway was omnipotent in the 1880s, labelling whatever they chose to," said David. "Donald Smith christened the survey camp Siding 29 in honour of Banffshire, where he and George Stephen had been born in Scotland."

Nancy said, "More appropriately, the park's name, Yoho, comes from the Cree word for *wonder*."

"Mount Stephen was named around the same time," said David. "At least George Stephen was the first president of the CPR, so it was a tribute."

Nancy said, "The Mount Stephen Hotel in Field was the first deluxe accommodation in the Rockies, built two years before the Banff Springs Hotel."

"So why *this* lodge? Why here?" I asked. The high ceilings gave a woody comfort; the glass-everywhere in log walls reflected warmth from the fireplace.

"You're staying on the grounds of what was Altman's Auto Court," said Nancy.

"What's an auto court?" asked Riley.

"It's a roadside rest place. Like a motel," said Julie.

"Miners stayed here," said Nancy. "Construction workers called it home. It wasn't fancy. But it was one of the most beautiful places in the world to wake up. Still is."

Riley slipped away from the table with a nice bow of thanks and walked to our cabin. When I joined him an hour later, he showed me the tooth that had finally given way and ended up in his hand. I told him the Rocky Mountain Tooth Fairy paid out a dollar, tops. He pocketed the tooth and smiled at my inability to pull off a joke, or maybe it was at my cheapness.

"You're going to miss me when this trip's over," I said. "You'll be having grampa withdrawal."

Riley had a wink in his words. "I'll be singing Halleluiah. Halleluiah..."

MORNING CAME, our last of the journey. Bears awoke in the mountains not a hundred yards from our cabin. Surely there were cubs. Deer that had stood all night half asleep and half alert began to graze. Mountain goats, stable on the steep mountainsides, opened their eyes to the early light. Somewhere within a mile of our safety lurked a nocturnal cougar marking the end of its night's 30-mile (almost 50-kilometre) circuit of foraging. A rabbit's head poked out from a hole. Riley's head poked out from the blankets. Each was convinced that this was one of the most beautiful places in the world in which to wake up.

Returning from the lodge, I pushed open the cabin door as Riley ducked back under the covers. I waved two steaming mugs at him. His nose rose up from the pillow, twitching like a rabbit's at the smell of hot chocolate.

"I'll be outside with these... Bring a blanket."

Riley came onto the porch, blanket in tow. He slipped into the wooden chair, pulled the blanket around him against the chill, and reached for his mug. He poked where his tooth was missing. I drew my thumb and forefinger through my twelve-day beard. He smiled.

OVER US HOVERED the defining image of Cathedral Mountain. The name of the edifice exemplifies railway visionaries for me.

The notion of seeing visionary people as "cathedral thinkers" has been around for centuries but takes thirty seconds to understand. Say you were an architect in a European city in the fourteenth century, and the city elders commissioned you to design the town's new cathedral. You would begin that task knowing you would not live to see it completed. Perhaps a grandson or great-granddaughter would draw the final renderings for the spire, but you'd be dead by then. Cathedrals took decades—indeed generations, sometimes centuries—to complete. Those who began the work needed to do so with a long-term vision in mind so future generations could build upon their work.

I've come to realize that the philosophy of cathedral thinking is a way of life for some, often without the person talked about being aware of the concept. In that way, it is straightforward to view the railway visions of William Van Horne (1888), James Sherwood (1977), Rohan Vos (1986), and Peter Armstrong (1990) as those of "cathedral thinkers."

I tried to explain cathedral thinking to Riley. "If I was a stonemason laying the foundation blocks and putting the cornerstone in place to begin building a cathedral in the 1400s, I'd know I wouldn't live to see the cathedral finished. That thrill would go to you, as my grandchild working the same trade, building upon the solid foundation I set in place."

"What's a trade?"

"Job. You'd have the same job. If I was a stonemason, you'd be a stonemason."

"Not likely."

Cathedral thinking keeps the living generation tethered to the future. Sitting in a crafted wooden chair on a veranda at a log cabin beneath Cathedral Mountain, I wondered if I was helping to lay a strong foundation for Riley's future, perhaps even providing one of its cornerstones.

You'll find a cathedral thinker behind every railway and train design that lasts, albeit modified, to this day—from Trevithick's steam locomotive throughout the railway age and on to sleek bullet trains. There was a cathedral thinker behind the designs of the coaches pulled by *The Mountaineer* out of Chicago and through the Rocky Mountains in the 1920s through to the 1950s, and those of today's *Seven Stars* out of Tokyo. Not all the train world's cathedral thinkers live on with name recognition—Pullman or Nagelmackers are examples of those who do. Many sought only the certainty that their ideas would last for generations and do well for humankind.

On this trip, I tried at various points to understand four cathedral thinkers, two of whom I had met in the early 1990s when their visions were unfolding and gaining attention from train travellers around the globe; the third was my railroad boss; and I had stood by the graveside of the fourth.

I'd met James Sherwood thirty years ago, when his *Venice Simplon-Orient-Express* was enjoying a revival of popularity and I was working for Rocky Mountaineer. He and his wife had been invited to Canada specifically to travel the Rocky Mountains to Vancouver in a heritage business coach owned by the chairman of CNR. CNR's loan of the coach was what clinched Sherwood and his wife's willingness to travel along, hauled behind the *Rocky Mountaineer* train, but nonetheless separate. It was oak-panelled and well-appointed; private varnish at its best. An attendant was on constant call to answer their needs, and their meals were prepared by the train's chef, who worked to a requested menu. The *Rocky Mountaineer* did not have dome cars to show off in those days, so what was most special was the scenery, and the ambitions of the train's owners. Sherwood was gracious and forthcoming. He saw the difficulties of attracting sufficient customers to pay the fare that would cover investment in new dome coaches. He offered advice about working with track owners CNR and CPR. "It is a challenge to run over tracks owned by others," he said. "That has costs that get complicated and are difficult to manage, let alone reduce." He talked about the need to build beyond one train journey, as his own company did. "The original *Orient Express* had multiple excursions and was constantly improving. So are we." Sherwood envisioned his enterprise being built to last forever. His company had a long-term vision; it branched into hotels, created a new train experience in Thailand, and established high-end river cruises. James Sherwood was a cathedral thinker.

I'd met Rohan Vos in the early 1990s at World Travel Market in London, and at Internationale Tourismus-Börse in Berlin, two significant gatherings of owners, sellers, marketers, train companies, and tour operators. I attended, representing the brand new Rocky Mountaineer company, and Rohan representing his nascent Rovos Rail and its *Pride of Africa*. With Rovos Rail he was creating something that would last for decades, to be inherited and operated by his grandchildren. He had a clear vision that would require future generations to build upon it by constantly making it better. Rohan Vos was a cathedral thinker.

THEN THERE ARE the third and fourth of the cathedral thinkers I contemplated while looking at the namesake mountain. A dozen years ago, I travelled in a convertible Mustang with a friend searching for all the old parts of Route 66, finding 20-mile (30-kilometre) stretches of gravel that had lasted only a few years under that route's designation, or major lengths that had been bypassed by politics, pavement, and progress. We got stuck in the mud on a left-behind road no longer much needed. We drove a lot of dead ends, knowing they were once part of the vision for Route 66. That mattered to us. We wanted the experience of travelling abandoned roads that were once someone's dream about the future.

We'd begun our eight-state trip where Route 66 begins: Chicago. On our first day on the old road we stopped in Joliet, Illinois, where discarded sections of the road are visible. While munching ice creams, it dawned on us that one of Canada's great railwaymen was laid to rest in Joliet. We searched out the Oakwood Cemetery and parked our car near large boulders that mark the man's plot. We walked over to confirm the name on the headstone. I was travelling with one cathedral thinker and standing at the graveside of another. For several peaceful minutes I stood in silence beside Peter Armstrong at the grave of William Van Horne. I wondered what they would have said to one another.

ON OUR LAST morning in the Rockies, Cathedral Mountain's omnipotence clarified something about the future for me. The homeward jot of our journey was nigh. Riley had travelled on the cusp of becoming an adult, and I hadn't always acted like one. I had taken for granted that we were starting our trip with a base of love and respect, yet by day two had realized that legacy travel (which I accept as a better term for "intergenerational travel") tests such attributes. Only now as it neared completion did I realize that surviving such a test had been my ambition.

Until the end-point in a trip, there is always more to come. A summit is the start of a mountaineer's way down; a cave's bottom is the spelunker's notice to find a way out; a trail's fork is a choice about moving onward. But when travel has drawn a fully inked circle (or nugget) on a map, as had ours, it's over, except in the way memories leave any physical trip an unfinished journey. It seems irrelevant to squiggle a line eastward because an airport and flight lay in wait. Such a separate jotting takes you outside the journey's story. In that way, Riley and I were about to leave the Rockies and let some things about us stay behind.

Travel can be about old clothes, contemplation, growing a beard, playing a video game, or food, a loose tooth, or the sudden sighting of a bear can define it. It may be about revived memories, eagles overhead, or late arrivals. It can be about dancing on a train. And smoothies. New friends come to mind, along with their tales, laughter, and secrets. Good travels blend silly expectations, misremembered history, and little dramas. Put most simply, travel is about moments strung together, their buffed connectors unseen.

But I am naïve. Every ending is an imagination, recalled as we wish it to have been. Riley and I thought our once-in-a-lifetime journey was behind us, but it was starting anew—and not just because of our new-found understandings of one another.

As we stood beside raging waters in the wilderness, my hip against a boulder, Riley leaned into my shoulder. (Had he grown taller since we left home?) He breathed deeply for both of us, surely knowing I was sad; maybe he was, too. (I didn't dare ask.) The air was sharply cool—an amalgam of river mist, the smell of red cedar and hemlock trees, of dung and dawn. The sun glanced off the face of Cathedral Mountain, the massif daring us to think of it as anything but the strong wall of a medieval cathedral—enchanting and proud, elegant and dreamy.

Riley saw it first. Westering through the trees at the foundation of the mountains across from us, a train was beginning its journey with travellers aboard. Like the mountains that back-dropped it, the train was enchanting and proud, elegant and dreamy. Riley waved at the train. "Grampa, there goes our *Rocky Mountaineer*."

I mused aloud, "Ahhh, the best luxury of all."

"What is?" asked Riley.

*Time*, answered the mountains.

# — ACKNOWLEDGEMENTS —

T HERE WOULD BE much less of a story, far fewer insights, and not nearly as many patches of absolute fun without my travel companion Riley Antonson, grandson, adventurer, and fellow storyteller. His most subtle contributions are often only visible between the lines of this book, wherein he taught me about the hidden truths of train travel, family, respect, and the art of sarcasm.

As with many travel books, this one started with talk about an unforgettable journey. Having been my companion on a Route 66 jaunt that forms the narrative backbone for one of my travel books, Peter Armstrong asked, "Why don't you write a book that contributes to the conversation about the *Rocky Mountaineer*?" That was the only intent I heard from him in the two years during which this book was written; he kept a railroad mile of editorial distance, which I respect. His anticipation was that a book popular with the general public could be one that the Rocky Mountaineer company would like copies of during their anniversary year and beyond.

On the publishing side, there are many fingerprints on the resulting book, and I begin with a thank-you to Tricia Finn as development editor on behalf of Greystone Books, and a side role researching a handful of vignettes for me. Founding Publisher and CEO Rob Sanders encouraged the idea from our first exchange, with a keen eye on the international market for the resulting book. As the manuscript evolved, it fell under the editorial care of Jennifer Croll and Lesley Cameron, who made marked improvements in the flow of writing and storytelling. I thank Lenore Hietkamp for undertaking copyediting and Alison Strobel for proofreading, and making a difference. Jess Sullivan oversaw the book's lovely design, which earlier benefitted from the ideas of Nayeli Jimenez, and Fiona Siu created the impactful jacket. Eric Leinberger saw to the maps' ability to inform readers, as he has for my earlier books. (He adapted (with permission) the fifth map, "Railway routes in the western provinces," from a fuller map appearing in *Whistle Posts West*.)

I benefitted from research, interviews, and suggested storylines by journalist Martha Perkins, who also gave the manuscript an editorial comb early on. Richard Thomas Wright and my older brother, Brian, also delved into pockets of research, and shared ideas on how such stories might be told here. All three patiently reviewed what I created from their framing.

This is my fifth travel book, and I know having trusted readers involved at various iterations of the manuscript improves the resulting work, particularly when they bring intelligence and a dose of skepticism. I am indebted to Jess Ketchum, Jon Hutchison, and Darren Johner for again accepting that responsibility. Joining them for this book was historian and author Mary Trainer, whose fascination with all-things-train provided helpful insights. Graham Bell brought experience and humour to fact-checking, saving me from oversights. Dania Sheldon was permissions editor, once more providing her respected thoroughness and guidance.

Nicole Ford of Rocky Mountaineer brought a wealth of knowledge and a keen eye to her readings and recommendations. I also thank Steve Sammut, then CEO of GCRC, for taking a look at the evolving story. Paula Salloum, formerly of Rocky Mountaineer, kindly gave helpful opinions. And I tip my hat to staff onboard the *Rocky Mountaineer* for their information and professionalism. I trust my characterization and quotes ring true. My thanks to Geoffrey Litherland, who cast a legal eye over the manuscript when requested. Polly Tracey sorted out the train reservations for Riley and me, and her efficiency proved a good omen for our journeys. And Carolyn Rohaly became a welcomed Rocky Mountaineer team member drawing attention to the book.

This book finally published under the guidance of Greystone's new publisher, Jen Gauthier, and benefits from the exceptional marketing experience of Greystone's Megan Jones, and Makenzie Pratt. Publicist Wendy Underwood has been a constant friend for my books, and I deeply appreciate her talent in nurturing my presence on social media and in promotional undertakings.

Once again I benefitted from the "Antonson focus group" (brother Brian and my sons, Brent and Sean) on everything from title debates to content to assumptions. I wouldn't want to publish without their input. Also, I thank Riley's parents, Hilary and Sean, for lending me their son.

Howard Jang of the Banff Centre for Arts and Creativity spent helpful time with Riley and me and provided introductions to Monte Greenshields and Lindsay Stokalko, who in turn furthered my understanding of the Whytes and early American artists in the Rockies. My thanks to Nancy Stibbard and her colleagues for enabling an extraordinary experience for Riley and me in the Rockies at their lodges and surroundings. And to George Game, who enlivened Riley's understanding of trains in Vancouver on his walkabout at the Engine 374 Pavilion at Yaletown's Roundhouse.

Others took a look at portions of the manuscript to ensure I was in line with facts and inferences. Thank you, Jos Beltman; Wade Bush and Robin Jha from the *Rocky Mountaineer*; and Rohan Vos and James Sherwood.

Fellow travellers spoke of other train journeys or history I was unfamiliar with, prompting research, and I attributed the resulting information to them when it felt in keeping with their comments and intentions. I've exercised artistic licence in amalgamating some settings for continuity, changing a few character names when I could not track them down for confirmation, and blending personalities from my rail journeys with the sole intent of such composites moving along the narrative in the interest of the reader rather than bogging down with an extended cast.

## ACKNOWLEDGEMENTS

My wife, Janice, was as always the first reader of my manuscript, the first to advise where I could take a different tack or tone to improve it, and the first to encourage me to write the book after Peter sparked my consideration of the idea. Invaluable.

I realize that in a full-length book, there may be writerly mishaps, but hopefully no derailments of fact. If there are, they are my responsibility.

# — NOTES —

1 Train talk is usually in miles, even in Canada, where metric is the order of the day. However, I'll use both imperial and metric measures to keep all international readers comfortably informed throughout.

2 Train names appear in italics, like the title of a book or name of a play, while rail lines or companies are only capitalized, with no italics. Rocky Mountaineer, however, will sometimes be italicized, sometimes not, depending on whether the name refers to the company or the train.

3 For a comparison most people will recognize: *Polar Express* is pulled by a "2-8-4," a Berkshire locomotive, in the movie.

4 This name has held from 1881, with the aberration of 1946 to 1979, when it was renamed Mount Eisenhower, in honour of Dwight D. Eisenhower. After some public pressure, the name returned to its prior designation, though not far enough back to its original Siksika name, Miistukskoowa.

5 Amtrak (the brand name for the National Railroad Passenger Corporation, once Railpax) operates a passenger rail service, run by the federal government, in every state except Hawaii, Alaska, South Dakota, and Wyoming. It operates over 22,000 miles (35,000 kilometres) of track and connects 500 stations.

6 It is said that Nagelmackers previously ran a test train from Paris to Vienna in October 1882, calling it "Train Éclair de Luxe"— literally, "lightning luxury train."

7 The French National Railway, the SNCF, holds the rights to the name, and it has tightened permission controls in the past decade. James Sherwood's use of Orient Express as the brand for his trains and company was affected by these restrictions and the company name was changed to Belmond in 2014.

8 Trail gossip also considered François Decoigne, who was in charge of Rocky Mountain House in 1814 and later years, as possibly being Tête Jaune.

# SOURCES AND
— RECOMMENDED —
READING

T HE BIBLIOGRAPHY SNAPSHOTS at the end of a book always feel aloof to me, absent the smudge of fingerprints on the actual books, missing the musty smell for older editions, and lacking the individuality of their covers or annotations about how they came to the author's interest. I have therefore written this section instead. It is about materials I had at hand while writing *Train Beyond the Mountains*, books that helped set my tone or brought back details I'd forgotten, or added atmosphere for my storytelling by letting me turn their pages. A few of them I've not yet touched but knowledge of them through their authors was helpful. Each in their way influenced the book you hold in your hands.

My first railway book was *The Real Book About Trains*, by Davis Cole (illustrated by David Millard; New York: Garden City Books, Doubleday & Company, Inc., 1951), with a greyish cover depicting an engineer looking out from the cab of his train, and kid-sized type throughout, a gift from Mom and Dad when I was ten years old, Riley's age on our trip. When not being thumbed for details about how a locomotive worked or about my dream job as an engineer controlling the throttle and whistle blowing (though later I wished to be the conductor once I understood that position was actually "in charge" of the train consist), it sat on a shelf in a bedroom I shared with my older brother, near *The Map-Maker*, by Kerry Wood (Toronto: Macmillan, 1955) with its celebratory story of explorer David Thompson.

During the following fifty years, my collection of railway books grew in spurts of interest or opportunity. For five years in the mid-1980s I was vice-president and general manager with Douglas & McIntyre publishing, and during that time the house released important works, including *Trail of Iron: The CPR and the Birth of the West, 1880–1930*, by William Carey McKee. I kept my copy, which proved important to my current writing. Books from all over the world inform my sense of trains. One came my way while I was attending the Frankfurt Book Fair, on behalf of Douglas & McIntyre, and where I acquired Jack Simmons' *The Railways of Britain* in the then brand new Pan Macmillan edition of 1986, though the book was first published in 1961; it was a gift from the London publisher, and I was smitten as much by its cover art of a steam train pulling into a station with waiting passengers as its title.

When heading out on the Trans-Siberian railway with my two sons in the 1990s, I came across Eric Newby's *The Big Red Train Ride* (New York: St. Martin's Press, 1978), curling and tearing its cover with my fingers as I ploughed through it in search of travel advice. A writer will read portions of a biography or travelogue and end up with only a partial quote to be used in their own work, and such was the case with me and *The Great Trains*, by Bryan Morgan and Edita Lausanne (New York: Crown Publishing Group, 1988), which I'd picked up in New York's Rizzoli Bookstore decades back.

When living in Europe, I began researching and writing about the *Rocky Mountaineer*. I came across James Sherwood's autobiography, *Orient-Express: A Personal Journey*, written with Ivan Fallon (London: The Robson Press, 2012). Titles related to that train used to bend my bookshelves: *Orient Express: The Birth, Life, and Death of a Great Train*, by Garry Hogg (New York: Walker & Co. Library, 1969), and *Orient Express: A Century of Railway Adventure*, written by Jean Des Cars and Jean-Paul Caracalla and translated from the original French by George Behrend (London: Bloomsbury Books, 1986), only two of many.

A while ago, I donated my personal train-related library to the West Coast Railway Association's museum park at Squamish, B.C. I did so over two visits to introduce the museum's refurbished coaches and locomotives to each of my grandsons separately. Among those books were ones I later needed for writing *Train Beyond the Mountains*. The first visit with Riley was to deliver 173 titles about international trains, which included my dented and roughed-up *The Lore of the Train*, a lovely sense of the past told by Cuthbert Hamilton Ellis (New York: Madison Square Press/Grosset & Dunlap, 1971). The delivery also included a battered hardcover, *The Ways of Our Railways*, by Charles Grinling (London: Ward, Lock & Co., 1911), which I'd found in a rare-books store in England. A month later, Declan and I dropped off 147 books, their cardboard boxes labelled "Trains in Canada," including *The Romance of the Canadian Pacific Railway*, by R. G. MacBeth (Toronto: Ryerson, 1924), and a mouldy-smelling *The Life and Work of Sir William Van Horne* (Walter Vaughan, New York: Century, 1920). It also included dog-eared volumes of Pierre Berton's classic duo, *The National Dream: The Great Railway, 1871–1881* and *The Last Spike: The Great Railway, 1881–1885*, along with a slip-cased edition of his annotated pictorial collection, *The Great Railway Illustrated*. All three were published in Toronto by McClelland & Stewart, respectively released in 1970, 1971, and 1972, bringing strong Canadian and world interest in the story, followed by the CBC television series based on the books, in 1974.

As I got into the preparation of this book's vignettes, I borrowed back a few dozen of those books, including G. R. Stevens's two-volume *Canadian National Railways* (Toronto: Clarke, Irwin, 1960—with library markings on the spine, indicating whomever I bought them from had perhaps not returned them... or was that me?). And I found my first edition of *George Dawson, the Little Giant*, by Joyce C. Barkhouse (Toronto: Clarke, Irwin, 1974), which was given to me the year of its publication with the request that I review it for TV Week magazine.

When I returned all the borrowed books to their rightful place at the museum in Squamish, I did so with my brother Brian, to once more walk in silent awe around the restored *Royal Hudson #2860*, the 4-6-4 steam engine we'd found neglected in the old Yaletown rail yards in the 1960s. On that day, I took the occasion to donate train miscellany (clutter, actually) that I'd gathered over the years, such as the cast iron door off a 1950s caboose stove with an embossed engine graphic that a railway worker gave me forty years ago for my bookshelf, plus an iron "clip" that used to hold down a track in Port Moody and to which I'd added a felt bottom so it could serve as a bookend, along with a handful of railway spikes, one adorned with a miniature train spot-welded on one side. Each artifact represented a story of which I was no longer the custodian, and they belonged with the books for others to enjoy, though the inspiration of seeing them on my desk while writing this book hopefully made some descriptions more vivid.

Mary Trainer, my brother Brian, and I wrote *Whistle Posts West: Railway Tales From British Columbia, Alberta, and Yukon*, published in 2015, and it sparked my retelling about the train horn farm story, a longer version of which appears in that book. A friend, Fred Braches, shared the lost gold story in his inimitable style in his 2019 book, *Searching for Pitt Lake Gold: Facts and Fantasy in the Legend of Slumach*. Heritage House Publishing of Victoria released both titles. And Sumas Lake's demise has a proper accounting in *Before We Lost the Lake*, Chad Reimer's 2018 book (Caitlin Press of Halfmoon Bay, B.C.), with a heartrending story told more fully than I tell it here. *Flapjacks and Photographs: A History of Mattie Gunterman, Camp Cook and Photographer* is a book I'd have loved to help research for the sheer joy of participation in something important, but the job was admirably completed by Henri Robideau (Victoria: Polestar Book Publishers, 2002). Though I've not visited the Madeline Gunterman Collection at the Vancouver Public Library, I intend to see the photographs taken by Mattie between 1890 and 1920. At the Whyte Museum I came across *This Wild Spirit: Women in the Rocky Mountains of Canada*, edited by

Colleen Skidmore (Edmonton: University of Alberta Press, 2006), teeming with stories I wished to recount but lacked space to do so.

Of course, trains were but a part of the necessary thinking; books aplenty were scattered about my dens in Europe and in Vancouver, and later in our home at Predator Ridge, where I'm writing this section. One of those books was about centuries-old breaking news: *The Secret Voyage of Sir Francis Drake 1577–1580*, by Sam Bawlf (Vancouver: Douglas & McIntyre, 2003). Alongside it was Derek Hayes's splendid sharing of little-known images, seldom-viewed maps, and a narrative that breathes at the pace of exploring: *First Crossing: Alexander Mackenzie, His Expedition Across North America, and the Opening of the Continent* (Vancouver: Douglas & McIntyre, 2001).

On some topics, many sources were tracked and I offer you a sampling by way of the following. Stories like that of William Irving came from pamphlets and archives identified by New Westminster's Irving House. Many books have faded from public sight, as have the images on their jackets, such as for *Paddlewheels on the Frontier* (Art Downs, Langley, B.C.: BC Outdoors Magazine, 1967). *Golden Miles of History: The Chinese in Lillooet* (a District of Lillooet publication) and *Jade Fever: Hunting the Stone of Heaven*, by Stan Leaming with Rick Hudson (Victoria: Heritage House Publishing, 2005), were two publications I'd not known existed prior to research for this book. Of similar help were materials about telegraph services, including *My Sisters Telegraphic: Women in the Telegraph Office 1846–1950* (Thomas C. Jepsen; Athens, Ohio: Ohio University Press, 2000) and *Railway Telegraph and Telephone*, found through the Canadian Railroad Historical Association (Robert G. Burnet; publication No. 425, November–December 1991).

A problem for this researcher is "getting into a book," such as George Behrend's *Luxury Trains: From the Orient Express to the TGV* (New York: The Vendome Press, 1977) and finding that hours have passed, my seeking a sliver of information having been enveloped by the enjoyment of reading a good book. That is also true for my evening by the fireside with a glass of wine and *The History of Trains*, by Massimo Ferrari (New York: Crescent Books, 1990).

Two earlier books about the *Rocky Mountaineer* need mentioning. I count the authors of both as friends, and respect their work. *Trip of a Lifetime: The Making of the Rocky Mountaineer,* by Paul Grescoe (Vancouver: Hurricane Press, 2000), captures the early years of the company and recounts dozens of interviews with staff or associates, many of whom have now passed away, making their recollections priceless. *All Aboard! The Canadian Rockies by Train,* by David Joseph Mitchell (Vancouver: Douglas & McIntyre, 1995), lets wilderness adventures rattle alongside the tracks of the Rocky Mountaineer's development.

Richard Thomas Wright's *Overlanders: The Epic Cross-Canada Treks for Gold, 1858–1862* is the seminal work on those brave people, their journeys, and the aftermath of their arrivals. It was a book I watched him write, as we spent time together over his maps and research—and coffees. At one point I hoped to be its publisher, though life intervened, and the book was published by Western Producer Prairie Books in Saskatoon, in 1985; subsequently, it was released as a Winter Quarters Press edition (Wells, B.C., 2000). Richard contributed a piece about this trek for an edition of *Canadian Frontier* magazine, which I was involved in publishing with my brother Brian and our friend Mary Trainer (Nunaga Publishing in New Westminster, 1974 to 1978), edited by Brian, and then Gordon Stewart. (And it was when flipping through the pages of those magazines from forty years ago that I came across an article by Vera Fidler, about the runaway train on the Big Hill, and recalled our decision to publish her piece in *Canadian Frontier.* We never met, she and I, but I sure want to thank her.) Richard wrote two other books that helped me: *Barkerville and the Cariboo Goldfields* (Victoria: Heritage House, 2013), and *In a Strange Land: A Pictorial Record of the Chinese in Canada, 1778–1923* (Vancouver: Douglas & McIntyre, 1988). Amy Newman and Richard created bonepicker.ca, innovative diggers in history that they are. They provided unpublished material, drafts of video commentary, and research, along with conversations that enhanced the dialogue in my storytelling.

Richard introduced me to Lily Chow, whom he knew from Barkerville, and while she validated information I was using, she told me about her two books, *Blood and Sweat Over the Railway Tracks: Chinese Labourers Constructing the Canadian Pacific Railway (1880–1885)* (Vancouver: Chinese Canadian Historical Society of B.C., 2014), and *Blossoms in the Gold Mountains* (Halfmoon Bay, B.C.: Caitlin Press Inc., 2018), which proved instructive.

The British Columbia historian, author, provincial minister of tourism, and my friend, Bill Barlee (1932–2012) researched, wrote, and published twenty-nine issues of *Canada West* magazine (Summerland, B.C., 1969 to 1982) and I'm fortunate to have an entire set of them, along with his books. Though he has left us, many today catch reruns of his wonderful television show that ran nationwide from 1986 to 1996, *Gold Trails & Ghost Towns*. In researching B.C.'s history and preparing early drafts of this book, I benefitted from the colour and commentary of Bill's first-hand accounts about pioneer personalities and ghost towns he tramped around before the buildings collapsed, his infectious love of discovery evident in his every footstep.

I mention E. Pauline Johnson's book, which I found when stepping (gently, as I'd had a lot of wine) off the *Napa Valley Wine Train* and into a second-hand bookstore in California. While the leather binding was tailored and the artwork intriguing, it's the book's current version you'll be able to track down if interested: *Legends of Vancouver*, by E. Pauline Johnson (Tekahionwake), in a 1997 edition released by Douglas & McIntyre.

Over four decades, I built a small library of books about Indigenous Peoples of North America, with a focus on B.C., Alberta, and Canada's north. For years I had the art and history and storytelling books in my office at Tourism Vancouver. One afternoon before I left that role, Gibby Jacob, Hereditary Chief of the Squamish Nation, was in, and I asked him where I might donate those 180 titles so they'd be available to students and researchers, rather than in a private collection. He introduced me to the Squamish Lil'wat Cultural Centre in Whistler, and that is where the books went. Worth separate mention as helpful in my research are sites about Indigenous languages, first among them being native-languages.org. I also enjoyed canadiangeographic.ca for "Mapping Indigenous languages in Canada." A source of perspective as well as referral to other sites is hellobc.com, under Indigenous Languages in British Columbia.

As I write this, I'm reading the third Jenny Willson mystery by Dave Butler. It was the first of his series, *Full Curl* (Toronto: Dundurn Press, 2017), that led me to interview him to bolster my perspective on wildlife poaching.

The aforementioned Derek Hayes is a prolific map compiler and author, with half a dozen unusual books under his literary belt, each packed with stories, anecdotes, visual memorabilia, and the best of maps (collected and newly created). I value his *Historical Atlas of the North American Railroad* (Vancouver: Douglas & McIntyre, 2010) as a resource, but I value it even more for the satisfaction of an armchair evening's slow page turning. The same is true for any railway book by Barrie Sanford, starting with his *McCulloch's Wonder: The Story of the Kettle Valley Railway* (North Vancouver: Whitecap Books, 1977). Wendy Wickwire's *At the Bridge: James Teit and an Anthropology of Belonging* introduced me to a man I did not know and his working with Indigenous Peoples as they battled for rights against colonizing governments, and his field research often repurposed by Franz Boas.

The public's taste for train books has been furthered by, among books by other train travel adventurers, Paul Theroux's *Great Railway Bazaar: By Train Through Asia* (Boston: Houghton Mifflin Company, 1975) and his retracing of the route told in *Ghost Train to the Eastern Star: 28,000 Miles in Search of the Railway Bazaar* (Boston: Houghton Mifflin, 2008), which I, too, appreciate for their flavour. However, my favourite bit of writing about being a passenger on a train is near the beginning of Bram Stoker's *Dracula* (London: Archibald Constable and Company, 1897), as the train heads into Transylvania; it's unparalleled for making you want to be aboard with the writer.

Nothing quite puts me in the mood to write about trains as does *100 Years of Classic Steam*, by Colin Garratt (Surrey, U.K.: Bramley

Books, 1997), though I'm always motivated when I have a chance to hunker down on a rainy day with J. B. Hollingsworth's *Atlas of Train Travel* (London: Sidgwick & Jackson, 1980).

A writer of non-fiction benefits from fictional work as they are writing, as did I from works such as Peter Haining's anthology, *Murder on the Railways* (London: Artus, 1996). I recommend one read (or reread as I have on occasion) Agatha Christie's *Murder on the Orient Express* (London: Collins Crime Club, 1934), or, as its first U.S. edition was titled, *Murder in the Calais Coach* (New York: Dodd, Mead & Company, 1934).

I should add a handful of train magazines that held articles or snippets of information that helped my thinking or provided factoids. Among them were *The Railway Magazine, Railway Preservation News, Passenger Train Journal,* and *Classic Trains,* and the tattered copies of *Railroad Magazine* I had in my collection that, though dated, brought atmosphere to my writing about older trains.

In the last weeks of this book's preparation, I was challenged to find a photograph of Chinese workers building the railway—because there are so few that will reproduce in good quality—and then I was introduced to author Jim Cooperman who was revising his book *Everything Shuswap* (Salmon Arm, B.C.: Shuswap Press, 2017). Jim had found a wonderful image he intends to use and was willing to share it for my purposes, which both surprised and impressed me.

No recommendation about travel experiences stands up to the impact of "word of mouth," and so it was that trains mentioned to me by fellow passengers aboard the *Rocky Mountaineer* meant I needed to research further. Books I was happy to have handy for clarifications included *Great Railway Journeys of the World: An Encyclopedia of the World's Best Locomotive Journeys,* by Max Wade-Matthews (London: Lorenz Books, 1998), and *Luxury Trains of the World,* by Geoffrey Freeman Allen (New York: Everest House, 1979).

There are as many websites and blogs devoted to trains as there are miles of trackage, or so it seems, and to sort them out (indeed, to accurately recall which ones I bounced among) would be difficult. What I can recommend, however, is the satisfaction of searching under snippy headings such as: "Trains, international, beautiful" or "Trains, refurbished locomotives" or "Railway routes never built" or... well, you get the picture(s)... Of course, blog pieces like *Hollywood in the Canadian Rockies* provided retroactive bits that I found fascinating. As I have done for each of my earlier books, I made an appreciative donation to the incomparable—and not-for-profit—Wikimedia Foundation. Where would fact-based writers be in today's "I need to confirm something right now!" atmosphere without them?

# CREDITS AND
## — PERMISSIONS —

EVERY REASONABLE EFFORT has been made to identify the copyright holders of text and lyric excerpts and photographs used in this book that do not belong to the author. We ask that any errors or omissions be sent to the publisher so they can be corrected in the next printing.

Epigraph on page v is from Paul Theroux, *Sunrise With Seamonsters: Travels and Discoveries 1964–1984* (New York: Houghton Mifflin, 1985). Reproduced by permission of Houghton Mifflin Harcourt. SUNRISE WITH SEAMONSTERS: TRAVELS AND DISCOVERIES 1964–1984 by Paul Theroux, copyright © 1985 by Paul Theroux. Used by permission of Penguin Random House LLC. All rights reserved.

Epigraph on page 15 is from Timothy Morton, *Humankind: Solidarity With Nonhuman People* (London: Verso, 2017). Reproduced by permission of Verso, an imprint of New Left Books.

Epigraph on page 27 is from a letter written by Mary M. Vaux to Dr. Charles D. Walcott, published in *This Wild Spirit: Women in the Rocky Mountains of Canada*, edited by Colleen Skidmore (Edmonton: University of Alberta Press, 2012). Reproduced by permission of University of Alberta Press.

Excerpt on page 44 is from "The Canadian Mountain Peak That Feeds Three Different Oceans," by Ken Jennings, *Condé Nast Traveler*,

October 7, 2013. © Condé Nast. Reproduced by permission of Condé Nast.

Lyric excerpt on page 99 is from
Time In A Bottle
Words and Music by Jim Croce
Copyright © 1971 Time In A Bottle Publishing and Croce Publishing
Copyright Renewed
All Rights Administered by BMG Rights Management (US) LLC
All Rights Reserved Used by Permission
*Reprinted by Permission of Hal Leonard LLC*

Epigraph on page 133 is from *The Will of a Nation: Awakening the Canadian Spirit*, by George Radwanski and Julia Luttrell (Toronto: Stoddart, 1992). The author has been unable to locate the copyright holder. Additional information will be welcome and provided in subsequent reprints or editions of this book.

Photographs on pages 148 (top), 149 (left), 150 (below), 151 (above and logos on left), 154 (above and left), and 155 courtesy of Rocky Mountaineer.

Photograph on page 148 (left) of Joe DiMaggio and Marilyn Monroe, August 1953, first appeared in *Marilyn, August 1953: The Lost LOOK Photos by John Vachon* (New York: Calla Editions, 2010). Reproduced by permission of Anne Vachon.

Photograph on page 149 (above) of Mary Vaux photographing wildflowers in the Canadian Rockies is courtesy of the Smithsonian Institution. The quoted text in the caption is from Mary Vaux, "Camping in the Canadian Rockies," *Canadian Alpine Journal* 1, no. 1 (1907), 67–71. This work is in the public domain.

Photographs on pages 150 (left) and 152 (left) of Riley Antonson by Rick Antonson.

Photographs on pages 152 (below) and 153 (top) of the Last Spike are reproduced by permission of the Canadian Pacific Railway.

Lyric excerpt on page 228 is from
Rocky Mountain High
Words and Music by John Denver and Mike Taylor

Lyric excerpt on page 235 is from CANADIAN RAILROAD TRILOGY.
Words and Music by GORDON LIGHTFOOT. © 1967 (Renewed) WC
MUSIC CORP.

Lyric excerpt on page 240 is from MORNINGTOWN RIDE by The
Seekers. Words and music by Malvina Reynolds. © 1957 Malvina
Reynolds.

# — INDEX —

*Maps and photographs indicated by page numbers in italics*

# ABOUT
# — THE AUTHOR —

RICK ANTONSON HAS travelled on trains in more than thirty-five countries and is co-author of a book of railway stories, *Whistle Posts West: Railway Tales From British Columbia, Alberta, and Yukon.* He and his two sons, Brent and Sean, circumnavigated the Northern Hemisphere by train over the course of five trips, travelling through countries as varied as Belarus, Mongolia, and North Korea. Rick and his wife, Janice, became engaged on a train in Alabama en route to New Orleans. Rick is the former president and CEO of Tourism Vancouver, and served as chair of the board for Destinations International, based in Washington, D.C., and vice chair of the Pacific Asia Travel Association, based in Bangkok, Thailand. He was vice-president of Rocky Mountaineer during its start-up years in the early 1990s. *Train Beyond the Mountains* is his fifth travel narrative.

**ALSO BY RICK ANTONSON**

*To Timbuktu for a Haircut: A Journey Through West Africa*

*Route 66 Still Kicks: Driving America's Main Street*

*Full Moon Over Noah's Ark: An Odyssey to Mount Ararat and Beyond*

*Walking With Ghosts in Papua New Guinea: Crossing the Kokoda Trail in the Last Wild Place on Earth*

*Slumach's Gold: In Search of a Legend* (with Mary Trainer and Brian Antonson)

*Whistle Posts West: Railway Tales From British Columbia, Alberta, and Yukon* (with Mary Trainer and Brian Antonson)

*The Fraser Valley* (with Bob Herger)